BOMBER SQUADRON

BOMBER SQUADRON

MEN WHO FLEW WITH XV SQUADRON

MARTYN R. FORD-JONES

Dedicated to Valerie Ann Ford-Jones

In appreciation of her love, devotion, help, support, and sacrifice

over the last fifty-three years

Fonthill Media Language Policy

Fonthill Media publishes in the international English language market. One language edition is published worldwide. As there are minor differences in spelling and presentation, especially with regard to American English and British English, a policy is necessary to define which form of English to use. The Fonthill Policy is to use the form of English native to the author. Martyn R. Ford-Jones was born and educated in London; therefore, British English has been adopted in this publication.

Fonthill Media Limited
Fonthill Media LLC
www.fonthillmedia.com
office@fonthillmedia.com

First published in the United Kingdom and the United States of America 2019

British Library Cataloguing in Publication Data:
A catalogue record for this book is available from the British Library

ISBN 978-1-78155-708-2

Typeset in 10pt on 13pt Sabon
Printed and bound by CPI Group (UK) Ltd, Croydon CR0 4YY

Foreword

History with its flickering lamp, stumbles along the trail of the past, trying to reconstruct its scenes, to revive its echoes, and rekindle with pale gleams the passion of the former days.

Winston Churchill, 12 November 1940

All too often, the makings of aviation history and heritage are not recorded formally until many years later. By that time, memories have faded, key personnel have passed away, and the opportunity to present the 'human element' has been lost. Martyn Ford-Jones has certainly not stumbled along the trail of the past as Churchill mused. He has reconstructed vividly personal stories and scenes that are part of our recent history. He has succeeded in reviving echoes of characters now past, but whose legacy lives on; he has rekindled the passions of those former days admirably.

Since the dawn of aerial combat in the First World War, the heroism of the men who put their lives at risk in the air has known no bounds. When war once more broke out in 1939, it was clear that much of the battle would be in the air and as war progressed, air strikes would become increasingly important. There were no more heroic airmen than the fighter pilots and bomber crews of the Second World War. These men awoke every morning knowing that this day could be their last; many sacrificed their own lives in order to save their crewmen and others. In telling these stories of individuals, Martyn has sought to paint a picture of courage in adversity and allow us to celebrate the extraordinary feats of ordinary men.

To attempt to define courage alone involves a myriad of variables of circumstance, opportunity, the ability of an individual, their motive, and determination. It follows therefore that in any part of aerial warfare, to single out specific people is naturally problematic. In the Second World War, many fighter pilots were known by name to the general public through their reported exploits, particularly during the Battle of Britain: it resonated in the public psyche; they had saved the nation. By contrast, only a few bomber pilots were accorded the same accolades by the press of the time: Guy Gibson and Leonard Cheshire being prime examples. Their exploits and truly outstanding flying careers, both culminating in the award of the Victoria Cross, became the stuff of legend. However, there were of course many thousands of bomber aircrew who remained anonymous save in the hearts of their families and friends. The bomber aircrews of XV Squadron were just some of these men. They were a small percentage of the aircrews across Bomber Command who carried out their duty as members of an air force seeking to save Britain from the potential annihilation of the life and freedoms that the nation had come to represent. In this book, Martyn has sought to recognise those men and to show that each and every member of the bomber aircrew cadre contributed in their way to making the whole triumphant.

In putting this series of stories together, Martyn has been acutely aware and clearly mindful that he is seeking to produce a retrospective record of the exploits of individuals. Fortuitously though, he has not had to rely solely on written historical accounts; he has been able to glean verbal accounts directly from some of those who took part in the innumerable missions flown by XV Squadron crews during the Second World War. I believe that he has succeeded admirably in striking a balance between recording the historical facts while also conveying the spirit of the time and ensuring an accurate portrayal of the lives and experiences of the men recognised in this book.

I have been privileged to serve on XV Squadron twice in the forty-three years I served with the RAF. It was my first operational squadron which I joined as a young flying officer pilot flying the Buccaneer in October 1974 at RAF Laarbruch in Germany. The following year, it was the Diamond Jubilee of the formation of XV Squadron. At the associated celebrations, I was privileged to meet some of the men mentioned in this book. They were of course still only sixty years of age or so at that time and their memories remained sharp and detailed. They still retained the graphic images and the details of the exploits of their younger lives. Such experiences obviously created deeply engraved images that lasted a lifetime.

When I returned to XV Squadron in 1994, it was as a wing commander. I had been accorded the great honour of command of this illustrious squadron now equipped with the Tornado GR1 and based at RAF Lossiemouth in Scotland. Time had of course moved on by some twenty years and many of those that I had met in 1975 were no longer with us, but some were. Once again, this time at the eightieth-anniversary celebrations in 1995, it was a privilege to meet those who had earned their place in history. As CO, and also by virtue of being a little older, I became even more aware of the importance of history and the men and women who made it. Therefore, when Martyn approached me with his burning passion for aviation and XV Squadron in particular, it was my great pleasure and my duty to support him. Since then, Martyn's role as the official historian of XV Squadron has reaped enormous rewards. The squadron's record in the RAF's history has been enhanced immeasurably; I commend his commitment and determination.

By taking the decision to record the events surrounding the lives of the men in this book who fought and died for their country and ensured the freedoms that we enjoy today, Martyn has produced a record which future historians will find of value; he has grasped the moment and redressed any potential shortfall of fact through time. It is abundantly clear that within every squadron, there were brave men who plied their 'trade' in the face of great adversity. Such bravery was linked firmly to the qualities that Britain values so highly: loyalty, duty, sacrifice, service, and patriotism. The tales within this book cover heroism, tenacity, survival, escape, and capture—I commend them to you.

Graham Bowerman
Greetham, Rutland
December 2017

Acknowledgements

The majority of those whose stories appear in this book, and with whom Valerie and I became friends, originally met at the Mildenhall Register reunion in 1981, where the idea for this work was first formed. As those friendships grew, Valerie and I had the pleasure of visiting their homes, staying with them, and enjoying their hospitality; some of them came and stayed at our home. Many a happy hour was spent sharing a beer or two while listening to, and recording, their respective stories. Unfortunately, the passage of time has taken its toll and most of these illustrious gentlemen are no longer with us, but that does not prevent me from thanking them again for allowing me to record and publish their stories. I know they would all be pleased and delighted to learn there is still an interest in the part they respectively played in Bomber Command in the Second World War. In the first instance, I must name Corporal Don Clarke, MBE, stalwart of the Mildenhall Register (who later became its president), who afforded me a very warm welcome to RAF Mildenhall all those years ago. Others who also accepted my approaches and whose stories are included in this book are, in alphabetical order, Squadron Leader Peter Boggis, DFC; Flight Lieutenant Oliver Brooks, DFC; Flight Sergeant Harry Bysouth, DFM; Pilot Officer Graham Cullen, RNZAF; Warrant Officer Bernard Dye; Sergeant Douglas Fry; Flight Sergeant Gilbert Marsh; Flight Lieutenant Len Miller, DFC; Sergeant Frederick Stevens; Air Vice-Marshal Stewart Menaul, CB, CBE, DFC, AFC, MiD; Flight Sergeant D. A. 'Pat' Russell; and Group Captain Michael Wyatt, DFC. Others who contributed stories and who have also passed on are Sergeant George Allom; Flight Lieutenant Frank Diamond, DFC; Flight Sergeant Ken Pincott, DFM; Sergeant John Sparrow; Flight Sergeant Frank Watson; Pilot Officer George Wright; and Flight Sergeant Kay Godfrey, WRAF.

There are three new chapters in this edition, the first being that relating to Pilot Officer Leonard O'Hara. I never had the privilege of meeting this young

American officer as he was to pay the supreme sacrifice for volunteering to join a war, which at that time his country was not involved in. Little thought is given to those left behind when a loved one is lost, but Leonard's story gives an insight into one family's long journey, over many years, to find out what really happened. I must therefore express my most sincere thanks to Leonard O'Hara's family, Tom and Barbara Lowe, Mary and Roger Lowe, Cathie and Dave Lange, and Patrick Bump, for agreeing without hesitation to my request for help and allowing me through Tom's personal research and privately published work *Finding Leonard* as well as access to personal documentation and photographs relating to their relative. Although resident in various states across America, this close-knit family have been an inspiration, and Valerie and I have both been honoured to be welcomed into their respective homes and to spend many happy and memorable occasions in their company. Valerie and I were also extremely privileged to have known Harriett Bump, sister of Leonard O'Hara, and mother and grandmother to the family named above. Harriett, a gracious and charming lady who passed away at the age of 102 years, never gave up hope of finding out what had happened to her brother.

The second new chapter is the story of Arthur Edgley who was quite a character in his own right—a true country boy and a consummate gentleman. Although I knew Arthur for a number of years, and we often talked about his exploits, I knew little about his early background. It is with that thought in mind that I must extend my grateful thanks to Diane Chester (*née* Edgley) for filling in some of those blanks. In later years, Diane accompanied her father to the Mildenhall Register reunions where Arthur would meet and chat with many of his friends over the three-day event.

The third of the new chapters is that relating to Group Captain Michael Wyatt, DFC, whose story I am extremely pleased to include in this revised edition, especially as it gives a different aspect to the operational life of a bomber pilot and his crew. Michael Wyatt's story is one of those stories recorded shortly after the original publication of *Bomber Squadron*.

Having first met him shortly after he took command of XV (R) Squadron in May 1994, I am deeply honoured and delighted that Group Captain Graham Bowerman, OBE (RAF, Ret'd) agreed to write a foreword for this book. When Valerie and I were gathering material prior to writing *Oxford's Own: Men and Machines of 15/XV Squadron, Royal Flying Corp/Royal Air Force*, Graham responded to my request for help by inviting Valerie and me to RAF Lossiemouth, where he extended every courtesy to us, allowing us access to squadron albums, files, and ephemera; it was the start of a warm and lasting friendship.

Others to whom my thanks must be extended are my good friend Sean Strange, BA (Hon), ARPS. Sean, a professional photographer, has been of immense help and support with regard to ensuring the photographs selected to illustrate this work were all of perfect quality. Sean's help, advice, and input throughout have been greatly appreciated.

Again, as with previous publications of mine, David Green has taken time away from his wife Bernadette and his two daughters, Lisa and Emma, as well as his demanding job, in order to proofread the manuscript; he tells me it gives him a break, but he does not say whether it is from his work or his family.

My thanks are also extended to Alan Sutton for his continued acceptance of my work, as well as Jay Slater, Jamie Hardwick, and the staff at Fonthill Media for their help and support along the way.

I would like to take this opportunity to express my thanks to my two daughters and their partners—Emma and her husband Looey, and Alex and her husband Grant—and our grandchildren Sonny and Loulou for their continued love and support.

Valerie was by my side, helping with the research, writing, providing constructive criticism and moral support when this book was first being written and prepared for publication; now, over thirty years later, she is doing the same thing all over again. By rights, the name of Valerie A. Ford-Jones should be alongside mine as co-author, but she refuses to be acknowledged as such. Therefore, all I can do is just say a huge, heartfelt thanks for all Valerie has done for me, not only on this book, but also over the years.

Martyn R. Ford-Jones
Wiltshire, England

CONTENTS

Introduction

At 10.54 a.m. on Friday, 31 March 2017, XV (R) Squadron paraded its standard in front of approximately 700 invited guests at RAF Lossiemouth. At the end of the Reviewing Ceremony, the standard was marched out of the hanger, accompanied by its armed escort, followed by a lone piper who played 'Sands of Kuwait', a tune written to commemorate XV (R) Squadron's last battle honour. As the squadron piper disappeared from view, and the sound of the pipes dissipated on the wind, a total of 102 years of service were brought to a close.

No. 15 Squadron ranks among the oldest squadrons in the Royal Air Force, having been formed as part of the Royal Flying Corps at South Farnborough, Hampshire, on 1 March 1915. Personnel were drawn from No. 1 Reserve Squadron and the Recruits Depot. The squadron's first commanding officer was Captain P. B. Joubert de la Ferté, who later became Air Chief Marshal Sir Philip Joubert de la Ferté, KCB, CMG, DSO, and was twice commander-in-chief Coastal Command.

Initially equipped with an assortment of aeroplanes, 15 Squadron re-equipped with BE.2c biplanes for army co-operation duties during the late summer of that same year. The squadron relocated to France during December 1915 where it flew photographic and artillery ranging sorties. The assistance 15 Squadron rendered to the Fifth Army during the attacks on the Ancre salient in January 1917 was recognised by Field Marshal Sir Douglas Haig, the commander-in-chief of the Expeditionary Force. At the end of May 1917, the squadron converted to RE.8 aeroplanes, or as the machines were more commonly known, 'Harry Tates'. For the remaining eighteen months of the war, 15 Squadron continued in its allotted tasks of aerial photography and artillery spotting. Although the Great War finished in November 1918, the squadron remained in France until February 1919, before being disbanded at Fowlmere, England, in December that same year.

On 20 March 1924, 15 Squadron was resurrected at Martlesham Heath, near Ipswich, Suffolk, as part of the Aeroplane and Armament Experimental Establishment. Its equipment consisted of de Havilland DH.9As, one Vickers Vimy, and two Bristol F.2b fighters, all of these machines being used in experimental roles as part of the work undertaken by the A&AEE. During its ten-year association with the A&AEE, the squadron carried out a wide range of experimental trials including bomb ballistics, trialling bombing cameras, use of parachute flares, and high-altitude gunnery tests.

On 1 January 1934, 15 Squadron reformed as a day bomber unit under Squadron Leader Thomas Elmhirst, AFC; it was equipped with Hawker Hart Mk I aircraft, which were delivered to the squadron's new base at Abingdon, in Oxfordshire, between 2 June and 8 August. Wanting 'his' squadron to become known to the general public, Squadron Leader Elmhirst sought and gained official permission for the aircraft under his command to be adorned with the letters XV. Applied to each side of the rear fuselage, the large, blue-painted Roman letters could be easily seen when the aircraft were in the air or on the ground.

March 1936 saw another change of equipment when the squadron converted to Hawker Hind aircraft. It was as a result of converting to this type of aircraft that XV Squadron decided to change the hart's head displayed on the unit's badge to a hind. This amendment was approved by King Edward VIII during the summer of 1936 when the first set of squadron badges were officially approved. By the end of September, the hind's head was proudly displayed on the tail fins of all the squadron's aircraft.

The Air Defence Command of Great Britain was reorganised during July 1936, as a result of which the formation of four new Commands were formed; these being Training, Coastal, Fighter, and Bomber Commands. As part of the No. 1 (Bomber) Group, XV Squadron was absorbed into the latter command and began its long association with RAF Bomber Command.

During June and July 1938, XV Squadron gave up its Hind aircraft in exchange for Fairey Battle bombers, with which it was to go to war in 1939. The monoplanes were escorted into RAF Abingdon by the outgoing biplanes.

As Squadron Leader Elmhirst had done four years earlier, in 1939, the Government decided to foster good relations between the RAF and the general public, as a result of which the Air Ministry approved a scheme which affiliated some squadrons to certain cities and towns throughout Great Britain. The scheme, which commenced in April 1939, linked XV Squadron with the 'City of Dreaming Spires', Oxford. Although the name was not officially adopted, for a short period during the early part of the Second World War, XV Squadron was known as 'Oxford's Own' Squadron.

When a state of emergency was declared at the end of August, the squadron changed its identification code letters of EF, which it had worn on the fuselage since the spring of 1939, to LS, which it retained until 1951.

Pre-empting the declaration of war, which was expected at any time, XV Squadron relocated to France on 2 September 1939 one day before the official declaration of war was announced. It was to remain on the continent until December that same year, during which time it undertook armed daylight reconnaissance flights over the Siegfried Line. Over 9 and 10 December, XV Squadron returned to England, flying its now outdated Fairey Battle aircraft back to RAF Wyton, where it converted to twin-engined Bristol Blenheim bombers. RAF Wyton, a 2 Group station, was to become XV's home until August 1942, although it did move to RAF Alconbury (a satellite airfield) for a month between April and May 1940.

As the war progressed, so did the technology, and XV Squadron re-equipped twice during its stay at Wyton: first in November 1940 with the twin-engined Vickers Wellington bomber, which carried a crew of five, and then in April 1941, when it became the second squadron to receive the Short Stirling bomber. The Stirling, which carried a crew of seven, was the first of the four-engined heavy bombers operated by Bomber Command. While at Wyton, the squadron participated in many major raids against enemy targets, including the first Thousand Bomber Raid on the night of 30 May 1941, followed by the second Thousand Bomber Raid two nights later.

Following receipt of an Air Ministry signal on Thursday, 13 August 1942, XV Squadron relocated to RAF Bourn in Cambridgeshire from where it continued the fight against Germany. The squadron's stay at Bourn was a relatively short one as, after almost nine months to the day, XV redeployed to Mildenhall in Suffolk. RAF Mildenhall reopened as an operational station in April 1943, after being closed during the winter months for refurbishment and the installation of concrete runways. This move proved to be the last one made by the squadron during the war years, although another change of equipment came in December 1943 when XV converted to Avro Lancaster bombers.

On Tuesday, 10 August 1943, the personnel and equipment of 'C' Flight were moved across the airfield at Mildenhall and renumbered as 622 Squadron. For the duration of the war, the two squadrons operated alongside one another, until 622 were disbanded two years later in August 1945.

During the Second World War, XV Squadron acquitted itself in a credible manner, not only through the men who flew with XV, but also the members of the ground crew who serviced the aircraft and made them ready for operations, and the ground staff who worked in the various associated offices.

Apart from dropping a high tonnage of bombs, incendiary devices, and mines, at the end of the war, the squadron participated in the 'Manna' operations, dropping food parcels to the starving Dutch population, and carrying out both 'Exodus' and 'Dodge' sorties. 'Exodus' was the codename given to the operations whereby former British prisoners of war located in

Germany, were flown back to England, while 'Dodge' was the codename given to flying prisoners of war home from Italy.

Many of those who served with XV later attained a higher rank in the post-war RAF, including Lord Elworthy, GCB, CBE, DSO, MVO, DFC, AFC, MA (1935), who became Marshal of the Royal Air Force. The squadron also fostered four air chief marshals, four air vice-marshals, and eight air commodores.

A number of members of aircrew who trained or served with XV Squadron were later awarded decorations for courage or acts of outstanding bravery with other squadrons, including four recipients of the Victoria Cross: Second Lieutenant William Barker, who trained with XV Squadron in July 1916 and flew BE.2cs in France; Sergeant Thomas Gray who served as a Leading Aircraftman during the pre-war years 1933–36; Air Commodore Hughie Edwards who, in 1936, flew Hawker Hinds at Abingdon; and Group Captain Leonard Trent, who was serving with XV Squadron the day war was declared, and saw action with XV during the Battle of France.

1

Three Times Fifteen: Air Vice-Marshal Stewart 'Paddy' Menaul

Stewart Menaul, who was born in Northern Ireland on 17 July 1917, was to receive the benefit of a peacetime training when he was accepted as an apprentice with No. 2 School of Technical Training, RAF Cranwell, in 1931. Three years later, in 1934, he was awarded the Hyde-Thomson Memorial Prize—a prize for non-commissioned officers who excelled in wireless telegraphy examinations. The following year, Flight Cadet Menaul was posted to 'C' Flight, RAF College, and a further year later was promoted to the rank of flight cadet sergeant.

On leaving, Cranwell Paddy was posted to 19 (Fighter) Squadron based at RAF Duxford, Cambridgeshire. The posting was probably one of the shortest on record and brought forth a home truth as the young airman commented:

> When I left Cranwell I was sent to 19 Squadron at Duxford. I reported for duty, but before I had time to unpack my kit I received a telegraph directing me to XV Squadron based at Abingdon. I duly made my way to the Oxfordshire base where I was welcomed by Flying Officer 'Sam' Elworthy, the 'A' Flight Commander, who later became a group officer and personal assistant to the AOC-in-C; he retired from the RAF as Marshal of the Royal Air Force, The Lord Elworthy, KG, GCB, CBE, DSO, LVO, AFC, MA. At that time XV Squadron was flying Hawker Hind aircraft, which I flew two or three times during the first couple of weeks I was there. I had only been at Abingdon about a month, and was just getting to know the area, when I received a telegram instructing me and another officer to report to 21 Squadron, at Lympne, Kent. With all this changing about I suddenly realised the truth in the old RAF cliché, why bugger about by yourself when you can join the RAF and be buggered about by experts.

With the posting came a promotion to a commission in the rank of pilot officer. Another bonus for Paddy was the fact that, like XV Squadron, No. 21

also flew Hawker Hind aircraft so he did not have to worry about converting to a new type. Training took place at a leisurely pace and the location of the airfield had, in those closing years of peace, a distinct advantage as Paddy remembered with nostalgia:

> Lympne was a marvellous place. The Cinque Ports Flying Club was based on the airfield and I, along with another pilot from the Squadron, would hire a de Havilland Puss Moth aeroplane and fly, with two young ladies, to Le Touquet for the weekend. The whole damn thing would cost ten shillings [approximately £29 in 2018], including the fuel for the aircraft.

During August 1938, 21 Squadron moved to Eastchurch on the Isle of Sheppey, converting to Bristol Blenheim Mk I twin-engined bombers at the same time. Seven months later, in March 1939, a further move was made, this time to a new base located at Watton in Norfolk. No. 21 Squadron was still at RAF Watton in September that same year when Neville Chamberlain, the Prime Minister of the day, made his now famous speech to the nation, declaring that Britain was at war with Germany. Initially, the squadron was employed in photographing enemy airfields, but its main task was anti-shipping operations in the English Channel and the North Sea. Some targets on the continent were also attacked. Commenting on those raids, Paddy Menaul remembered:

> Those first attacks, during the early part of the war on places like Kiel, were absolutely suicidal. Some of the boys almost blew themselves up with their own bombs, going in at low level. Furthermore the Blenheim aircraft we flew were slow, lacked proper armament and were totally unsuitable. They were hacked down like butterflies by the Messerschmitt Bf 109s.

The qualities of his leadership soon showed through and Paddy was appointed to a higher rank. By the time he was posted from 21 Squadron, during the summer of 1940, he was an acting squadron leader. His association with XV Squadron, which was now based at Wyton and had also converted to Blenheim Bombers, was resumed later in the year when he was posted there in early September.

The first operational sortie he carried out with XV Sqn occurred on the evening of 22 September, when ten aircraft were detailed to attack a new tidal basin and dock facilities at Ostend. The attacking force was led away from Wyton by Pilot Officer Robert Megginson, who was piloting Blenheim bomber L8800. One by one, the other aircraft raced across the airfield until the last Blenheim, T2227, piloted by Paddy, lifted gently into the air.

Having arrived over the target unscathed, Robert Megginson carried out a shallow diving attack on the new tidal harbour. He was unable to observe the results, unlike Paddy whose bombs were seen to start large fires after he had made a high-level attack. On this raid, both flak and enemy fighters were conspicuous by their absence, enabling all XV Squadron aircraft to return safely to base.

Two nights later, the squadron dispatched nine aircraft to attack the docks at Le Havre. Paddy was first away, again flying T2227. Over the target, the weather was clear with 2/10th cloud at 10,000 feet. Paddy Menaul executed a high-level attack on the docks but, on this occasion, his ability to observe the results was interrupted by the approach of two enemy fighters. The fighters, which according to the Blenheim pilot seemed to signal their approach by having their landing lights on, were not prepared for the swift reaction of the Blenheim aircraft; the latter quickly and easily evaded the enemy's intended attack. Likewise, the flak defences put up a weak barrage, which did little to deter the attackers. By comparison, four nights later on 26 September, the enemy flak positions defending Boulogne harbour put up a heavy and accurate barrage of steel, which the Blenheim crews found more worrying. Six aircraft from XV Squadron were detailed for the attack, which took a similar pattern as previous raids, with Paddy leading the operation and making a high-level attack. Searchlights assisted the German flak batteries by scanning the night sky, weaving back and forth in an endeavour to latch on to a bomber. For one heart-stopping moment, Paddy's aircraft was caught by a single beam but, by throwing the aircraft into a skilful evasive manoeuvre, he managed to escape from the blinding ray.

An identical raid, utilising the same number of aircraft, was carried out against the same target on 7 October. Again, the flak barrage was heavy but the German gunners' efforts were in vain and all the aircraft returned safely.

Three nights later, on 10–11 October, XV Squadron assisted the Royal Navy in a combined operation against Cherbourg. The squadron detailed twelve aircraft for the operation, one of which did not take off; of the remaining eleven aircraft, nine were detailed to bomb the town and docks in an effort to create a diversion which would allow HMS *Revenge* to get within range. The bombs would hopefully start fires which in turn would give the navy gunners an aiming point. The two remaining aircraft, piloted by Wing Commander Joe Cox, OC XV Squadron, and Paddy Menaul, were to bomb any shore batteries, which endeavoured to return the Navy's fire.

A large fire was started, as planned, by the exploding bombs in the main target area, on which the Royal Navy did not hesitate to capitalise. The German shore batteries opened fire in retaliation, which was the cue Joe Cox and Paddy had been waiting for. Wing Commander Cox swung into the attack and unleashed his bombload on some gun emplacements, quickly followed by Paddy who released his first stick of bombs on the same position, adding to the intensity of the fires already burning. Although the second stick of bombs was seen to explode in the area of the docks, unfortunately, the results were not observed due to the two RAF pilots directing their attention to, for them, a more important matter, as Paddy remembered:

> I well remember flying over Cherbourg whilst the Navy were bombarding it. It was quite a remarkable performance. Joe Cox and I were supposed to cruise around dropping flares and bombs on the gun emplacements below, whilst the Navy pumped shells into the town. I considered this a very unhealthy pastime. Keeping one eye on the instruments and the other on what was going on around me, Joe Cox and I circled separately over the target area; at one point we bloody nearly collided head-on, but saw each other just in time.

Hauling back on the control column and kicking the rudder bar at the same time, Paddy hauled the Blenheim out of its path to destruction. Joe Cox obviously took the same course of action and the two aircraft skimmed past each other, a hair's breadth from disaster:

> It was remarkable that we didn't collide. Fortunately too, we didn't turn in the same direction; if we had the aircraft would most certainly have met! On the way home my wireless operator tuned his set into the BBC wavelength and picked up a dance band playing one of the popular compositions of the day, a number entitled, 'Fools rush in where angels fear to tread'. When I got back to Wyton, I told Joe Cox, stating that the title of the tune could not have been more appropriate.

The operation proved a great success and the Royal Navy, by way of thanks, commented on the excellent co-operation it received from the RAF, thus enabling the raid to be carried out according to plan.

The last major operation carried out by XV Squadron before it relinquished its Blenheim bombers, occurred on 29 October 1940, when seven aircraft were detailed for an attack against a fuel plant near Hamburg; take-off time for the raid was set at 6.15 a.m. The flight out was undertaken without incident with little or no cloud, but on arrival over the Hamburg area, the target could not be located due to severe ground haze. Even though flares were dropped to assist the bombing, a decision was taken to abort the attack on the primary target and attack other installations such as searchlight batteries, harbours and docks. The order to abort having been issued, Paddy Menaul wasted no time in looking for a suitable alternative on which to unleash his bombload; he found the ideal target in a troublesome searchlight battery in the Ruhr area.

On 1 November, both XV Squadron and the RAF airfield at Wyton, which had been part of 2 Group Bomber Command, were transferred to 3 Group. At the same time, the squadron converted to Vickers Wellington Mk Ic bombers. The conversion period, which involved taking on new, larger, more powerful twin-engined bombers, also necessitated the training of existing and new squadron members to fly as five-man crews, instead of the three-man crew they had with the Blenheim aircraft. The whole of November, together with the first two weeks of December, was given over to the conversion programme.

The new aircraft had the distinct advantage over its predecessor of having rotating front and rear Frazer-Nash turrets. Another advantage came with the two additional crew members who flew, respectively, as second pilot and rear gunner; the front turret position was operated by the observer as an extra duty.

With the increase in numbers of aircrew, there were many new faces to be seen at Wyton at the end of 1940. On 14 December, another new face arrived when Wing Commander Herbert Dale was appointed to take command of the squadron, which was declared ready for operations.

On the night of 16 December, Paddy's crew and three other crews were placed at readiness to attack Boulogne, but the attack was cancelled due to the weather. The weather during the third week of December continued to preclude the squadron from participating in any operations. Eventually, on the night of 20 December, one aircraft managed to take off on an operational sortie in which the crew bombed a petrol dump in Antwerp. Originally, four crews had been detailed for the attack but, at the last minute, three of the aircraft were grounded for modifications to the flaps; one of the grounded machines being that assigned to Paddy.

Two days after Christmas, Paddy took off, accompanied by four other aircraft, for an attack against the docks at Le Havre. Piloting Wellington bomber R1280, he struggled through inclement weather conditions, hoping the 10/10th cloud would break up by the time they reached the target. Although the conditions remained hopeless, searchlights scanned the clouds and gun batteries sent up the familiar barrage of flak. The searchlight beams, giving an indication as to their location on the ground, allowed Paddy and two other crews to bomb the batteries estimated positions, while one crew bombed Saint-Inglevert, in Pas-de-Calais; the final crew took their bombload home.

With the New Year came a change in the weather conditions. On 1 January 1941, the cloud that had been hanging around during the day began to dissipate as the evening wore on. The change enabled 141 aircraft of Bomber Command to carry out a highly successful raid against Bremen that night. XV Squadron detailed five aircraft to participate in the operation, their allotted target being the docks. Paddy Menaul, piloting Wellington bomber R1280, took off at 4.45 p.m. closely followed in turn by Pilot Officer Robert Gilmore, Pilot Officer Cuthbert Raymond, Flying Officer James Manahan, and Pilot Officer Leonard Giles.

Visibility over the target was excellent, although there had been light haze at the start of the attack. The target was identified and successfully bombed by all crews, with the exception of Pilot Officer Raymond whose bombs blasted the railway junction at Lesum, to the north-north-west of Bremen. For the part he played in this attack, Squadron Leader Menaul received a mention in dispatches. Although the ground defences responded to the attack, all the participating aircraft returned; four, however, were known to have crashed on reaching England. Two of the four aircraft, operated by 301 (Polish) Squadron, were shot down by German intruder aircraft, with the loss of twelve members of aircrew, while one aircraft from 50 Squadron and one from 78 Squadron, also crashed with the loss of one crew member from the latter aircraft.

Over the following few weeks, the squadron detailed crews to participate in a number of scheduled operations, but Paddy's name did not appear on any of the battle orders; he explained why this was:

> As a flight commander my name was not on the battle order every night, unlike some crews. Due to certain commitments associated with the position of flight commander, one's operational tour took longer to complete.

A full twelve days were to pass before Paddy flew operationally again. On the night of 16 January, he led eight aircraft on an attack against Wilhelmshaven, taking off from RAF Wyton at 5.30 p.m.; their allotted target was the railway marshalling yards. Although the weather was recorded as perfect, Pilot Officer Dove was forced to return to base his aircraft having endured severe icing while flying in heavy cloud. The remaining seven Wellington bombers flew on and carried out a successful attack, despite the numerous searchlights and heavy barrage of anti-aircraft fire. The cold beams of light swept back and forth across the night sky, while the flak threw up heavy barrages of hot steel in the form of bursting shells. Regardless of the action going on all around them, the bombers continued with their allotted task, dropping mixed loads of 500-lb high-explosive and incendiary bombs. The returning crews later reported seeing numerous explosions and large fires burning in the target area. All aircraft returned safely to base, including that of Pilot Officer Whittet, who had been detailed to attack Emden that same night.

The continual strain of operational flying was occasionally broken by an evening of drinking, dancing, or sometimes both, when operational and other duties permitted, as Paddy recalled:

> When the Squadron was stood down we would jump into a car or van and tear off in search of some amusement. Cambridge was, of course, a favourite place, especially at weekends, because there was an officers' club there. The only thing that really spoilt our enjoyment on these occasions was a ghastly chap who

> insisted we wear our gas mask in the action position. One Sunday afternoon he came into the club while we were dancing, and started 'cutting up rough'! Imagine trying to dance with a girl with this bloody box between you, especially if she was big-bosomed. We were thoroughly brassed-off with this individual and decided to get our own back. The following weekend he was found in the local drain culvert. He wasn't hurt but he was certainly wet; that experience certainly put an end to his jaunts into the officers' club. Nobody liked him and he really was an objectionable sod. We all felt he could be more usefully employed, especially after we had been on 'ops' the night before and wanted some relaxation.

Returning to operations on the night of 7 February, Paddy participated in an attack against Boulogne harbour for which eight crews were briefed, with Wing Commander Herbert Dale named as leading the assault. The outward flight went without incident, but when the attacking force approached the target area all hell broke loose. Paddy saw three large explosions as his bombs exploded with force across the gates of Dock No. 4 with fires starting as his incendiary bombs fell in the same area. Having unleashed his bombload, instead of turning for home, he pushed forward on the control column of Wellington bomber R1280, and dived to an altitude of 2,000 feet towards two searchlights at Cap Gris Nez, in order that his gunners could hopefully extinguish them with machine gun fire.

While Paddy was trying to distract the searchlight batteries, Wing Commander Dale, piloting Wellington T2624, remained at a high level and bombed from 10,700 feet. The latter saw his bombs detonate along the western edge of the dock starting a dozen or so fires, one of which rapidly developed and could be seen from many miles away.

The flak continued to arc up into the sky as the remaining crews of XV Squadron added to the conflagration below. Pilot Officer Dove's aircraft, T2847, was fitted with both a camera and a 4.5-lb photographic flash in its bomb bay, this enabled the squadron to make its first attempt at night photography; the results of this were, unfortunately, not recorded.

Three nights later, on 10 February, a total of 220 aircraft, including nine Wellington bombers from XV Squadron, were detailed for an attack against Hanover, but not all of them were to return. When the first crews arrived over the target the sky was clear, but very quickly, 9/10th cloud made observation very difficult. Paddy dropped his bombs from a height of 13,000 feet, but the intruding cloud made observation very difficult. Seemingly, as if by way of retaliation, a flak shell penetrated the cloud and exploded very close to Sergeant Fougere's aircraft. Although holed by hot metal fragments the Wellington Bomber remained airworthy and landed safely at Wyton. Sergeant Garrioch and his crew were not so lucky; having sent a 'task completed' signal at 9.35 p.m., he and his crew were not heard from again. It later transpired that William Garrioch survived being shot down by *Hauptmann* Walter Ehle and, along with four other members of his crew, was taken as a prisoner of war. Unfortunately, Sergeant Glyndwr Reardon, the rear gunner, was trapped in his turret and was lost along with the aircraft. A total of four Bomber Command aircraft were lost that night, together with a further three which were shot down by German intruder night fighters over England.

On the night of 15–16 February, Bomber Command ordered an attack against the Holten oil plant at Sterkade, for which XV Squadron detailed ten crews. Included on the battle order were the names of Paddy Menaul and his crew. Observation over the target was hampered by both ground haze and the glare of numerous searchlights penetrating through the haze. Paddy released his bombload in two sticks, from an altitude of 12,000 feet, and saw them explode in the target area. As Wing Commander Dale released his bombload, he was informed by his rear gunner that they were being followed by an unidentified twin-engined aircraft. The rear gunner fired a warning burst and the suspect aircraft peeled off to the starboard side and dived away without making any form of attack. Having unleashed his bombs on a concentration of searchlights between 2 and 3 miles to the north-west of the target, Sergeant Fougere was followed by a formation of five aircraft, which he estimated were 600 yards astern. One aircraft broke away from the formation and closed up to a range of approximately 200 yards. Deciding discretion was the better part of valour, Sergeant Fougere took evasive action and all the unidentified aircraft were lost to view without a shot being fired by either side.

During the period of time that Paddy had been with XV Squadron, he had made a number of friends—two in particular were Cuthbert Raymond and Bob Gilmour. The trio was, however, split up when the latter was posted to No. 20 Operational Training Unit, based at RAF Lossiemouth, on 21 February.

The night of Monday 24 February, Paddy took part in his last attack for that month, when he was detailed to join seven other XV Squadron crews for an attack on a German *Admiral Hipper*-class cruiser berthed at Brest. Brest was a dangerous target with no less than fifty searchlights reportedly in the area. Attached to the searchlight concentration were batteries of both heavy and light flak, which proved fairly accurate. As predicted, when the Wellington bombers flew in over the target area flak burst all around them, while searchlights scanned back and forth across the night sky. Paddy released his bombs from a height of 10,000 feet and saw them burst in an area adjacent to the dock where the German warship was berthed; photographs taken the following day indicated that the cruiser had received two direct hits.

During the first two weeks of March, Paddy made three operational sorties to Germany. The first attack was on the first night of the new month, when a total of eight crews were detailed for a sortie against Cologne. The second

Above: A flight of six XV Squadron Hawker Hind bomber aircraft photographed at RAF Abingdon, Oxfordshire, in March or April 1937. (*Author's collection*)

Below: Wing Commander Joe Cox buckles on his parachute, while Sergeant Trehearne climbs up into the turret of Bristol Blenheim R3594.
(*Author's collection, via Patricia Banks neé Cox*)

Above left: Vickers Wellington Mk Ic bomber T2961 at RAF Wyton in March–April 1941. This aircraft was adopted by Sqn Ldr Paddy Menaul as his personal aircraft. (*Author's collection*)

Above right: Wing Commander Paddy Menaul, DFC, assumed command of XV Squadron on 7 December 1942. (*Author's collection*)

Below: Photographed under the forward fuselage of Wellington bomber T2961 are (*left to right*) Fg Off. L. Downes; Sgt H. Cossar, AG; Sqn Ldr Paddy Menaul, pilot; Flt Lt Archie Cochrane, observer; and Sgt John Warner, wireless operator/air gunner. (*Author's collection*)

raid was against Kiel on the night of the 11th, and the third attack was two nights later when the crews of XV Squadron raided Hamburg. For the latter operation, the squadron detailed eight crews who joined a total force of 139 Bomber Command aircraft. Conditions for bombing were good, with a full moon and clear visibility, but were not so good with respect to evading night fighters. Some crews encountered thin layers of cloud at 20,000 feet, against which their aircraft were silhouetted.

When the crews from XV arrived over the target, they saw many fires burning, both in the north and eastern areas of the city. As was always the case, searchlights were in evidence weaving back and forth across the sky. One picked out Wing Commander Dale's aircraft, but this experienced pilot managed to evade the probing beams with skilful evasive tactics, before the exploding shells from the gun batteries opened fire. Unfortunately, Paddy, who was on his bombing run, ran the gauntlet of the exploding steel from both the heavy and light flak, the former being very intense. His bombs cascaded down to the conflagration below and exploded 600 yards north-east of the northern end of Außenalster, a large lake. At that precise moment, the tenacious beam of a searchlight engulfed his aircraft and shrapnel burst all around the Wellington bomber, puncturing the fabric skin in several places. Like the squadron boss, Paddy was also an experienced bomber pilot and he too managed to evade the beam by skilful and evasive flying. Another pilot, flying in the same section of sky, was not so lucky when the same beam locked on to his aircraft. The pilot threw his bomber into violent turns, but the beam stayed with him, focussing the flak which exploded around him. As Paddy watched, he saw the aircraft slowly peel over into a dive and plunge vertically earthwards, of this incident he commented: 'Hamburg was always fierce for action you could see the flak exploding just off your wingtip. Sometimes you could see it hitting an aircraft below or off to one side of you'.

Although all of XV Squadron's aircraft had been caught in the searchlight beams and six of the eight Wellington bombers had been hit by shrapnel, the raid itself was deemed a success with damage inflicted on the Blohm and Voss shipyard, a timber yard, the main fire station, and many other buildings.

Squadron Leader Menaul flew on only two other operations during March, the first on the night of the 15th when the squadron attacked the submarine base at Lorient, and the second two weeks later when he participated in an attack against Bremen. April was almost a repeat of the previous month with Paddy flying only two operational sorties, both against Kiel on the nights of the 7th and the 15th. Although the searchlights and flak were very much in evidence, Paddy and his crew returned to RAF Wyton unscathed on both occasions.

It was during this same period that XV Squadron began converting to Short Stirling bombers. The first of these four-engined bombers to reach the squadron was a dual-control machine from 7 Squadron, on 10 April. The following day, Flight Lieutenant Best arrived from RAF Oakington, where No. 7 was based, to give instruction to the crews in handling the huge aircraft.

The Stirling, as it was a new breed of bomber aircraft with more flying controls and defensive armaments, called for the addition of two extra crew members; these were a flight engineer, who would assist the pilot with flying the aircraft and managing its fuel consumption, and an air gunner, who would man the mid-upper turret.

During the conversion period, on 16 April, a signal was received immediately ordering seven of XV Squadron's crews, along with their aircraft, to Malta where experienced Wellington bomber crews were urgently required. The selected crews arrived on the Mediterranean island the following day. The change in the squadron's personnel strength did not hamper the conversion programme and, with the help of Paddy Menaul and Squadron Leader Morris, Wing Commander Dale declared the squadron ready for operational duties by the end of the month.

The allotted target for XV Squadron's first operation on the night of 30 April came as a shock to the participating crews when they saw the battle order for that night; instead of being broken-in gently, they were heading for the 'Big City': Berlin. Unfortunately, it was somewhat of an inauspicious start for various reasons.

Although a total of ten Stirling bombers were detailed for the attack only three managed to reach the target which was, unfortunately, cloud-covered, thus preventing accurate bombing. Among the aircraft which did not reach Berlin was Stirling N6015, piloted by Paddy. Squadron Leader Menaul's problem was not a navigational one but one of mechanical failure. On the outward journey, both starboard engines ceased to function, thus forcing him to jettison his bombload into the sea 5 miles north of Borkum before turning for home. On the return flight, the outer starboard engine picked up, enabling the pilot to keep better control of the aircraft, even though the motor was not giving full power. Eventually, after a fraught and tiring flight, he landed safely at RAF Wyton. Paddy did not hold a high opinion of the new four-engined bomber, as he recalled:

> The Wellington bomber was slow and vulnerable; its successor the Stirling was probably worse. It was an aeroplane designed by a committee and built from bits of other aircraft. It had part of the wings of a flying boat, a ghastly gangling undercarriage and the first of the exactor throttle controls which were inherited from the Empire flying boats; the latter were a constant cause for concern as they would not stay in place but would move to the 'closed throttle' position of their own accord. Another problem was its climb rate, the bloody thing just refused to climb, but my method of getting the aircraft to climb was to take her up, which took an awful long time, then lower the nose and go into a short descent. Having gained speed in the dive I would open the throttles wide and then pull up again.

> The momentum gained in the dive could give as much as a thousand feet extra height. Some of today's military aircraft [during the 1980s] use a similar method to gain extra altitude.

At this period of time, XV Squadron was fully operational with Stirling bombers, but there was still one Wellington bomber, R1498, recorded as being on squadron strength. This machine, flown by Sergeant Leggate and his crew, undertook an attack against Rotterdam on 2 May. The operation was successfully completed and the machine returned safely to Wyton. Four nights later, on the 6th, Sergeant Leggate and his crew were detailed to fly this same aircraft on another raid, this time against Hamburg, accompanied by three Stirling bombers. On this occasion, due to adverse weather conditions, Sergeant Leggate failed to locate the target and returned to RAF Wyton with his bombload. This raid brought XV Squadron's association with the Wellington bomber to a formal conclusion.

Paddy, flying on this same raid, also experienced problems with the weather. For a brief moment, through breaks in the cloud, he saw one or two fires burning which he took to be dummies. Suddenly, flak came up through the cloud and exploded in the vicinity of his aircraft. Without further ado, he ordered the release of the bombload, which rained down to detonate below the clouds. Although the crew were not able to see the explosions, the rear gunner reported the reflection of a terrific glow on the clouds after the first stick had exploded.

A further four nights later, Wing Commander Dale was lost during a raid against Berlin, his aircraft having been subjected to eight separate fighter attacks. Dale's replacement, as officer commanding XV Squadron, Wing Commander Patrick Ogilvie, arrived at Wyton a week later, on 16 May 1941.

Flight Commander Duties prevented Paddy from undertaking any further operational sorties until 27 May, when he participated in an attack on the German cruiser *Prinz Eugen*. Although the search covered a wide area, no trace of the ship could be found and the bombers returned to base.

On the night of 10 June, Paddy was detailed for an attack against Düsseldorf, but encountering further problems with the weather, turned his attention to the secondary target at Duisburg, where he was later able to report bombing a large building in the dock area which instantly burst into flame. The operation was a relatively quiet one, but sorties were not always like that, as Paddy commented:

> The Ruhr was one of the most disliked target areas. It was always fierce for action. You were being shot at from the moment you crossed the Dutch coast on the way in, until you crossed the coast again on the way out. It was a never ending barrage of bursting flak and sweeping searchlights. The Ruhr really was most heavily defended.

In mid-June, a number of the operational sorties Paddy participated in were hampered by either thick cloud or ground haze. Having been recalled on 13 June from an attack against the German pocket battleship *Lützow* due to weather conditions, later that same day Paddy and the three other crews flying with him found the target, three German cruisers in the French port of Brest, obscured by 10/10th cloud. Initially flying at 20,000 feet, he took the formation down to 13,000 feet in the hope of getting a clearer view, but then found the target concealed by ground haze. Not wishing to return to Wyton with his bombload, Paddy dropped his bombs in what he thought was the appropriate location, taking a photograph as he did so. Unfortunately, the image later showed that the first stick of bombs fell into the sea just off Lanvéoc, where there was a seaplane base, while the second stick of bombs fell inshore at Anse de Morgat.

On the night of 20 June, Paddy led seven aircraft on an attack against Kiel. The weather over the target was much the same as it had been the week before, with heavy and persistent cloud, but this did not prevent the enemy defences from opening up. An intense barrage of heavy anti-aircraft fire penetrated the cloud and exploded among the bombers. To add to their woes, German twin-engined fighters entered the fray, one such aircraft turning in to attack Stirling N6021, piloted by Sergeant Frank Needham, but fortunately, Needham's rear gunner was alert and quickly opened fire at the enemy machine. The latter withdrew to search for a new victim which it found in the shape of Stirling bomber N6015, piloted by Paddy Menaul. Using the same tactics, the fighter endeavoured to creep up behind the bomber, but to the German's misfortune, Paddy's rear gunner, Pilot Officer Jack Bushell, DFM, was also alert and saw the fighter approaching. Opening fire, Bushell claimed hits on the fighter, which was last seen diving earthwards with flames trailing fiercely from one engine.

Earlier, back in January 1941, Air Marshal Sir William Sholto Douglas, C-in-C Fighter Command instigated the idea of undertaking daylight raids, carried out by a small number of bomber aircraft that would be escorted by a large number of fighters, to targets within the escorts fuel range. The object of this form of attack, named 'Circus' operations, was to entice Luftwaffe fighters into the air so that the RAF fighters could attack and hopefully destroy the former. When this idea was first put into practice, vulnerable, twin-engined Bristol Blenheim bombers were used as the 'bait'.

On Saturday 5 July, Paddy was detailed to lead Flight Lieutenant Gilmour and Flying Officer Thompson on Circus No. 33 to the Fives-Lille steelworks, France. The day was bright with good visibility and Paddy had no difficulty joining up with the close fighter escort from Northolt and Kenley. The Biggin Hill and Tangmere Wings, led by Wing Commander 'Sailor' Malan, were flying as target support. The latter group arrived over Lille ahead of the bombers as planned and circled the target until the Stirling bombers arrived. Messerschmitt Bf 109s could be seen some distance away, forming into small groups, getting ready to attack.

Paddy Menaul led Gilmour and Taylor over the French coast at Dunkirk, where the enemy flak batteries burst into life, peppering the blue sky with shrapnel. Paddy commented: 'It seemed strange to see the flak bursts in daylight; at night one mostly only felt them'.

As the bombers approached the target area, the German fighters dived into the attack, a manoeuvre Malan was waiting for. He chased after two Bf 109 fighters, selected one of them as a target and opened fire from a range of 300 yards. Both cannon and machine gun fire raked the Messerschmitt's fuselage before it dived away.

The German fighters endeavoured to draw the close escort Spitfires away from the bombers by diving between the latter. While 610 Squadron stayed in position to protect the bombers, 312 Squadron, a Czechoslovakian unit, gave chase and claimed a Bf 109.

Paddy declared the first bombing attempt a dummy run, due to the 5/10th cloud over the target forcing the three Stirling bombers to run the gauntlet of intense flak for a second time. With exploding steel peppering the sky around them, the three XV Squadron aircraft dropped their respective loads, fifteen 1,000-lb and thirty 500-lb bombs, on the factory below. The steelworks shook as the bombs detonated on impact on the target, which was left severely damaged. The following afternoon, XV Squadron detailed six Stirling bombers to attack the same target in two formations. Paddy led the first three aircraft, while Squadron Leader Piper, who had been posted to the squadron three weeks earlier, led the second formation; on this occasion, Wing Commander Malan's Spitfires provided the close escort.

As the main force, flying at 20,000 feet, approached Lille, Malan spotted a number of Bf 109s. In anticipation of the ensuing dogfights, he ordered his flight of Spitfires into two sections, but in the heat of battle, all four Spitfires got separated. While Malan extricated himself from the *mêlée* and went on to shoot down a Bf 109, the bombers, having descended to an altitude of 14,000 feet, continued towards the target. The German fighters again dived down through the formation in an effort to destroy the bombers.

Sergeant Ward, Flight Lieutenant Gilmour's front gunner, got an enemy fighter in his sights and opened fire; strikes were seen to hit the machine which was later claimed as damaged. Although Sergeant Needham's aircraft was attacked from behind by a Bf 109, the rear gunner was unable to respond due to two of the escorting fighters being in his line of fire.

As the heavy barrage of flak spewed hot metal around the sky trying to destroy the bombers, twenty-four 1,000-lb and fifty-six 500-lb bombs whistled down and exploded on the steelworks, adding to the damage created the previous day. Although many direct hits were claimed, some bombs were known to have struck the adjacent railway marshalling yards.

Things were to get even hotter when, for the third day in a row, on 7 July, Paddy piloting Stirling bomber N3656 was to lead Flight Lieutenant Gilmour and Flying Officer Thompson on yet another raid on a daylight 'Circus' operation. On this occasion, their target was the Kuhlman Chemical Works at Chocques, west of Béthune, France. The lack of enemy fighter intervention was compensated for by the heavy and intense flak thrown up by the 88-mm artillery batteries below; it was a raid Paddy would remember:

> The one raid I distinctly remember was the one during which we got some good photographs. It was a daylight attack against the Kuhlman Chemical Works on 7 July 1941. There was flak bursting all over the place, as a series of pictures taken at the time show. In one of them you can see flak bursting around Bobby Gilmour's aircraft; he seemed to get more of it than I did, and some of it was pretty damn close. However, we hit the factory fair and square, and left it burning like hell. It was still burning when the results of our work were later photographed by a Spitfire.

Almost every one of the fifteen 1,000-lb and forty-two 500-lb high-explosive bombs dropped struck the target, creating huge clouds of smoke, dust, and debris.

The raid was such as success that the following day Paddy, and the other participating crew members, were all able to read about it in the newspapers. For his part in the attack, Squadron Leader Menaul was awarded a Distinguished Flying Cross, and with this raid being his thirty-second operational sortie, he was declared 'tour expired' and posted from XV Squadron to 3 Group Headquarters, on 19 July 1941.

During the period from July 1941 to the first week of December 1942, Paddy not only instructed novice pilots in the art of flying Stirling bombers at a conversion unit, he often flew with them and their crews on their first operational sorties; this work eventually earned him the award of the Air Force Cross.

On completion of his time at conversion unit, Paddy returned to operational flying; he explained how that came about:

> I was sitting in the 'ops' room one morning, early, about half-past-eight, when Air Vice-Marshal 'Jacky' Baldwin, the 3 Group AOC, strode into the room, after his early morning ride across Newmarket. He pointed his riding crop at me and told me I was going to take over a squadron and that was that.

On 7 December 1942, with a DFC ribbon displayed above the left breast pocket of his tunic, and a third full tape on the cuffs of both sleeves, Acting

Wing Commander Stewart Menaul, DFC, reported to RAF Station Bourn, Cambridgeshire, where he was to take command of XV Squadron. This was his third posting to the squadron, which was still equipped with Stirling bombers.

Ten days after his arrival, Paddy flew his first operational sortie, which was successfully carried out but almost came to grief at the very last moment. Seven aircraft had been detailed for mine-laying operations, two aircraft to the Friesian Islands and five to the Bay of Biscay. Paddy was flying with Squadron Leader Faulkner in Stirling BF356, which was one of the original Mk 1 aircraft. During the four-hour flight, the port outer engine cut out due to the failure of the exactor throttle. On the final approach to the airfield, in full landing configuration, Paddy found he was unable to throttle back. Without hesitation, he opened up the throttles with the intention of aborting and making another circuit, but as he did so the port inner engine also cut out. With the Stirling settling on the runway, Paddy throttled back, the aircraft continued to roll, overshot the end of the runway, collided with a tree and burst into flames; fortunately, only one injury was sustained.

On 14 January 1943, Paddy flew his second sortie, another mine-laying operation, but was forced to return early due to severe icing. He fared better the next night when he was able to complete an attack, along with six other XV Squadron aircraft, on the town and docks at Lorient. Three weeks later, on 7 February, he led a further attack against Lorient, when fifteen aircraft from the squadron joined a maximum effort raid. Despite the heavy German defences, a devastating attack was carried out, leaving many large fires burning. In retaliation, the flak accounted for the loss of seven RAF bombers, but all XV Squadron's aircraft returned safely to base. Following this raid, Paddy was engaged in making the necessary preparations for XV Squadron's proposed move to RAF Mildenhall, which was to reopen following renovations and the laying of three concrete runways.

The actual move to Mildenhall was made on 14 April with the assistance of two Airspeed Horsa gliders, which airlifted some of the personnel and ground equipment. The Stirling bombers were flown in by their crews who were then stood down and given twenty-four hours to settle into their new quarters, before commencing operations.

Paddy Menaul's long association with XV Squadron came to an end on 7 May 1943, when he was appointed to the rank of Acting Group Captain and posted to command RAF Station Bourn. His distinguished service to the Royal Air Force continued into the post-war years, the defence of his country ever present in his mind. He retired as Air Vice-Marshal Stewart Menaul, CB, CBE, DFC, AFC, MiD.

2

MacRobert's Reply: Squadron Leader Peter J. S. Boggis, DFC

The recommendation for the immediate award of one Distinguished Service Order, seven Distinguished Flying Crosses, and two Distinguished Flying Medals by the air officer-in-chief, Bomber Command to His Majesty King George VI read:

> On 18 December 1941, in daylight, a strong force of Stirling and Halifax bombers carried out a determined attack on the German warships *Gneisenau* and *Scharnhorst* at Brest. The operation was carried out in the face of extremely heavy and accurate anti-aircraft fire, and determined attacks by enemy fighters. Nevertheless, the aircrews engaged pressed home their attacks to the utmost and succeeded in scoring direct hits on their objectives. Many enemy aircraft were shot down. The success of the operation, which demanded the highest degree of skill and courage, reflects the greatest credit on the efforts of the following officers and airmen who participated in various capacities as leaders and members of aircraft crews.

Among the ten men recommended for an award were four members of XV Squadron, these being Wing Commander Patrick Ogilvie, RAF; Flying Officer Peter Boggis, RAF; Flying Officer Cyril Verneux, RAFO and Flight Sergeant Richard Hardy, RAF.

For Squadron Leader Boggis, this attack, his fifty-fifth operational sortie, marked the completion of his second operational tour with Bomber Command, but not the end of his service career. Peter's association with the Royal Air Force began when he was accepted for a Short Service Commission in June 1937. By the time he was posted to XV Squadron, Peter was already an experienced bomber pilot. He held the rank of pilot officer and had completed a tour of operations with 38 Squadron at RAF Marham, Norfolk, flying

Vickers Wellingtons—twin-engined bombers. He had also completed a spell as an instructor at 11 Operational Training Unit based at RAF Bassingbourn, Cambridgeshire, and well remembers his arrival at Wyton:

> When I joined XV Squadron on 6 June 1941, there were only two Stirling bomber squadrons in service with the RAF, one at RAF Oakington [7 Sqn] and the other being XV at Wyton. Naturally, there was rivalry and friendship between the two and, unlike later in the war, when aircraft went missing there was sorrow at both stations. The odds were that the crew would be known to both squadrons; this was especially so with me, because prior to going to XV I had been an instructor at a Wellington bomber conversion unit and many of the pilots that passed through there went on to fly Stirling bombers.

Apart from feeling pleased about returning to flying on an operational basis, Peter was also pleased with his new surroundings and found the base well-situated:

> Wyton was a nice station with good pubs in the area of St Ives, and Huntingdon and Cambridge within striking distance. Cambridge in those days was a bright city and the Mecca for all aircrew within a reasonable travelling radius. Every 'night out' was a virtual reunion with our chums. Wyton was also fairly easy to find from the air because of two parallel canals that ran from the Wash almost to Huntingdon—a great asset when returning from operations in claggy weather. These canals were also part of our official low flying area. Looking back, we must have frightened no end of farmers, locals and cattle with our Stirlings roaring over their heads only a few feet up!

Apart from the main airfield, Wyton also operated from satellite airfields:

> We often operated from a satellite airfield, for dispersal and training, at Alconbury on the Great North Road. For a few weeks in September 1941 the Squadron also operate from Warboys whilst runways were being constructed at Alconbury. We used to be a bit apprehensive about flying from these satellite airfields because with all the activity going on, air tests, arming the aircraft with bombs and ammunition, and the general coming and going of transport etc., everybody in the vicinity knew 'ops' were on that night. It was a standing joke that if you wanted to know the target for that night the barmaids in the local pubs would tell you. It was not an uncommon sight to see cars stopped on the main road whilst Stirlings were being bombed up.

Peter also had mixed feelings about the massive, four-engined bomber he used to fly:

> My memory of the Stirling aircraft was of a huge aeroplane with the pilot's cockpit a long way off the ground due to the massive undercarriage that created a lot of drag, especially when taking off with a full load of bombs and fuel on board. It had a very poor heating system and an operating height that compared very unfavourably with that of Halifaxes or Lancasters. However, once airborne, with the undercarriage safely retracted, I found the aircraft pleasant to fly and quite manoeuvrable; fortunately, it could also take a lot of punishment from flak.

This was the picture that presented itself to Pilot Officer Boggis as he was about to start his second tour of operations during the summer of 1941. His first operational sortie, during which he flew as second pilot with Flying Officer Campbell, took place on 20 June, when XV Squadron detailed seven aircraft and crews to identify and bomb the *Tirpitz* at Kiel. Although a total of 115 Bomber Command aircraft were detailed for the attack on the German battleship, due to thick cloud and ground haze, the target could not be located. However, the attacking crews unleashed their respective bombloads over and around the city itself. Anti-aircraft fire over the target was reported as heavy and although two of the squadron's aircraft were attacked by enemy fighters, all seven Stirlings returned to Wyton safely.

The first four days of July saw Peter taking part in a blind-approach training course, held at Wyton, but he was back with XV Squadron in order to participate in an attack against Frankfurt on 7 July. Four days later, on the 11th, three aircraft were detailed for a daylight attack against the Fives-Lille steelworks and the name of the recently promoted Flying Officer Boggis was recorded on the battle order. The two other crews listed to fly the same sortie, known as a 'Circus' operation, were those of Squadron Leader Tim Piper and Pilot Officer Leggate; the latter had, recently, been granted a commission.

A thunderstorm over that area of France precluded the trio from attacking the primary target, so they turned their attention to the secondary target at Hazebrouck, where two of the three sticks of bombs, which rained down on the marshalling yards and station, are recorded as achieving direct hits:

> We did a few daylight raids during the summer of 1941, usually three Stirlings with a very large fighter escort of Spitfires and Hurricanes. We did not appreciate the fact at the time, but in hindsight these raids were presumably part of the general plan to obtain air superiority, and the Stirlings were the bait! It was nice to see so many of our fighters around, and crossing the Channel one felt like the King of England with an escort of Life Guards. We flew in at 15,000 feet which must have been an easy height for the German flak, and on each raid our Stirlings came back with flak holes, though I am glad to say we had no casualties in men or aircraft. We would watch, with baited breath [*sic.*], as the German fighters attacked from above, diving down through the fighter escort and being

> pursued by Spitfires and Hurricanes as they passed through the formation. It was difficult to sort out who was who.

The daylight raids ('Circus' operations) continued until 25 July, when the squadron returned to night operations, the first of which was an attack against Berlin. Five crews were briefed for the operation, including that headed by Peter Boggis.

Inclement weather conditions during this period of July had been hampering operations, with thunderstorms, 10/10th cloud and poor visibility hindering the aircrews involved. However, on this particular night, the 25th, it was Peter's aircraft, W7429, which caused the problems. On the outward flight, faults developed in both the front and rear turrets leaving the pilot, who had no defensive armament, no option but to abort the mission and head for home. As the bomber flew over the German city of Münster, a battery of searchlights suddenly illuminated the darkness and criss-crossed the night sky in search of the lone intruder. Peter took the opportunity to lighten the weight of his aircraft and dropped the contents of the bomb bay, which amounted to five 1,000-lb and seven 500-lb bombs, on to the city below. The crew were relieved that they experienced no opposition from either fighter or flak on the way home.

Operations against targets in Germany continued throughout August and September with raids on Berlin, Essen, Frankfurt, Hamburg, and Karlsruhe, with Peter and his crew participating in a good many of them.

On Friday, 10 October 1941, an unusual and moving ceremony took place on the airfield at RAF Wyton, when a Stirling bomber was officially taken on charge by XV Squadron. Normally, there would not be any ceremonial procedures when an aircraft was taken on charge by a squadron, but what made this occasion unusual and moving was that this particular Stirling bomber was purchased and donated by a mother who had lost her three sons in fairly quick succession. The mother was Lady Rachel MacRobert, the widow of Sir Alexander MacRobert, the first Baronet of Cawnpore and Cromer, who had died on 22 June 1922. Sir Alasdair, the eldest son, who inherited the title, was killed in a flying accident near Luton in 1938. The baronetcy passed to Roderic and then in turn to his younger brother Iain. Sir Roderic and Sir Iain, who were both pilots, were both killed in action flying with the RAF during 1941. In memory of her sons, Lady MacRobert donated a sum of money with which to purchase four Hurricane fighters, three of which would bear the names of her sons and the remaining aircraft being named *The Lady*. This grieving mother also gave the sum of £25,000 for the purchase of a Stirling bomber which, in response to the Germans whom she blamed for the death of her sons, was to carry the MacRobert family crest and was to be named *MacRobert's Reply*.

The aircraft, a standard Mk 1 Stirling bomber, had been allotted to XV Squadron on 15 September. It carried the serial N6086 and the squadron identification code LS-F 'Freddie'. During the formal ceremony, which was filmed by the Crown Film Unit, Wing Commander Ogilvie formally handed over the aircraft to Flying Officer Boggis. With the aircraft came a letter signed by Lady MacRobert, the content of which wished the crew good luck and asked them to strike hard, sharp and straight. The letter went on to thank all those who had care of her '*Reply*' and to prepare the aircraft for its missions. After the ceremony, for the benefit of the film cameras and the press, the aircraft was put through an impressive flying display. Peter only made one comment made about the ceremony and the display: 'I don't know why I was chosen to fly *MacRobert's Reply*. As I understood it, Lady MacRobert wanted a Scotsman to fly the aircraft and I was born in Barnstaple, Devon'.

Having been nominated as captain of the new aircraft, Peter piloted his Stirling on her first operational sortie two days later, when they joined a formation of 151 other bombers heading for Nuremberg. By the time the XV Squadron aircraft arrived over the target area, a considerable number of fires were burning. Peter circled the target for thirty-five minutes before taking N6086 in on the bombing run. At 1.15 a.m., five 1,000-lb and seven 500-lb bombs tumbled out of the aircraft's bomb bay and fell on to the burning city 16,000 feet below. The crew watched as the shimmering orange and red carpet of flame below emitted clumps of black cloud as the bombs detonated and added to the carnage. With her baptism of fire above a hostile target complete, *MacRobert's Reply* returned safely to Wyton, where she landed at 3.50 a.m. the following morning.

The squadron paid a price for its night's work when one aircraft crashed on landing at Wyton and another failed to return, the latter having been shot down by a night fighter. The lost aircraft, Stirling N6047, crashed at Mariembourg, Belgium, with the loss of Pilot Officer Colbourne and his crew.

Two nights later, XV Squadron detailed four aircraft, including *MacRobert's Reply*, for another attack on Nuremberg, but on this occasion, the crews were not able to locate the primary target owing to inclement weather conditions. All eighty aircraft participating in the attack, including the four from XV Squadron, were hampered by 10/10th cloud and severe icing, but these conditions did not prevent the German ground defences from sweeping searchlight beams back and forth across the sky, while anti-aircraft shells burst in its all too familiar pattern. Peter decided to bomb the flak and searchlight batteries at Mannheim, as did Flying Officer Nicholson who was piloting Stirling N3646, while the third aircraft jettisoned its bombload due to intercom failure, and the fourth aircraft landed at Stradishall.

During the rest of October and early November 1941 Peter took *MacRobert's Reply* on operations to Bremen, Cologne, the Skoda Works at

Above left: Lady Rachel MacRobert, the American-born benefactor of the RAF, reflects on the loss of her sons, in this post-war photograph, in the grounds at Douneside, her Highland home. (*Author's collection*)

Above right: Flying Officer Peter Boggis wearing the white flying suit and his crew take a final look at the map before boarding the aircraft, in this staged publicity photograph. (*Author's collection*)

Below: Flying Officer Boggis (right) and Pilot Officer John Ryan (left), look down from the cockpit of Stirling bomber N6086, LS-F, named *MacRobert's Reply*. Pilot Officer King can be seen over Ryan's left shoulder. (*Author's collection*)

Flying Officer Peter Boggis (left) and Wing Commander Patrick Ogilvie, Officer Commanding, No. XV Squadron, photographed at RAF Wyton shortly after the announcement of the award of a DSO to Wg Cdr Ogilvie and a DFC to Fg Off. Boggis. (*Author's collection*)

Pilsen in Czechoslovakia, and Brest. Brest was selected as the target for the night of 23 November, when XV Squadron detailed five Stirling bombers to participate in a small-scale attack by a total of eleven bombers. On this occasion, Peter was to pilot Stirling bomber N6098, and he has reason to remember the flight:

> In those days we were instructed to take bombs home if we could not identify the target. However, on this trip I dropped a 2,000-lb bomb on the estimated position and decided to take the remainder home. On the return journey, I experienced trouble with one of the engines and decided to feather it; I was running low on petrol. Considering my situation, I suddenly remembered a fighter pilot I had met somewhere saying we could always land at Exeter in an emergency [Exeter was a night fighter station]. I gave them a call on the R/T and although there was a raid on at the time, the controllers in the tower assisted me in every way, including putting their searchlights into a cone so that I could home onto them. They also turned on the minimum number of landing lights when I was over-head, warning me that as soon as I had landed the lights would go off. I turned the Stirling onto finals and lowered her onto the runway, easing the brakes on as I felt the aircraft touch-down. As pre-warned, the runway lights were immediately switched off and the Stirling rolled to a halt in the dark. I shut down the engines and waited for the tractor which, I was previously told, would tow N6098 to a dispersal area. Fortunately, the airfield escaped the air raid, but the city took a lot of punishment.

The Stirling was grounded for three days while repairs to the defective engine and general servicing were carried out, but Peter did not mind. Having been born in Barnstaple, only 40 miles away, he knew Exeter fairly well and was able to show his crew some of the local scenery, including a pub near the airfield where they added their respective signatures to those already on the ceiling of the bar, before returning to Wyton.

On the night of 14–15 December, Bomber Command ordered another small-scale attack against the *Scharnhorst* and the *Gneisenau*, berthed at Brest. Twenty-two Handley Page Hampden bombers and six Stirling bombers were detailed for the raid, all six of the latter aircraft being from XV Squadron. Yet again, the operation was hampered by the elements with 10/10th cloud rising to 16,000 feet. Thunderstorms and severe icing added to the problems already being endured by the participating crews, thus forcing the attack to be abandoned; Peter recalled:

> I decreased height down to 12,000 feet over the French coast and was still in cloud. There was some ack-ack (anti-aircraft fire) activity, but not enough to bother us. I dropped four flares but was still unable to see anything. On the basis

> I must hit something I jettisoned one 2,000-lb bomb over the area and turned for home with the rest of the load still on board.

Three days later, on 18 December, another attempt was made to cripple or destroy the two German warships. A total of forty-seven aircraft, comprising eighteen Halifaxes, eighteen Stirlings and eleven Manchester bombers were detailed for the attack. XV Squadron provided nine of the Stirling bombers, which took off from RAF Wyton just before 10 a.m. led by Wing Commander Patrick Ogilvie. Once airborne, they formed themselves into three 'vee' formations and headed towards St Ives, near Wyton, where they were to rendezvous with 7 Squadron, who provided the remaining nine Stirling bombers. The two squadrons flew west towards Lundy Island where the Halifaxes and Manchester bombers from 10, 35, and 76 Squadrons were to join the formation for the flight south, over Land's End. During this leg of the flight out, the weather changed dramatically, then the cloud dissipated and presented a clear blue sky with bright sunshine and clear visibility.

As the bomber force approached the target, the enemy fighters pounced, with 7 Squadron taking the brunt of the initial attack. The German fighters, who had been warned of the raid by the incoming aircraft on their ground-based radar screens shot down two of 7 Squadron's aircraft and damaged many more, some of which crash-landed at their home base.

The raid had been planned so that each flight would be over the target at one-minute intervals, and XV Squadron was detailed to be the second wave. Each flight was to approach the target at 17,000 feet, dive down to 14,000 feet in order to release its bombs and climb back up to regain formation. The enemy fighters were determined this would not happen and peeled over to attack the bombers as they dived. The bombers pressed home their attack even though there was intense fighter and anti-aircraft opposition. Flak bursts peppered the sky in a continuous barrage of anti-aircraft fire. As each salvo exploded, the black smoke dissipated on the wind, as if to make room for the next barrage; the staccato rattle of machine gun fire was audible over the straining roar of aircraft engines as fighters and bombers twisted and turned in evasive manoeuvres around the sky. The whole action was punctured by the whistle of cascading bombs which rained down to explode, with forceful impact, on or near the target.

Most of the bombers were attacked by the fighters, including *MacRobert's Reply* which managed to escape the attention of three separate German fighters, one of which was later claimed as damaged. However, the German pilots were successful in their endeavours elsewhere in the *mêlée* and shot down two of XV Squadron's aircraft. Flight Lieutenant Gilbert Heathcote, piloting Stirling N3665, was reported to have crashed at Plouguerneau, approximately 14 miles north-west of Brest. Gilbert Heathcote, who was the son of Brigadier General Charles E. Heathcote, CB, CMG, DSO, was killed along with his crew. Likewise, Stirling bomber W7428, piloted by Flying Officer Gordon Bunce, was last seen over the sea with its port wing totally ablaze, while still fending off attacks by at least five Bf 109s.

In the confusion of diving aircraft, anti-aircraft fire, and black smoke rising up from the dock below, Peter became separated from the rest of the squadron, but, having completed his bombing run put the nose of *MacRobert's Reply* down and headed north out towards the Channel.

With so many German fighters around, Peter warned his crew to be vigilant. A short while later, the rear gunner reported a formation of aircraft approaching from behind them. Instinctively, the crew tensed and waited for the impending fight, which to the crew was inevitable, but before the gunners could get their sights on the aircraft, the 'intruders' were recognised as a formation of Halifax bombers who had the same idea of flying low out over the sea. As the formation caught up with the lone Stirling bomber, it opened sufficiently to allow *MacRobert's Reply* to join its rank and together they flew back to England.

Behind the homeward bound formation lay the results of a successful raid. The bombs were dropped with great accuracy and the ships were left billowing black smoke high into the air. Two enemy fighters were shot down and others damaged. The following day, a signal was received from the Chief of the Air Staff thanking all those who had taken part in the raid. The signal went on to state that the CAS had the greatest admiration for the skill with which the raid was planned and the gallantry with which it was carried out.

The operation marked the completion of Peter's second tour of operational duty. The recommendation for his DFC award was approved on 31 December 1941. Nearly one month later, on 21 January 1942, Flying Officer Boggis, DFC, was posted to No. 15 Conversion Flight, as an instructor, before moving to 1651 Conversion Unit at RAF Waterbeach in May the same year. While undertaking instructional duties, Peter flew a further six operational sorties, including the first two Thousand Bomber Raids, on Cologne and Essen. In total, he completed sixty-one operational sorties.

Peter retired from the RAF in the rank of squadron leader, but *MacRobert's Reply* was not so fortunate. Stirling bomber N6086, F—Freddie, was written-off following a collision with a Spitfire at Peterhead, in January 1942. The MacRobert family crest and nameplate were quickly removed from the damaged fuselage and applied to Stirling bomber W7531, also coded LS-F, which was to serve as the second *MacRobert's Reply*. Unfortunately, this aircraft was to crash in Denmark, on the night of 17–18 May 1942, after being hit by fire from German flak ships; all but one member of the crew perished.

3

The Quest to Find Leonard: Pilot Officer Leonard O'Hara

The men who flew with XV Squadron were many and varied; they came from different backgrounds, cultures, and countries. The majority of those who came from overseas came from the Dominion Countries, Canada, Australia, and New Zealand, but others came from South Africa, Rhodesia, the Caribbean, and America; one of the latter was a young man named Leonard O'Hara.

Leonard William O'Hara was born on 2 August 1918 in Des Moines, Iowa, in America's Midwest, in the home of his parents Leonard and Katie O'Hara. Having been preceded by two sisters, Harriett and Kathryn, Leonard received a warm welcome into the family and was the pride of his parents and became much-adored by his two sisters.

As the early years began to roll by, Leonard became very mischievous and adventurous, and arrived home on more than one occasion to a warning from his grandma regarding his dirty and dusty clothes. On a warm summer's day, his fifth birthday to be exact, Leonard decided that he was now big enough to jump off a chair, which he used as a diving board, into a bucket of water; the caper ended with him breaking his arm. A year later, while riding a new cart down a hill adjacent to his home, his 'vehicle' overturned and he broke his other arm.

The Des Moines neighbourhood in which Leonard lived became his playground and, as a result, the loveable rascal became known to many of the residents. On one occasion, the young scallywag was recorded as having clambered up the wall of a building and straddled the rooftop of a friend's house. One of Leonard's favourite pastimes was climbing trees, leaving his dog 'Bozo' at the bottom to bark at him for hours—generally having fun, along with playing baseball with his friends, became his way of life.

By the time he reached high school age, Leonard was becoming, what the British people of the time would have called, a 'typical young American boy';

he was clean-cut, hair combed back, and good-looking, with a star-quality about him. Likewise, by the time Leonard graduated from North High School, he was driving a battered Ford Model A motor car. Riding in the back seat of the car was not without its dangers as, in order to maintain continued engine power and mobility, those brave enough to accept a ride were required to ensure the ends of two sets of wires were in constant contact with each other, by holding them together. There is no recorded documentation as to what happened when they relaxed their grip on the wires, or there were no back-seat passengers.

In November 1938, Leonard secured employment in Washington. Having passed the necessary civil service test, he was accepted for employment with the Government Printing Office (more commonly known in America as the GPO), where he worked in the bindery department. On the 20th of that month, Leonard sent a night-shot photograph picture postcard of the Capital Building home to his mother, on which he wrote:

> Dear Mom, [*sic.*] Arrived here 04.50 Sunday morning. First thing I saw was the dome of the capital. Looking kinda [*sic.*] rugged in the night. I don't think that this town will be hard to learn as it seems that the capital is in the center [*sic.*] and the streets lead out from the capital. Leonard.

Leonard acquired accommodation, sharing an apartment with three other young men, at the strangely addressed, 327, A Street, N. E., Washington DC, which was the home of Miss Eve, an elderly lady who, according to one report, 'ran a very tight ship', thus allowing no entertaining of young ladies on her property. However, it would seem that Leonard had no time to pursue young ladies for when he was not working in the GPO, he spent his free time learning to fly; after all, if he got a pilot's licence, he could put all the young ladies in a spin—literally. To achieve his aim, the would-be pilot enrolled for a course of lessons with a flying club based at Beacon Field, an aerodrome in Alexandria, Virginia, south-west of the capital.

Leonard was not alone in wanting to fly, his like-minded friends joined him and in order to finance their hobby they set up a round-the-clock taxi service; taking it in turns to take a shift at driving. In due time, their venture enabled them not only to learn to fly, but also to invest in a Piper J-3 Cub, single-engine, light aircraft. In 1939, having passed the various required tests, Leonard was awarded a civil pilot's licence which he put to good use by flying to locations such as Cuba in the south and Ottawa, Canada, in the north. Unfortunately, on an August day in 1941, the Piper Cub aircraft which Leonard and his co-owners had nicknamed 'Suzy', and in which he had gained over 200 hours of flying experience, came to an undignified end, when a flying club member made an extremely heavy landing causing the machine to crash and break up.

Having previously annexed Austria a year earlier, 1939 was the year that Adolf Hitler's military forces annexed Czechoslovakia, before making an all-out assault on Poland, the latter being an act of aggression that was to ignite the Second World War. Many of the airmen who managed to escape the Nazi thrust into Czechoslovakia and Poland made their way to England, where they joined the RAF, as did some of the Belgian, Dutch, and French aviators a year later after Hitler's forces overran the Low Countries and France. Although America was not involved in the conflict at the time, a number of brave young American airmen were lured across the Atlantic Ocean by a taste for adventure; Leonard O'Hara was one of those who volunteered to fight with the Royal Air Force.

With no hope of his own aircraft being rebuilt, and a continuing yearn to fly, Leonard saw an alternative opportunity, the Empire Training Programme. In signing up to join the RAF via this Programme, an American volunteer was required only to obey the orders of a commanding officer and not pledge allegiance to the king of the United Kingdom. In this manner, the volunteer avoided being stripped of his USA citizenship. Therefore, Leonard was recruited into the Royal Air Force.

When Leonard informed his friend Leo O'Grady that he had volunteered, the latter exclaimed, 'For Christ's sake, what made you do something like that?' to which Leonard nonchalantly replied, 'Well, they have cheap flying lessons.'

Leonard's RAF Record of Service (A. M. Form 1108) records that he had been 'Granted a commission, for the emergency, as Pilot Officer on probation, General Duties Branch, RAFVR, with effect from 13 October 1941'; the official announcement of this was published in the *London Gazette* dated 15 January 1942.

Although he had acquired a private pilot's licence, Leonard had to undergo full military flying training, and in a letter to Harriett, Kathryn, and the family, also dated the 13th, he wrote the following:

> My flying is going right along and I have learned a devil of a lot since I put in here [*sic.*]. I have completed the 'Primary' and am now on the 'Advanced' stage, flying a North American AT-6 advanced trainer; boy it's a sweetheart. I am supposed to solo tomorrow. We have to learn where everything is before we even fly, then pass a cockpit check—blindfold (to be able to put your hands on anything the instructor asks for). These ships [*sic.*] have absolutely everything that a modern Hurricane or Spitfire has on it, except guns! We go right from these [aircraft] onto P-40's, Spitfires or other high speed fighter.

Prior to flying the North American AT-6 trainers, Leonard is known to have undertaken some of his earlier flying training on Boeing PT-17 Stearman biplanes at Bakersfield, an airfield north of Los Angeles, in the Californian desert.

On or around 23 October 1941, having successfully passed his course flying AT-6 trainers, Leonard and his fellow cadets all posed for a group graduation photograph in front of one of their aircraft, before preparing to move north for further training with the RCAF/RAF in Canada. Before the move, copies of the photograph were duly distributed to the graduates, who promptly got their respective pictures autographed by their course mates. Three of those who signed Leonard's copy—George Middleton Jr, Dave Logan, and William Arends—not only travelled north with Leonard, but also stopped off with him at his family home in Iowa, where they were all interviewed by the *Des Moines Tribune* newspaper. When the reporter queried as to why American young men were joining the British Royal Air Force, Leonard replied that he had signed up for a little excitement. Less than one month later, the whole of America got more excitement than it bargained for, and the reporter got the true answer to his question.

Leonard reported to the RCAF recruiting centre in Ottawa on 19 November 1941. Having fallen asleep on the train on which he was travelling before it crossed the Canadian border, the young pilot had the strange experience of leaving one country and waking up in another. It would not be long before he would be waking up in yet another country, England, as he explained in a letter home to Harriett and the family, dated 5 December:

> I signed up for the 'duration' and will be shipped over [to England] any day now. We will have officer accommodation on the boat over, [be allowed] plenty of spending money and will be commissioned as a pilot officer on arrival in England. When the US enters the war, we will have the choice of staying on in England or returning home to the US Forces. This I intend to do. Our rating [*sic.*] as pilot officer is equal to a first lieutenant in the US Army Air Corps.

Two days after Leonard wrote that letter, on Sunday 7 December, aircraft from the Imperial Japanese Naval Forces attacked Pearl Harbor in Hawaii, taking America into the Second World War.

Having passed his medical, and completed all the other statutory requirements, Leonard was posted from Ottawa to Halifax, Nova Scotia; this was in preparation for embarkation to the United Kingdom, which took place on the 13th. A partial passenger list, compiled by fellow travellers, strongly implies that Leonard crossed the Atlantic on board SS *Letitia*, a single-stack, passenger liner built in 1924. The ship was requisitioned by the British Admiralty on 9 September 1939 and became HMS *Letitia*, before being reconfigured as a hospital ship and re-designated with the prefix HMHS.

Having survived the wrath of the North Atlantic and avoided the menace of the German U-boats, the ship docked at Liverpool on Christmas Day 1941. The following day, Pilot Officer O'Hara and his contemporaries were entrained to No. 3 Personnel Receiving Centre, based at Bournemouth, Hampshire, on the south coast of England, where they were processed before being transported to London for a period of leave.

The New Year period in London was spent wandering around taking in the sights Leonard had only read about or seen as images printed in books. The Americans were also able to see the results of the Luftwaffe bombing raids they had, again, only read about in the newspapers; the war suddenly became a reality. Leonard and his contemporaries were accommodated in the Regent Palace Hotel, just off Regent Street and adjacent to Piccadilly, the latter being where most newly commissioned RAF officers would go to visit Gieves Ltd, Burberrys Ltd, or some other high-class tailors in order to be measured for their 'Best Blue' uniforms.

For Leonard O'Hara the war took another step closer on 12 January 1942, when he reported to No. 3 Service Flying Training School, based at South Cerney, Gloucestershire, from where, on the 22nd, he wrote to his family:

> Suppose things are pretty worked up now that [the] US has gotten [*sic.*] into the war. I wish I had known she would be in it by now as I probably would have stayed and got into [the] US Forces. I certainly would love to get a sight on one of those Jap bombers. I believe they will be sorry for the little act [Pearl Harbor] as soon as the US gets rolling. Everything is rather quiet over England now. Very few enemy planes even venture over the Channel. While on the other hand our bombers are giving Germany quite a working over every night. Russia has turned the tables on the 'Jerries' haven't they? In fact that is the reason that England is getting a rest. Hitler is afraid to turn his back to the East for fear of Russian invasion. This little war maybe [*sic.*] over before we hope.

When reading the above, it must be remembered that the letter was written on a quiet, grassed airfield, situated just to the south of the small Cotswold town of Cirencester. It was at South Cerney that Leonard converted to Avro Anson, a twin-engined aircraft. Four weeks after his arrival at No. 3 SFTS, on 9 February, Leonard was posted to No. 1511 Blind Approach Training Flight at RAF Upwood, Huntingdonshire, where he converted to the Airspeed Oxford.

A further two weeks later, on 24 February, Leonard moved to No. 12 Operational Training Unit at Chipping Warden, north of Banbury. It was at the latter airfield that Leonard would form his crew and advance to becoming a bomber pilot and 'aircraft captain'. In the first instance, Leonard's crew had been selected, by him, in the usual method of mingling with the throng of men in the allotted hanger, engaging the appropriate candidates in conversations and, if you thought he or they would make a good crew member, inviting him or them to join your crew. Thus it was that, by the end of the procedure, Leonard had formed his crew consisting of Sergeant Ronald Mumford, navigator; Flight Sergeant Russell Hunter, wireless operator; Sergeant Thomas Orr, from South Africa, bomb aimer; and Sergeant Kenneth Forster, air gunner; a second air gunner and a flight engineer, possibly Sergeant Gunton and Sergeant Cross, would join the crew at a heavy conversion unit.

With reference to the aircraft 'our bombers' in the letter, No. 12 OTU flew Vickers Wellingtons, a twin-engined bomber aircraft, complete with front and rear turrets armed with twin 0.303-inch machine guns. Although this aircraft had, more or less, been relegated to the training role, occasionally it was put back into operational service for Thousand Bomber Raids or some other military operation. On reading the content of another of Leonard's letter home to the family, it gives the impression that he may well have participated in the first Thousand Bomber Raid, against Cologne, on the night of 30–31 May. While it is known that Wellington bombers from No. 12 OTU did participate in this attack, Leonard's name does not appear on any official crew listings; however, he wrote:

> [I am] almost fed up with all the war business. It's great fun and quite adventurous, but one minute you're scared silly and the next you are full of contempt for all the enemy's defences that he throws up at you. It's a funny way to live. I guess you have heard of our first big raid on Cologne, 1,000 aircraft over the target in two hours. I was very lucky that night. I will tell you all about it someday, I hope.

The letter was dated 31 May. However, it is known for certain that on the night of 25–26 June, Leonard did participate in the third and final Thousand Bomber Raid: an attack against Bremen.

With the war and all the training it entailed going on around him, Leonard still found time to think about his future after the war had finished and, with that thought in mind, penned a letter to the Civil Aviation Authority in Washington DC, enclosing his civil pilots flying licence for renewal. In the letter he expressed the desire to further his flying experience in the commercial sector, hoping his military flying would be taken into consideration.

While still undergoing training and during a leave visit to London, Leonard's name appeared in the pages of a local Des Moines newspaper back in America, reporting the fact he had been heard talking on a British radio programme. The report, from the unnamed and undated tabloid, read as follows:

> A Des Moines man, Leonard W. O'Hara, broadcast a message of greeting to his parents, Mr. & Mrs L. W. O'Hara, 1342 Harrison Avenue, from London, England, Saturday night. O'Hara, a member of the royal air force [*sic.*], said he was on leave, being well treated and was 'O.K.' His parents and two sisters heard the broadcast. O'Hara attended both East and North high schools and Dowling College. He had been working at Washington D.C., until eight months ago. He

> took some air training at Bakersfield in California, then went on to Canada and joined the R.A.F. He is now receiving advanced training [*sic.*] in London.

On 28 June, Leonard and his crew were deemed ready to convert to the four-engine, Stirling heavy bomber and were posted to No. 1651 (Heavy) Conversion Unit at RAF Waterbeach, Suffolk. During their six weeks at 1651 HCU, Leonard and his crew flew all manner of training exercises and air tests, culminating during the final week, on 4 and 6 August, with two cross-country and practice bombing exercises. Carrying a full war load, the first exercise was a daylight trip lasting five hours, while the second sortie was a night-flying exercise lasting four hours and fifteen minutes.

While at RAF Waterbeach, when time allowed, Leonard continued to write home. In the main, his letters contained comments asking what the family had been doing and where they had been. Occasionally, there were segments cut out of the correspondence, where the official censors had been busy with a pair of scissors. One item the censors did allow to remain was in a letter dated 27 July 1942:

> I am about to be transferred over to the U.S. Air Corp, as a Lieutenant (1st) I think. All papers have been rushed through at their request. They want us in a hurry now. [It] means about $300.00 per month instead of just $80.00. Sure will be a blessing at home I suppose.

The final entry in the 1651 Operational Record Book relating to Leonard reads, '8 August 1942—Pilot Officer O'Hara and crew posted to No. 15 Squadron'.

Having reported to RAF Wyton, Huntingdonshire, where XV Squadron was based, and paraded in front of Wing Commander Douglas Lay, DSO, DFC, who welcomed the 'Freshmen' to his squadron, Leonard and his crew were given two days to settle in and familiarise themselves with the layout of the airfield and the structures on it.

On Monday 10 August, Leonard's name was on the battle order for a mine-laying operation in an area codenamed 'Silverthorn', in the Kattegat, off the Danish coast; he was to fly as second pilot to Sergeant Richard Bebbington and his crew. Their designated aircraft, one of seven detailed for the operation, was Short Stirling serial N3669, coded LS-H.

Although the aircraft took off, and the crew were aware of their allotted duty, Sgt Bebbington was forced to abandon the task due to being unable to locate an aiming point enabling him to accurately drop the mines in the allotted position; he had no option but to return to RAF Wyton with the weapons still on board. Six months after Leonard had flown on the aircraft, during February 1943, Stirling N3669, having achieved a total of sixty-seven operational sorties, was displayed outside St Paul's Cathedral in the City of

London, during a 'Wings for Victory' exhibition, the idea behind the latter being to entice the public to donate money towards the purchase of similar aircraft to the one on display, thus supporting the war effort.

The night following his 'second dickey' trip, Leonard O'Hara flew as pilot and captain of his own aircraft, Stirling BF329, LS-A, which was one of eight aircraft detailed to attack Mainz. This city was easily identifiable from the air, given clear skies, as it was situated on the right bank, inside a bend on the River Rhine, at its confluence with the Main River. However, although there was 10/10th cloud, the target could be seen by the light of the fires burning below. It was by the light of those fires that Leonard was able to identify the target and unleash his bombload which exploded just to the south of the aiming point. Having taken off at 11 p.m., on the night of the 11th, he landed back at RAF Wyton exactly five hours later, at 4 a.m. the following morning.

A total force of 154 aircraft, comprising Lancasters, Stirlings, Halifaxes, and Wellington bombers had been detailed to participate in the attack, six of which failed to return from the operation. One Stirling bomber, N3756, LS-C, from XV Squadron was badly damaged during an attack by two Ju 88 night fighters, one of which was shot down by Flight Sergeant Egri, the rear gunner. The damaged Stirling made it back to Suffolk and was attempting to land at RAF Wattisham when it crashed into a pond at Potash Farm, Brettenham, about 4 miles away from the airfield. Flight Sergeant William McCausland, RCAF, and all but one of his crew were killed. William Egri, RCAF, was rescued from the wreckage, survived and was awarded a Distinguished Flying Medal, which was gazetted on 15 December 1942. In August 1944, William Egri had a second lucky escape from death while flying with 514 Squadron, when his aircraft was shot down and he was taken as a prisoner of war.

Although all of Leonard's crew completed their respective duties satisfactorily throughout the operation on the 11th, for no recorded reasons, Sergeant D. Cross, Sergeant R. Gunton, and Flight Sergeant Hunter, all ceased flying with Leonard's crew after the attack against Mainz. Sergeants Cross and Gunton completed their respective tours of operational flying with other crews, mainly Flight Sergeant W. Eby's crew, while Russell Hunter, the Canadian wireless operator, from London, Ontario, was to lose his life on the night of 21–22 June 1943, flying with Pilot Officer Eric Curtis. Their aircraft, Stirling BK815, was shot down by flak during an attack against Krefeld, Germany. Having been commissioned on 9 December 1942, Hunter was buried in Schoonselhof Cemetery, in Antwerp, Belgium, in the rank of flying officer; he failed to return from his twentieth operational sortie.

Over the period spanning Thursday 13 August to the morning of Saturday the 15th, there was a respite from operational duties, due to the fact XV Squadron relocated to RAF Bourn, south of Cambourne, Cambridgeshire. However, for Leonard and his crew, the relocation move gave them an extended period of leave, during which time Leonard returned to London. On his return to the active duty, he found the squadron on a 'stand down' period, between 19 and 23 August, while the majority of the squadron's aircraft underwent compass swinging procedures, ensuring that the aircraft were actually flying in the direction the navigators had specified to their pilots. It was during this unexpected leisure time that the American pilot caught up with some correspondence and wrote a lengthy letter to the family back in the States. It was written on official Officers' Mess, RAF Bourn stationery and dated 22 August 1942:

> By the time you receive this I will be in U.S. Air Corps uniform as a Lieutenant. I hope that my work won't be quite so [*sic.*] strenuous as it is at present. Although I expect to go along as a technical advisor or something in that capacity (Being an old experienced operator etc.). 'What Ho'. Well, I just finished a 6 day 'leave'. Of course—I went to London again—not so much because I like it that well because things are very high and its quite crowded, as all big cities are at this time, but chiefly because I had some business with the U.S. Air Corps [*sic.*]. While in London I chanced to be going through one of the rail depots and some British guards were herding some of the Luftwaffe airmen who were recently shot down or captured here in England. I was surprised to find they are very ordinary looking fellows. Just kids really and they looked at us and scanned our faces and appearance as curiously as we were looking at them. Somehow you just don't picture the enemy as just young fellows like that. Honestly you could take 5 of those guys an equal number of British or American chaps and mix them up in civilian clothes and not be able to tell the difference as to which was which. I guess they were thinking the same as we were when they looked us over. In fights in the air you don't see faces or personnel—you only see the aircraft as an enemy which must be destroyed. War is a hell of a business.

The six-page letter obviously covered other issues, including Leonard's thoughts on life after the war, what he had been doing when off duty generally, and enquiring how the family were getting along at home, especially now that America was at war on two fronts.

Pilot Officer O'Hara and his crew returned to operational duties on the night of the 24th–25th, when their names appeared on the battle order for an attack against Frankfurt. However, on this occasion, the names of Cross, Gunton, and Hunter, had been replaced by those of Sergeant Leon Cowen (flight engineer), Sergeant Robert Evans (wireless operator/air gunner), and Flight Sergeant Howarth (air gunner).

Bomber Command dispatched a total of 226 aircraft to the German city, which included eleven Stirling bombers detailed by XV Squadron. Short Stirling R9312 took off at 9.05 p.m. with Leonard at the controls and set course for the enemy occupied coast. Leonard and his crew were caught in searchlights, which they managed to evade without incurring any other problems, but two of the squadron's other crews incurred difficulties of a different nature. Pilot Officer Cyril Baigent, RNZAF, who was undertaking his sixteenth operational flight, abandoned the sortie due to the failure of one of the Stirling's engines; he returned to Bourn, taking his bombload back with him. Cyril Baigent, apart from becoming one of the RAF's youngest squadron commanders, at the age of twenty-two, rose to the rank of wing commander and was awarded a Distinguished Service Order, a Distinguished Flying Cross and Bar, and an Air Force Cross. He accumulated a total of 1,572 flying hours. The second crew who encountered problems during this operation was that headed by Bobby Gilmour, who jettisoned his load of incendiary bombs during combat with an enemy fighter. Squadron Leader Gilmour was an extremely experienced pilot who first joined XV Squadron, in the rank of pilot officer, when the unit was flying Bristol Blenheim, twin-engined bombers. Remaining with XV Squadron, he converted to Vickers Wellington bombers before converting to Short Stirling bombers; Robert Gilmour was awarded a DFC during November 1940, followed by a DSO in early November 1942.

Three nights later, on 27 August, Leonard was back in the pilot's seat of Stirling R9312, for an attack against Kassel; the squadron detailed twelve aircraft to join a total attacking force of 306 bombers. With one aircraft, Stirling R9351, being cancelled prior to take-off, it was to prove a costly night for XV Squadron. Two Stirlings, BF327 and W7624, failed to return, having been shot down by German night fighters. The former being shot down by *Hauptmann* Erich Simon, of *Stab* III./*Nachtjagdgeschwader* 2, at 11.35 p.m., while the latter fell to the guns of *Oberleutnant* Wolfrat Bauer, of 7./NJG1, at 12.26 a.m. Three Stirlings abandoned the sortie, two due to engine problems and one due to being hit by flak from British ships off the Suffolk coast near Aldeburgh, another crash-landed at RAF Oakington, due to undercarriage failure and two sustained flak damage over the target, one of the latter being Leonard's aircraft.

Damage to Leonard's aircraft must have been superficial, as it was back in the air the following night to continue the fight over Germany, although for Leonard and his crew the outward flight did not go as planned. The target for the operation on the night of the 28th was Nuremberg, with XV Squadron detailing eight crews to join the 151 other bombers dispatched by Bomber Command, although one of XV's allotted aircraft was withdrawn prior to take-off. Leonard took off at 8.50 p.m., but he, his crew, and Stirling R9312 were back down on the ground one hour and fifty minutes later, having abandoned the sortie and landed at RAF Oakington, due to low oil pressure; the following morning, the aircraft and its crew returned to Bourn. The squadron lost one aircraft on the Nuremberg raid, Short Stirling R9153,

LS-U, piloted by Pilot Officer Eric Patterson, RCAF. The aircraft crashed in France with the loss of the whole crew. One of those crew members was Sergeant John Ludgate, an air gunner who was undertaking his thirty-first, and possibly final, operational sortie. John Ludgate had been a member of Sergeant Bebbington's crew the night Leonard made his first operational flight as second pilot.

When any aircraft returned from a night's sortie, or indeed when they returned to base having landed away, as Leonard was forced to do, the ground crews would swarm over the aircraft for which they were responsible, checking for signs of battle damage or defects. Unheralded, they worked throughout the night and into the next day, if circumstances dictated so, to get the airframe ready for the next operation. Following her return to Bourn, Stirling R9312 had undergone the aforementioned procedure to ensure the aircraft was ready for her next flight, be it a flying exercise or an operational duty. For R9312, that next flight was to be an operational sortie specified for the night of 1 September. Bomber Command issued an order for an attack against Saarbrücken, on the German–French border. A total force of 231 bombers was detailed for the operation, which included seven Stirlings from XV Squadron.

Unfortunately, due to an error by the Pathfinders, who mistakenly illuminated the town of Saarlouis, situated 13 miles north-west of Saarbrücken, not one bomb fell on the intended target. Although no damage report was forthcoming, it is recorded that a total of fifty-two civilians were killed in the non-industrial town. The death toll would have been a lot higher had it not been for the unoccupied concrete positions of the Siegfried Line, the First World War German-built line of defences, which the local inhabitants used as air-raid shelters. The seven crews dispatched by XV Squadron, including Leonard and his crew, all reported bombing what they believed to be the north-east side of Saarbrücken.

The next night, the names of Leonard and his crew were again on the battle order for an attack against Karlsruhe, another target on the German–French border, south-east of Saarbrücken. On this occasion, the Pathfinders marked the city correctly and the ensuing raid was reported as very successful. A total of 200 aircraft, including six detailed by XV Squadron, participated in the operation, which culminated with the loss of eight aircraft. One of the aircraft which failed to return was Stirling bomber W7611, LS-F, piloted by Sergeant Richard Bebbington, the same pilot with whom Leonard had undertaken his 'second dickey' trip just over three weeks earlier. Apart from Sergeant William Shearer, the flight engineer, who was taken as a prisoner of war, the whole crew perished, leaving Leonard feeling very subdued, all the more so because flying with Bebbington, as second pilot, was Leonard's friend George Quinn. Pilot Officer Quinn had trained with Leonard at Bakersfield, California, and had signed Leonard's group graduation photograph. The two friends had taken the same route up to Canada, before embarking for the United Kingdom, where they were both posted to 1651 Conversion Unit. However, although their paths had taken the same route, for some unrecorded reason, George was posted to XV Squadron on 3 August, five days before Leonard. Another peculiarity concerning George Quinn was that, although he arrived on XV Squadron ahead of Leonard, George had to wait nearly a month before undertaking his first operational flight.

Two days after the loss of his friend, Leonard was back in the air undertaking a flight to Bremen, in north-west Germany; his aircraft being one of a total of 251 Bomber Command aircraft heading for the target. XV Squadron initially detailed eight Stirling bombers for the attack, but one was withdrawn prior to take-off. The remaining seven crews all reported large concentrated fires in the target area, which could be seen from over 100 miles away. Heavy bursts of light flak were also reported by the crews, along with the fact there were many searchlights scanning the sky. Leonard reported unleashing his bombs, from an altitude of 14,000 feet, over an area to the west of the old town. Having discharged his duty, Leonard turned Stirling R9312 on to a heading out of the target area and commenced his home run to Bourn, where he landed at 5.40 a.m. Although all XV Squadron's aircraft returned safely, a total of twelve bombers failed to return to their home bases.

On Sunday, 6 September, the day the German forces captured the Russian naval base on the coast of the Black Sea, at Novorossiysk, Bomber Command paid an early morning visit to Duisburg. A total of 207 aircraft were detailed for the raid, seven of which were from XV Squadron.

Leonard and his crew took off at 1.25 a.m. and headed east. Scattered patches of cloud were encountered along the route and over the target, but this did not obstruct the views of the fires raging below. Sergeant Thomas Orr, the bomb aimer, lay in the nose of the aircraft and guided his pilot to the aiming point. At the appropriate moment Thomas Orr pressed the bomb release 'tit' and called 'Bombs gone'. As the explosive weapons tumbled out of the bomb bay, the lanyard of the photo-flash which automatically took the aiming point photograph broke. It was not until the crew got back to Bourn, and the image had been developed, that they knew whether or not they had secured a photograph. The crew got their picture, but it resembled a tangled mess of car headlights twisting and turning every which way. The raid was considered a success, but it cost Bomber Command the loss of eight aircraft. Fortunately, all XV Squadron aircraft were back on the ground at RAF Bourn by 5.35 a.m.

Following the attack on the 6th, possibly due to injury, illness, or being posted to an air gunnery course, the name of Flight Sergeant Howarth, the mid-upper gunner, ceased to appear on any documentation relating to Leonard's crew; this meant that a replacement air gunner was assigned to the crew for

Above: A graduation photograph taken at Bakersfield Aero Centre, California, signed by the students on the same course as Leonard O'Hara (standing extreme left). George Quinn (kneeling extreme left) was also posted to XV Squadron. (*Courtesy of Tom Lowe, USA*)

Below left: Pilot Officer Leonard O'Hara (USA), Royal Air Force Volunteer Reserve, photographed on receiving his commission. (*Courtesy of Tom Lowe, USA*)

Below right: Harriett Bump (*née* O'Hara), sister of Leonard O'Hara, photographed on the occasion of her 100th birthday, with Valerie and Martyn Ford-Jones, at the Grand Haven Retirement Community in Eldridge, Iowa. (*Author's collection*)

Above: Stirling Mk I bomber N3669 on display outside St. Paul's Cathedral, London, during a 'Wings for Victory' week. It was on this aircraft that Plt Off. Leonard O'Hara made his first 'second dickey' operational flight. (*Author's collection*)

Right: The headstone in Amsterdam New Eastern Cemetery, which is thought to mark the last resting place of Pilot Officer Leonard O'Hara, RAFVR. (*Author's collection*)

Leonard's next operational sortie. That next raid came three nights later, on 9 September, when Leonard and his crew were detailed for a mining operation in the area codenamed 'Nectarines', in the Friesian Islands. For this sortie, the replacement air gunner was named as twenty-two-year-old Sergeant Charles Barrie, a Scottish lad from Dumfriesshire, who had flown his first operational sortie the previous evening with Squadron Leader Charles Fisher.

Six Stirling bombers were detailed to drop their mines into the sea in the area of Wangerooge Island, off the Germany coastline, near the ports of Wilhelmshaven and Bremerhaven. Leonard, piloting Stirling W7578, LS-A, took off from Bourn at 8.15 p.m. After a flight lasting five hours, and not being able to pinpoint the drop zone, Leonard landed back at base with the mines still stored in the aircraft's bomb bay. Four of the other aircraft are recorded as having dropped their mines, while the remaining Stirling crash-landed at RAF Waterbeach, due to engine problems, and minus four of its crew members who had bailed out over the Cambridgeshire countryside.

Sergeant Charles Barrie, who had flown with Leonard's crew as mid-upper gunner, returned to Squadron Leader Fisher's crew and was to undertake a further seven operational sorties before being killed in a tragic flying accident on 29 October 1942. Squadron Leader Fisher, piloting Stirling BF386, LS-Q, had taken off from Bourn, along with four members of his normal crew, to carry out an air test before that night's operational detail. Also on the aircraft, along for experience, was Sergeant Walter Hood, RNZAF, as second pilot, with two members of his crew and three members of ground crew, who were along for the ride. During its flight, the Stirling was seen to emerge from cloud, flying in a normal attitude, before executing a sharp, steep, turn and plunging into the ground. The aircraft burst into flame when it crashed at Salter's Lode, south-west of Downham Market, at 11.50 a.m., killing all on board. Sergeant Charles Barrie, son of Thomas and Mary Barrie, was buried at Bothwell Park (Bellshill) Cemetery, Strathclyde, Scotland. Squadron Leader Charles Gerald Fisher, who had been granted a commission in October 1939, was an experienced pilot with a total of 1,973 recorded flying hours; he was buried at Croydon (Queens Road), Cemetery, South Croydon, Surrey.

On the night of 10 September, Bomber Command ordered an attack against Düsseldorf, for which 479 aircraft were detailed, including eight from XV Squadron, although one aircraft was withdrawn prior to take-off. Checking the battle order that morning, Leonard found his name and those of his crew recorded, along with that of Flight Sergeant Page, who was to occupy the mid-upper turret. Flight Sergeant Page was another new air gunner who had flown his first operational sortie with Pilot Officer James Brown two weeks earlier, on 28 August.

Leonard took off from Bourn at 9.10 p.m. and settled into what was to be an uneventful flight to the target. On arrival over Düsseldorf, he found the city ablaze, with large fires raging; many structures, including public buildings, factories, and residential properties, were later reported as destroyed or severely damaged. While the gunners scanned the night sky for enemy night fighters, Leonard made his bombing run, following the instructions of Sergeant Thomas Orr, his bomb aimer, who guided him to the aiming point. With the bombload released from an altitude of approximately 12,000 feet, and the aiming point photographs taken, Leonard hauled the Stirling over into a turn away from the target area and set a new course for home.

Two of the aiming point photographs for this operation survive in the XV Squadron photographic archive, one of which shows ground detail with signs of explosions and fires. The second image is a mass of bright, latticework of criss-crossing lines. Alongside the image is a handwritten comment which reads: 'The many different criss-cross lines indicate that film was exposed for longer than 11 seconds—i.e. photo not taken with bombing'.

All XV Squadron aircraft returned safely, except for Stirling BF347, LS-J, piloted by Flight Sergeant Harry Bannister. The pilot and crew had managed to fly their crippled aircraft back to England, but unfortunately, it crashed at 2.55 a.m. while attempting an emergency landing at RAF West Malling, Kent, killing the entire crew.

During the rest period that the O'Hara crew were granted over the next few days, Leonard put pen to paper and spent some of the time catching up with correspondence, including a letter to Harriett and the family dated 12 September 1942:

> Glad to know you are all OK and happy. I am quite well and very busy as you probably know. My luck is still going strong and with the grace of God, a good crew and aircraft, I should finish with a lot to spare. I do enjoy hearing from you people, I feel rather lousy at times now that I am the last one of my gang left. Leo writes regular as heck and he is the same old Lee [*sic.*]. He wants to come along on a 'trip' with me. I sure wish that he could—I would like to hear him talk about it afterwards—that would be a classic. I am still in RAF and have not transferred yet. Incidentally I have an increase in rank in the RAF coming up October 1st. It will be Flying Officer (1st Lieutenant) instead of Pilot Officer (2nd Lieutenant) after that date.

Leo O'Grady, who wanted to experience a bombing sortie with Leonard, had grown up with the latter in Iowa and the pair had remained the best of friends. Leo, who had also been posted to England, was serving with an infantry unit of the United States Army. When their respective periods of leave coincided, they would try and meet up in London.

Two days after Leonard wrote his letter home, on the 14th, Leo wrote to his fiancée back in the States.

> Yes, I heard from Leonard quite often. He writes me that his transfer to U.S.A.C. has not yet went thru [*sic.*]. He is now a Captain and is in complete charge of a 4 motor bomber. He is really getting a work out over Germany at present—I hope his luck holds out. He has promised to take me on a raid with him if I can get down to see him. I sure hope I can make it.

The evening of 14 September saw Leonard and his crew back on operational duties. Along with five other crews, they were detailed for an attack against Wilhelmshaven. The squadron had originally listed seven crews for the raid, but one aircraft was withdrawn during the day, probably due to being unserviceable; the remaining six aircraft would join the 196 other Bomber Command aircraft detailed for this raid.

Flying with Leonard, occupying the mid-upper turret, was Sergeant Howard E. Johnson, a twenty-nine-year-old Canadian from Galt, Ontario, who was, as far as can be ascertained, flying his first operational sortie. Given his age, Johnson would have been considered as the 'granddad' of the crew but any reservations he may have had about the raid were probably smoothed over by the now experienced crew members with such comments as, 'It will be a piece of cake, you'll see'.

Sergeant Johnson's nerves may have been on edge at 7.45 p.m. when Stirling R9312, LS-C, piloted by Leonard began to creep forward, gather speed and lumber slowly into the sky. The outward flight went without incident and on approach the target could be clearly identified. Although a thick haze was reported, marking by the Pathfinders was recorded as being accurate, and Wilhelmshaven was subjected to its worst raid to date. The docks were in flames and many buildings were destroyed, including a number of residential areas. The return flight was without incident and when Leonard landed the Stirling bomber back at Bourn at 1 a.m. on the morning of the 15th, Sgt Johnson, without doubt, breathed a huge sigh of relief; he had completed his first operational sortie as Leonard had completed his twelfth sortie.

The weather during the first two weeks of September 1942 had been rather cloudy and unsettled, with small patches of rain falling in some areas. This weather pattern continued into the third week of the month, encompassing Wednesday the 16th. Having received a letter from a lady friend (known only as Irene), with whom he had worked at the Government Printing Office in Washington DC, Leonard spent that morning writing his reply:

> Dear Irene, I received your letter and was very glad to hear from you. Quite a nice card [*sic.*]. I am glad to hear that you are doing OK as well as all the rest. I am quite a bit behind in my correspondence at the moment. It's nice to hear from you girls. As you probably know I am busy as heck hitting Hitler these days. I suppose you are all quite busy at the GPO these days. Hello to all the girls and

> fellows for me. I must admit I miss you people and hope to see you all soon. My colossal luck is still holding out very well. (Knock wood)—CENSORED—[I am the only one left] ... out of [all] my buddies who came over together. This is a rough game that is being played over here. Buying Bonds and all the other work that you people are doing over there mean everything to winning the war. Keep up the good work.

Interestingly, although all the other letters that Leonard wrote home, on officers' mess stationery, passed through untouched, on this occasion the wartime censor deemed it necessary to also delete the name of the RAF Station printed on the letterhead.

Having written his letter to Irene, Leonard checked the squadron noticeboard and read the battle order. The typed document informed the reader that ten aircraft had been detailed for an attack against Essen that night, with a take-off time listed as 8.10 p.m.; it also informed Leonard that he would be piloting Stirling bomber BF353, LS-E, which had only been taken on charge by XV Squadron thirteen days earlier, on 3 September. The aircraft had undertaken its first operational sortie ten days later, on the 13th, and for Leonard this would be his thirteenth sortie.

During the day, prior to that evening's raid, all participating crews would take their allotted aircraft on an air test, to ensure that everything that should be bolted down was, and that all instruments were in good working order. The crew of each bomber, being satisfied, the respective pilots, including Leonard, signed the obligatory RAF Form 700; the document which confirmed every pilot was satisfied with the air-worthiness of his particular aircraft, although one aircraft was withdrawn prior to take-off. Later that night, at the appointed time, the crews were transported out to their individual aircraft, ahead of the pre-arranged take off time, to commence last minute pre-flight checks. On a signal from the ground crew chief, each aircraft slowly taxied out in preparation for take-off. At 8.25 p.m. that Wednesday evening, Leonard pushed the throttles forward, released the brakes and took off into the half-light of a mid-September evening sky. Stirling BF353 climbed laboriously into the darkening sky and was never seen again—neither was her crew.

A total of 369 bombers had been dispatched for the raid on Essen, of which thirty-nine failed to return, two of them being from XV Squadron. Leonard's aircraft was one of the latter, the other being Stirling R9318, LS-J, flown by Pilot Officer James Brown and his crew.

An official telegram conveying the news that Leonard was 'missing' in action was received with overwhelming sadness by the O'Hara family; it was a day Harriett would never forget. For a while, the family prayed for the possibility that Leonard may have been taken prisoner of war and that such news had not yet filtered through. Wing Commander Douglas J. Lay, DSO,

DFC, Officer Commanding No. XV Squadron, wrote to Leonard's family, offering sympathy at their loss, but also stated that their son and brother may well have been made a POW.

A number of weeks after his demise, on 1 November 1942, Leonard's last letter that he had written to Irene on the morning of the day he was killed was posted to Leonard's mother for her to keep in perpetuity.

Although three Luftwaffe night fighter pilots each claimed shooting down a Stirling bomber on the night of 16–17 September 1942, all of which are recorded as having crashed into the sea off the coast of the Netherlands, one of these claims has been amended to record Wellington bomber DV723 from No. 26 Operational Training Unit, which was shot down around the same time as Leonard's aircraft and crashed into the sea in the same area. The other two claims, filed by *Unteroffizier* Heinz Vinke of *5 Gruppe/Nachtjagdgeschwader* 2 (5./NJG2) and *Hauptmann* Horst Patuschka of 8 *Gruppe/Nachtjagdgeschwader* 2 (8./NJG2), both identify the bomber as Stirling R9318, piloted by Pilot Officer James Brown as the aircraft they each shot down; only one can be right. It is thought that Leonard's aircraft, which was probably hit by flak, crashed into the Ijsselmeer while undertaking its return journey to Bourn.

Nearly a year after the loss of Leonard's aircraft, the O'Hara family received a letter from the Air Ministry, in London, signed on behalf of the Director of Personal Services; dated 12 August 1943, it read in part:

> It is feared in view of the time which has elapsed that there is no hope that [Pilot Officer Leonard O'Hara] can be a prisoner of war. News of Air Force personnel made prisoner is normally received within two months of the date they are reported missing. Information has been received through the International Red Cross Committee that the body of Sergeant Forster was recovered from the sea at Urk Island on 25 September 1942, and the bodies of Sergeant Orr and Sergeant Cowen were recovered at the same place on 26 September. The body of Sergeant Evans was recovered at the Ijsselmeer on 19 September 1942. No further details were given, and no news has since been received regarding Pilot Officer O'Hara or of the other two members of the crew. The names of prisoners of war, and of allied personnel who lose their lives in enemy or enemy-occupied territory are reported to this department through the International Red Cross Committee, and in view of the information received regarding the other members of the crew it can only be concluded that the aircraft crashed into the sea and that the crew lost their lives.

Harriett, along with Kathryn Samuelson (Harriett and Leonard's sister, now married), and other members of the family were determined to find out more about the circumstances surrounding and leading to the loss of their brother's aircraft and its crew. Between them, they wrote many letters to government departments, military services, the United States Army Air Corps, the Royal Air Force, the Royal Netherlands Air Force, former military personnel who had served with or known Leonard, and anyone else they thought might be able to help in their search. Although they may not have realised it at the time, their endeavours were to set them on a quest to find Leonard, which would last for many years and raise many more questions.

Following the end of the war, the Dutch authorities commenced work on land reclamation in the areas of the Ijsselmeer. Trenching machines were used to excavate trenches 6–8 feet deep for use as additional drainage or runoff channels for the receding water; this achieved, the ground was then left to dry out. In 1956, a trenching crew unearthed some items of wreckage that, after inspection, were confirmed as being part of a Stirling bomber, but the question posed was which one; a vast number of bomber aircraft made their final 'landing' in the Ijsselmeer. The crash site coordinates were recorded and logged, and the site was left undisturbed for future investigation.

Knowing there were many more undiscovered crash sites, possibly containing human remains, the RNLAF created a special unit, to be known as the Royal Netherlands Air Force Recovery Department and Explosives Ordnance Disposal Command, who would have total responsibility for the removal and recovery of wreckage and casualties from the site.

Eleven years after it was first located, when the ground structure proved dry enough to undertake proper excavations, the site was reopened. By an unexplainable quirk of fate, the items retrieved from the dig ultimately proved to be from Stirling bomber BF353: Leonard's aircraft.

The recovery of the Stirling was not without its problems. As the men dug down, the ground became wetter and combined with the natural elements heavy lifting machinery began to get bogged down due to the weight of lifting undercarriage legs, propellers, engine parts and other associated items, all of which were transported to the Dutch air force base at Gilze-Rijen.

Although no sign of the missing three crew members—Pilot Officer Leonard O'Hara and Sergeants Ronald Mumford and William Johnson, RCAF—had been discovered during the excavations, Harriett, Kathryn, and the rest of the family continued in their task, even though their endeavours seemed, at times, an 'uphill' struggle.

During the late 1990s, a younger member of the family got very interested in the quest to find Leonard. Tom Lowe, Harriett's grandson and Leonard's great-nephew, took it upon himself to widen the search. Using the material gathered by his grandmother and other family members as a basis with which to work, Tom extended the search area by making contact with RAF historians in England and researchers in the Netherlands. Through these contacts, first in England, Tom learned more about his great-uncle's service with XV Squadron, the operations he flew and the places Leonard had visited in the United Kingdom; from the Dutch sources, he learned more about the circumstances of the crash and subsequent excavations. These investigations also led Tom to fly from California, where he lived with his wife Barbara and their two daughters, Megan and Caitlin, to both England and the Netherlands, where he met those with whom he had been corresponding for face to face conversations, and to follow in Leonard's footsteps. Visits to the former RAF training bases at Waterbeach, Cambridgeshire, and South Cerney, Gloucestershire, were followed by a visit to Bourn, also in Cambridgeshire, from where Leonard made his last take-off. It was at the latter airfield that Tom and Barbara experienced a strange phenomenon. On Sunday, 27 July 2003, having been shown around the few remaining remnants of the former RAF base, they were standing at the intersection of the two main runways discussing with the author the possible direction of Leonard's final take-off. Their conversation was interrupted by the obvious sound of the wind gathering momentum, gathering speed and seemingly heading down the runway towards them. As the noise of the wind grew louder, the trio was hit by a blast of warm air which momentarily engulfed them before continuing along the runway, the sound dissipating as it did so. With a look of some disbelief on his face, Tom asked the question, 'What the devil was that?' to which he received the reply, 'Leonard showing you the direction in which he took off'.

In September 2002, the family learned for certain that while four members of Leonard's crew—Sergeant Thomas Orr, Sergeant Kenneth Forster, Sergeant Howard Johnson, and Flight Sergeant Leon Cowen—were buried in Amsterdam New Eastern Cemetery, and that Sergeant Robert Evans was buried in Harderwijk General Cemetery, two were still listed as 'missing': Sergeant Ronald Mumford and Leonard.

During her ninetieth year, Harriett joined by nine other members of Leonard's extended family, flew from her home in Iowa, to attend the Remembrance Day service at the RAF Memorial, Runnymede, Surrey, on Sunday, 9 November 2003. At the appropriate moment, Harriett arose from her wheelchair and walked, with assistance, to the Stone of Remembrance, where she laid a wreath in memory of her brother. Two days later, on Tuesday the 11th (Remembrance Day), they visited the Royal Air Force Club in Piccadilly, Central London, where, on behalf of the assembled family, Harriett presented a copy of a book, relating the to the history of XV Squadron, to the Club Library; the book had been dedicated to the memory of Pilot Officer Leonard O'Hara.

Two years later, in May 2005, it was arranged for Tom and Barbara to attend the ninetieth-anniversary celebrations of the formation of XV Squadron, which was held at RAF Lossiemouth, Scotland. The visit gave Tom the opportunity to peruse some of the squadron's wartime documents and photographs. During his time at RAF Lossiemouth, Tom also met a number of XV Squadron veterans who had flown Stirling bombers in action during the period 1941–1943 and was able to gain an insight as to what it was like to fly the first of the four-engined heavy bombers, from those who had actual knowledge of the experience.

Thursday, 17 July 2014, was an extremely sad day for Harriett's family; it was the day this grand and gracious lady passed away, at the age of 102 years old. Apart from bringing up her family, she had dedicated a large part of her life in the quest to find Leonard; little did Harriett know how close the answer could be.

A Dutch historian, Nico Kwakman, had also been researching the loss of Leonard's aircraft and the remaining members of its crew, especially having noticed a headstone situated adjacent to those of Leonard's crew in Amsterdam New Eastern Cemetery. The inscription read, 'An Airman of the 1939–1945 War, A Pilot Officer, Royal Air Force, 25th September 1942'. The date was the same as that recorded when Sergeant Kenneth Forster's body was recovered from the sea near Urk island, and the day before the bodies of Sergeant Orr and Sergeant Cowen were recovered in the same area. Including this information with other documentary and photographic evidence he had gleaned, some from German sources, Nico Kwakman put together a convincing case which has been submitted to the Commonwealth War Graves Commission for consideration that Pilot Officer O'Hara has already been laid to rest in Amsterdam New Eastern Cemetery. If the CWGC agrees, an application will be made to have the existing headstone replaced with one bearing Leonard's full name.

At the end of March 2017, Tom and Barbara were back at RAF Lossiemouth for the formal disbandment of XV (R) Squadron, 102 years after its formation as a Royal Flying Corps squadron during the Great War. On learning that Tom's mother and his aunt were nieces of Leonard O'Hara, the officer commanding, Wing Commander Paul Froome, agreed it was in order for Roger and Mary Lowe (Tom's parents), Dave and Cathie Lange (Tom's aunt and uncle) and Pat Bump (brother of Mary and Cathie), to fly across to Scotland in order to attend the event too. The solemnity of the disbandment ceremony during the day was matched, in the evening, by one 'hum-dinger' of a hanger party, attended by approximately seven-hundred guests.

On Sunday 1 April, having said goodbye to XV Squadron, the group flew from Inverness across to the Netherlands where they undertook a pilgrimage to Amsterdam New Eastern Cemetery, and stood in front of the headstone identified by Nico Kwakman. Such was the interest in this visit by the locals, that throughout the whole of the four-day visit to Holland, the family was 'shadowed' by a Dutch documentary film crew; their visit, along with interviews given by the family members, was shown on a Dutch television news programme.

The family also visited Harderwijk General Cemetery, where Sergeant Robert Evans, the wireless operator/air gunner was buried, the Dronten Air Gunners' Museum and the crash site of Stirling BF353, LS-E, now part of a farm on the reclaimed land, where they found various fragments of metal, Perspex and bullet casings, all of which induced further discussions, thoughts and theories. However, the most poignant part of their visit was standing in front of that headstone in Amsterdam New Eastern Cemetery. After years of writing letters, searching records, and travelling hundreds of miles to Europe and the United Kingdom, the O'Hara family finally feel their quest to find Leonard has been completed.

4

Sojourn in Spain: Group Captain Michael Wyatt, DFC

By the time Squadron Leader Michael Wyatt reported for duty at RAF Bourn, in Cambridgeshire, he was already a very knowledgeable bomber pilot with a wealth of flying experience and a two-year detachment to Australia behind him.

Young Michael grew up wanting to be a pilot, like his father before him, with hopes of going to RAF Cranwell straight from school, but when his father was killed in a flying accident, while waiting to be demobilised at the end of the First World War, Michael's mother expressed her concerns about her son joining the Royal Air Force. Not wanting to give up his dream, Michael promised his mother he would not join until he was twenty-one years of age; it was an oath he kept and was in fact twenty-two when he joined the Reserve of Air Force Officers.

Having completed his initial flying training course at the Blackburn School of Flying at Brough in Yorkshire where he flew Blackburn B-2 aircraft, Michael was granted a commission in the rank of pilot officer, in the RAFO, and presented with his 'wings' on 23 March 1934.

Over the next two years, Michael undertook his annual refresher flying courses at Desford Civil Flying Training School in Leicestershire. However, for his annual service flying training, he was attached to No. 99 Squadron, flying Handley Page Heyford, open-cockpit night bombers out of RAF Mildenhall. The Heyford was the last of the RAF's biplane heavy bombers.

In 1936, Michael decided to transfer to a short service commission in the regular air force. On completion of the service flying training syllabus, he was posted to No. 12 (Day Bomber) Squadron based at Andover. The squadron was equipped with Hawker Harts, but shortly after Michael's arrival at the Hampshire base, the squadron re-equipped with Hawker Hinds; both aircraft also were open-cockpit biplanes. Approximately fourteen months later, during

February 1938, No. 12 was re-equipped with Fairey Battle aircraft; Michael flew his first solo on one of these single-engine, enclosed cockpit machines two months later on 9 April. Later, when war came, Michael yearned for those earlier open cockpit years:

> They were happy days and it was rather like being in a friendly and exclusive club. However, there was much talk about a possible war with Germany, and in September 1938 we were put on special alert whilst the talks in Munich, between Mr Chamberlain and Hitler, were in progress. That particular scare died down and we resumed our normal training.

With all the talk of war going on, an insignificant moment to the rest of Europe was overshadowed on 8 January 1939, when Michael was promoted in the rank of flying officer.

In the build-up to possible hostilities, No. 12 Squadron was assigned to the Advanced Air Striking Force (AASF); it was also given a predetermined airfield in France, at Berry-au-Bac, north-west of Reims, to which it would mobilise immediately in the event of war. A similar directive applied to all squadrons flying Fairey Battle aircraft, with each squadron flying to its own designated airfield. In the meantime, on 9 May 1939, No. 12 relocated to Bicester airfield in Oxfordshire.

It was around this period of time that the political situation started to deteriorate, and with it the knowledge that war was becoming inevitable. With the latter thought in mind, part of the flying training took on the necessity of formation flights over France, with each squadron ensuring it flew over the airfield it was to occupy so that crews could familiarise themselves with the location and surrounding territory. Michael remembered another preparation for war that the squadron made:

> Earlier I had specialised in navigation and was appointed Squadron Navigation Officer. Soon after our arrival at Bicester large stocks of maps of France and Germany started to arrive and I was instructed to make them up into sets and hold them in readiness for our possible move to France. I prepared two sets for each aircraft and one set for the principal officers in the Squadron—the O/C and flight commanders etc.

Sometime around 15 August 1939, Michael was not only ordered to distributed the sets of maps he had made up, he was also instructed to organise briefing sessions in which he was to explain the route they were to fly, the salient points relating to surrounding landmarks, and other relative information.

At 2 p.m. on 1 September, No. 12 went on to a war footing when the squadron's aircraft took off for Berry-au-Bac, but to the crews, who had practised this scenario so many times, it was quite routine. Having arrived at the French airfield and picketed their aircraft the crews made their way to their billet, a chateau in Guignecourt, owned by the Marquise de Nazelle, who also owned the cellars of Veuve Cliquot.

Initially, the aircrews were kept busy practising formation flights, familiarisation flights, and undertaking a number of reconnaissance flights along the Maginot Line and around Metz; the latter counted as war operations and were therefore recorded in the individuals flying logbooks. However, the phoney war, as it was now becoming known, amounted to nothing and the crews were getting rather bored. Luckily for Michael, he had been selected to attend a specialisation course, at the School of Air Navigation, RAF St Athan, and was posted home on 9 October. On completing and passing the course, the 'N' symbol was applied after his name in the Air Force List. He was then posted on detachment, to Australia as part of a thirty-strong team of specialists who were to assist the Royal Australian Air Force set up training schools under the Empire Air Training Scheme. Having sailed 'down under' on RMS *Strathnaver*, Michael and his fellow officers arrived in Australia on 20 April 1940.

Apart from helping set up navigation training schools at Point Cook, Cootamundra, and Mount Gambia, Flying Officer Wyatt also helped establish flying training schools at Wagga Wagga and Adelaide, and armament training schools at Sale and Amberley near Brisbane.

While in Australia, the RAAF started to receive consignments of Fairey Battle bombers, dismantled and in crates. A decision was taken to assemble these aircraft at the Massey Ferguson tractor factory at Geelong, south-west of Melbourne, in the State of Victoria. As there was no one in Australia who had any experience of assembling these aircraft, it was all done by trial and error. Then came the bit Michael was most concerned about:

> As I was the only pilot in Australia who had ever flown Fairey Battles I was asked to test fly them as they were completed. It was the most hair raising flying I had ever experienced, firstly because the grass field we used for an airfield was much too small, and secondly because some of the aircraft would go more or less out of control as soon as you got airborne because they had been assembled incorrectly with the wings or the tailplane assembled out of alignment. Luckily we did not have any accidents, and I managed to get the aircraft back on the ground, although not always on the airfield. After a while an RAF squadron leader engineer arrived at Geelong to supervise the assembly of the aircraft and, as he had all the required instruments for the angles etc., flying became the proverbial piece of cake from then on.

Although he enjoyed his time in Australia, Michael felt he could have been more usefully employed back in England with regard to the war effort, following events such as the Battle of France, the Battle of Britain and the Blitz, occurring in the northern hemisphere. Obviously, he was able to read about the situation at home but was frustrated by the Australian press who seemed to single out the exploits of their own countrymen and never mentioned the RAF contribution to the war effort.

The last eight months or so of Michael's tour of duty in Australia was as Group Navigation Officer, No. 1 (Training) Group, RAAF, based in the Toorak suburb of Melbourne; he had, by this time, been promoted in the rank of squadron leader. In the spring of 1942, he was posted home and had a number of reasons to remember the voyage:

> On 16 May 1942 I was posted back to England and embarked on a small modern liner in Sydney docks for the journey home. Our route took us between the North and South Islands of New Zealand via the South Pacific to the Panama Canal, from there to Liverpool via the Azores. Our ship was a Dutch vessel called the *Ruys* and it was fast enough to be allowed to travel alone which was much nicer than being in a convoy; she could do 26 knots for short periods. The voyage was uneventful apart from being shadowed by a Focke-Wulf Fw200 Condor [a German four-engine, maritime patrol] aircraft, as we passed west of the Bay of Biscay. The ship's captain piled on the speed and we were left alone. As we approached the Azores we came across the crew of a Norwegian tanker in an open boat. They had been torpedoed about six weeks earlier and were making for Flores in the Azores. They knew exactly where they were and refused all offers of help. However, in an exchange of radio messages with the U.K. our captain was ordered to arrest the Norwegians and take them on board along with their boat. On being informed of these orders the Norwegian skipper said he had no intention of obeying as this was the second time he had been torpedoed in less than two years, he was going to settle in the Azores and stay there for the rest of the war. Our captain said he was going to obey the orders he had been given, particularly as we were in a very dangerous position stationary in the middle of a submarine infested sea. So he ordered his crew to secure the Norwegian's boat and hoist it aboard, with them in it if they would not come aboard normally. This was done amid much abuse and shouting. As I was manning one of the Oerlikan [*sic.*] ack-ack guns at the time, I was ordered to train it on the Norwegians as a means of persuading them to comply. As soon as they were on board we were on our way again at fairly high speed.

On his arrival back in England, Squadron Leader Wyatt immediately noticed that things had changed in the two years he had been away. Austerity was very much in evidence, a fact he saw all around after having lived in the land of plenty.

He returned home with orders to report to the Air Ministry Personnel Department where he would be given a posting. On reporting as instructed, he was informed that after he had undertaken operational training at an OTU, and heavy aircraft conversion at HCU, he would be posted to an operational squadron in 3 Group, Bomber Command.

Obeying orders, Michael reported to No. 10 Operational Training Unit at Abingdon, which was equipped with obsolete Whitley Mk V bombers. Having been at the base for three weeks, during which time hardly any flying was achieved due to the persistent adverse weather conditions, the airfield was closed down for concrete runways to be laid.

It was on his arrival at Abingdon that Michael was introduced to a crew that had been selected for him; he found them to be six pleasant and co-operative people with whom he looked forward to flying, and he hoped the feeling was reciprocated. The crew was made up Pilot Officer H. Daborn, navigator, Sergeants Gordon Clary, wireless operator, E. Henry, air gunner, J. Heal, T. Kemp, and A. Ames. From Abingdon, the newly formed crew went to No. 12 Operational Training Unit at Chipping Warden, where they were to fly Vickers Wellington, Mk III bombers. On completion of that course, they were posted to No. 1651 Heavy Conversion Unit at Waterbeach, where Michael and his crew converted to the four-engined Stirling Mk I bomber. The next stop was a posting to that operational squadron in 3 Group:

> At last, having completed the HCU course we were posted to XV Squadron at Bourn in Cambridgeshire, which was a satellite airfield of RAF Oakington, the home of No. 7 Pathfinder Squadron. On arrival at Bourn, the Commanding Officer, Wing Commander Douglas Lay, DSO, DFC & Bar, MiD, informed me that I was to take over as flight commander of 'A' Flight. The Squadron was equipped with Stirling Mk I and Mk III aircraft. Operational life on the Squadron was very carefree and at times extremely rowdy; the spirit was very good, and everyone thought highly of the C.O., who was clearly very efficient at his job.

Michael arrived at Bourn on 26 October 1942 and flew his first operational sortie, as second pilot to Warrant Officer Sayers, on Stirling R9192 the next evening. Six aircraft were detailed for a mine-laying operation in the estuary of the Gironde River. It was a clear moonlit night and all crews except one, which returned early due to a defective turret, saw their parachute mines float down to the water.

Although all but one of the operations detailed for the first week of November were cancelled, Michael flew his second operational sortie on the night of the 7th. On this occasion, he was to fly as second pilot to Flight Lieutenant Baigent, on an attack against Genoa, Italy. Cyril Baigent, a New Zealander by birth, was an experienced bomber pilot who was undertaking his thirtieth operational sortie that night. He was to rise to the rank of wing commander, and was to be the recipient of a DSO, DFC and Bar, and an AFC.

He was to die, almost eleven years to the day later, on 10 November 1953, while on active service with the Royal New Zealand Air Force.

The attack was deemed successful with all crews having clear views of the target on approach, and all being able to see the marker flares. Two aircraft returned early, one of which was Stirling BK595, whose pilot, Flight Sergeant Frank Hamilton, RCAF, reported that the port inner airscrew was unserviceable and that the starboard outer engine oil pressure had dropped.

The next night, Michael flew a third operational sortie as second pilot; on this occasion, he flew with Flight Sergeant Hamilton, who ten days later was to be recommended for the immediate award of a Distinguished Flying Medal, on a 'Nickel' (leaflet dropping) raid over Marseilles, in the South of France. The mission went well and all aircraft returned safely to base, even though Flight Sergeant Alexander Halkett, RCAF, affectionately known to his crew as 'Porky', is recorded as having flown back on two-and-a-half engines.

Two nights later, Michael flew as captain of the aircraft in his own right when he took his crew on a mine-laying sortie in the Friesian Islands; the results of their labours could not be recorded due to the cloud base being down to 2,000 feet. There was no fighter or enemy opposition, and they returned to Bourn with little to report.

Another mine-laying sortie was detailed for the night of the 16th, when Michael made a return visit to the estuary of the Gironde River. For the crews who took part in the raid, it was a repeat of the sortie to the same area three weeks earlier, with a low cloud base, no fighters, and no flak.

Part of Michael's duties, as a flight commander, was to prepare the battle orders for the operations dictated by Bomber Command HQ and select the aircrews that would carry them out; the task obviously meant putting his own name on this document. Having given himself four days off operational flying, but still having to deal with admin duties, Michael added his name, those of his crew and that of Pilot Officer Crich, a relatively new pilot who would be undertaking his second 'second dickey' trip, to the battle order for the night of 20 November, an attack against Turin.

> I had already been down to Italy when I bombed the docks at Genoa on the 7th, so knew the drill fairly well. We took off at 18.00 hours in Stirling BK595 and set course for the French coast, which we crossed at Fécamp. The Germans gave us the usual welcome for a few miles either side of the coastline but did not bother us again. It was the full moon period and as we flew over France the moon rose up fully and the sky was just like early daylight with excellent visibility. We were due to cross the Alps near Grenoble but as we got there, and whilst I was admiring the staggeringly beautiful sight of the snow-covered mountains bathed in soft moonlight, the starboard inner engine suddenly cut out. It seemed like an ignition failure and as if the switches had suddenly been put in the 'off' position.

Right: Wing Commander (later Grp Capt.) Michael Wyatt, DFC, MiD, joined XV Squadron, in the rank of Sqn Ldr, on 26 October 1942. (*Author's collection via the late Grp Capt. M. Wyatt*)

Below: The crew of Stirling BK595: *standing left to right*: Plt Off. H. Daborn, navigator; Sgt Gordon Clary, W/op; Sgt A. Ames, F/E; Sqn Ldr M. Wyatt, pilot; Sgt E. Henry; Sgt J. Heal; and Sgt T. Kemp. (*Author's collection via the late Grp Capt. M. Wyatt*)

Above: Spanish mechanics search the shattered remains of Stirling bomber BK595 on a beach at Playa de Aro. (*Author's collection via the late Grp Capt. M. Wyatt*)

Left: The tangled components that once kept Stirling BK595 in the air lay strewn across a Spanish beach. (*Author's collection via the late Grp Capt. M. Wyatt*)

The pilot called for the flight engineer and the second pilot to check all the obvious mechanisms and circuits that might have caused the failure, but they both reported back with negative responses. Michael then decided to feather the propeller but for some reason it did not fully respond, but when he tried to un-feather the airscrew to see if it would feather fully on a second attempt, it simply refused to budge either way. While all of this had been going on, Michael had tried to keep the aircraft on course, but found with the drag caused by the partially feathered propeller, he was not able to maintain height—certainly not enough to get them over the Alps on the planned course. The navigator was ordered to produce a new course which would take the aircraft slightly off to the west, in order that it might cross over the lower mountains in that region. While the navigator plotted a new course, the pilot informed his crew of the situation:

> I called up the whole crew and explained what had happened so far and told them that once we had got rid of the bombload we should be able to maintain height and return safely to base on three engines. I also explained that as we were less than 100 miles from the target I considered that it would be best to get rid of the bombs in the proper way over the target, rather than jettison them where we were. They seemed to agree as they did not raise any queries when I asked if anyone had any doubts about my decision.

The Stirling droned on towards Turin and although the remnants of the Pathfinder marker flare were still burning, they could not be seen clearly because of the smoke from the earlier bombing. Due to her engine problems, Stirling BK595 was late over the target area.

Their allotted duty done, the pilot asked the navigator for a reciprocal course for home. When the latter responded, he sounded very glum as he stated that the flight engineer was very concerned about the fuel consumption and that they possibly had insufficient fuel to get back. Michael instructed the navigator and second pilot to go over the calculations with the flight engineer. When the answer came back it was not good news, there was definitely not enough fuel to get them back to England, let alone Bourn.

After a further discussion with the navigator, the pilot informed his crew he was going to head for Spain, as it was much nearer than England. He added that if they made it, he could either ditch in the sea or crash land on a beach. The second pilot, who had already experienced ditching in the North Sea, expressed his concerns and feelings about being subjected to a similar episode. The rest of the crew individually expressed their preference, if given the choice, as being for a crash landing. Michael assured his crew that, if possible that is what he would endeavour to accomplish, he then concentrated on doing his best to keep the aircraft airborne.

Flying parallel with the French coast just south of Marseilles, the port inner engine began showing signs of losing power and, as the only remaining generator in use was powered by this engine, Michael had no intention of losing it, he kept it going by reducing the revolutions as much as possible as he had no desire to put his aircraft down in the South of France. The aircraft was, at this stage, flying at an altitude of approximately 8,000 feet, but it was gradually losing height. Michael had calculated that he wanted to be about 1,500 feet when he was over the Spanish coast. As the aircraft approached the small coastal town of Portbou, in the most north-eastern corner of Spain, adjacent to the French border, the pilot addressed his crew:

> I made sure they knew their positions and drill for a crash landing. I also ordered the bomb aimer to activate the explosive charges on the GEE and IFF sets and instructed the wireless operator to smash the radio set. The noise of the explosive charges was quite deafening and the smell of cordite was most overpowering. As soon as I spotted a suitable beach with plenty of sand and not too many rocks I ordered the crew to take up crash positions. I did one quick circuit and then went in and put the aircraft down on a deserted beach. The landing was very smooth but just before the aircraft skidded to a halt the port wing hit some low rocks that ran down the beach at right angles to our landing path. The impact swung the aircraft to port and the fuselage broke in half just behind the wing root.

The fact the fuselage broke in half assisted the crew in effecting a quick and easy escape from the wreckage, all of whom clambered out unscathed but looking shaken, bewildered and with the sounds of tearing, twisting and wrenching metal still ringing in their ears.

Having accounted for everyone, the pilot explained that their first responsibility was to set fire to the aircraft using the two incendiary bombs provided for that purpose. Two of the crew members went back into the wreckage but, although they operated the incendiaries correctly, neither of them would ignite, a fact they related to their captain. On hearing of this debacle, the second pilot immediately volunteered to go back in and set a fire in the cockpit utilising maps, charts and instruction manuals for the purpose. To aid the second pilot, the flight engineer had also gone aboard and opened the fuel jettison valves to release any remaining amounts of fuel. Soon there was a good fire going, with smoke issuing out of the broken fuselage, accompanied by the sound of exploding ammunition.

It was at that moment that Michael became aware of four figures, all dressed in black or dark uniforms approaching the crew from behind, shouting and firing rifles over the Englishmen's heads. Thinking of his crew's safety, the pilot told them to stop what they were doing, raise their hands above their heads, and follow him up the beach.

The aggressors turned out to be members of the *Guardia Civil*, all of whom started talking at the same time in a very guttural tongue, which was later identified as Catalan, a dialect of Spanish. Unfortunately, no one could understand what anybody else was saying. With two of the uniformed guards positioning themselves in front of the crew members, and the other two taking station behind them, it became obvious the Englishmen were being escorted up the beach to a cliff face which, surprisingly, had a café at the top of it which was still open at four o'clock in the morning.

While three of the guards sat around drinking coffee and brandy, the fourth guard made a number of telephone calls, presumably to find out what to do with their captives. As no drinks had been offered to the 'prisoners', Michael did his best to get refreshment for his men:

> I indicated by mumbo jumbo that we would like a drink too but without result. I did however recognise the word '*Dinero*' which clearly meant money and it became obvious that unless we had money we could not have a drink. We sat around for an hour or so feeling very fed up and longing for both a wash and some sleep. Our guards seemed to be quite happy drinking brandy and smoking foul smelling cigarettes. They kept giving us furtive glances and, occasionally, made loud remarks directed at us in their strange language.

An army officer who spoke reasonably good English eventually appeared, and it was obvious from his agitated and terse manner, when he spoke to the squadron leader, that he was very annoyed at having his sleep interrupted. He informed the English officer that as he and his crew had entered Spain illegally, without papers, they would all be incarcerated in the international internment camp at Miranda near Gerona; this news horrified the crew as a whole.

During escape and evasion briefings, all RAF aircrew were warned by the intelligence officers of the pitfalls of being sent to Miranda. The camp was notorious for its squalid conditions, meagre food rations, and (more concerningly) its high death rate. When Michael remonstrated with the army officer, the latter informed the captives that they had better do as they were told or they would regret it. The RAF officer stood his ground and said they had the right to talk to the British Consul General in Barcelona, to which he received the response, 'You have no rights at all'.

Much against their will and with their protestations falling on deaf ears, the crew were informed they would be going to Gerona and, as there was no available transport, they would have to walk there. The continuing protests of the crew, which got louder as the crew were forced to march in uncomfortable flying boots, received attention from an unexpected quarter:

> We must have been making a noise as lights came on in several houses and a man wearing pyjamas and a dressing gown came out of one of the houses to see what was going on. He asked in perfect English if we were British airmen, which I immediately confirmed as being correct. I hastily informed him of our predicament and he in return confirmed the *Guardia Civil* had no right to deny us access to the British Consulate or make us walk to Gerona. He then quickly turned to the army officer and his men and told them to escort us to the council offices in St Feliu, where we were to spend what was left of the night. The Spanish guards were obviously in awe of this gentleman, and sheepishly did as they were instructed. He then informed me that he had read law at Oxford and was a solicitor with a practice in Gerona and another in St Feliu. He concluded by telling us that he would arrange for our proper treatment under International Law; this intervention altered the course of our lives [while] in Spain.

Having arrived at the council offices and been shown where to bed down for the night, the rawness and unreality of what had happened to them began to hit the crew. Several of them had never been away from England before and in the shaken and emotional state they found themselves, one or two of them broke down and sobbed uncontrollably in the darkness of that room.

Michael and his crew were awoken by the arrival of the office workers who, even at 8.30 a.m., gave the Englishmen red wine to drink and dry bread to eat. Although they were given breakfast, no opportunity to wash or shave was offered; they were allowed to go to the toilet, one at a time, under armed guard.

Mid-morning, an English-speaking Spanish Air Force officer arrived. Having introduced himself as Captain Matamoros-Scott, his English mother's maiden name being used after his father's surname (as was the Spanish custom), he then dismissed the *Guardia Civil* before explaining to the bemused airmen that he was to be responsible for them for the time being.

Captain Matamoros-Scott took his charges to a local café where they had breakfast, including hot, black coffee and the opportunity to have a wash. He then took them back to the beach to see the wreckage of their crashed Stirling in daylight. Michael wondered about the Spaniard's motive for doing this:

> By the numerous questions he asked, it seemed Matamoros-Scott was cross-examining us but I had previously reminded the crew of their obligation to give only 'name, rank and number' and when he realised that his questions were a waste of time, he said we would continue our journey.

The group was taken to Barcelona in two antiquated cars, with cloth sacking where there should have been tyres; this journey, not surprisingly, took approximately two hours. Michael travelled in the front of the lead car, along with the captain, who persisted in trying to engage the former in what was supposedly casual conversation, but was in reality, mild interrogation. It also became obvious to the RAF officer that his 'interrogator' had made a close inspection of the wreckage of the Stirling as he kept referring to the 'Identification Friend or Foe' (IFF) equipment, which of course the crew had destroyed.

On arrival in Barcelona, the crew were taken straight to the British Consulate, where they were introduced to Mr Harold Farquhar (possibly later, Sir Harold Farquhar, KCMG, MC), to whom the crew related their story. After a lengthy period of questioning and cross-examination, the crew were offered the opportunity to wash and shave, presented with food and drinks, and informed they would be allowed to spend the night in the Consulate. The unwelcome news was that under international law, they would all be handed back to the Spanish authorities the next morning.

At 8.30 a.m. on the morning of 23 November, Captain Matamoros-Scott collected the airmen and took them in the same two cars to Zaragoza, where they were to be interned in a small hotel near to a large Army Area HQ to which they would have to report once or twice a day. Due to the makeshift tyres on the cars, the journey took ten hours, at an average speed of 10 mph.

Throughout the length of the journey, the captain engaged the squadron leader in more of that seemingly casual conversation, which Michael had become wise to, leaving him to believe his assumption that Matamoros-Scott was in fact a highly-trained and experienced interrogator.

Having arrived at their destination and spent the night in the hotel, the next morning the crew were taken shopping to purchase new civilian clothing along with a selection of toiletries and shaving equipment, for which the Captain instructed the shops to submit the bills for payment to the British Embassy in Madrid. Looking more presentable, the British airmen were taken to the Army HQ, where they were introduced to a general and two colonels. Using the Captain as an interrupter, the general told Michael that it might be helpful if he learned a little Spanish, if only to pass the time, he also put the crew on their honour not to try to escape.

Back at the hotel, the Captain informed the crew that he would not be seeing them anymore but before leaving warned them that their every move would be shadowed by plain-clothed agents. It was shortly after this final meeting that Michael started taking Spanish lessons every afternoon except Sunday. Most days, he was joined by Pilot Officer Daborn and Pilot Officer Crich, both of whom decided to also learn some of the language.

At the end of the first week, the colonel to whom the crew had been reporting every day, asked Michael to stay behind after the others had left. The colonel explained to the British officer that there were between thirty and forty allied airmen interned in Spain, usually at or near the locations the *Guardia Civil* had apprehended them. One example he cited was the apprehension of a complete crew of a Halifax who had ditched close to the beach at Alicante and were interned in a military establishment in or near the city. The crew to whom the colonel referred could well have been that headed by Flight Lieutenant A. Dowse, DFC, whose Halifax Mk II bomber, W1063, ditched into the sea approximately 5 miles off the Spanish coast, between Alicante and Valencia, on the night of 7–8 November 1942. The crew were apprehended and interned in the city of Albacete, which obviously had a military presence.

The colonel then explained that as allies of the Germans, Spain did not intern any member of the German services entering the country but allowed them to return to Germany without undue delay. Putting these two factors together, the colonel described how the Spanish authorities had worked out an exchange rate that for every thirty Germans who were allowed to go free, one British serviceman would be released. Listening to the colonel, Michael wondered where this conversation was actually going and then the former got to the point:

> The colonel explained how he had managed to commandeer two large spa hotels at a place called Alhama de Aragón. He said that as I was the senior British internee in Spain at that time and as my crew were obviously well disciplined, he would like me to form a proper internment centre at Alhama, run on service lines. I replied that I would be prepared to take on the responsibility provided that there was some kind of recompense for me. When he asked what I had in mind I immediately replied that my crew and I should be allowed to go free as soon as the centre was running to his complete satisfaction. Implying it was a reasonable proposition, he agreed and much hand shaking ensued.

The next communication Michael received from the colonel was on 7 December, instructing him and his crew to be prepared for a move on the 9th, when a car would collect them and drive them the 75 miles to Alhama de Aragón.

It was only when they arrived at the hotel that Squadron Leader Wyatt was glad he had taken the opportunity to learn some Spanish as neither the manager nor his staff spoke any English. Having had a light lunch, followed by a quick look around the facilities, Michael sat down with the manager and explained his thoughts and plans. He decreed that officers and NCOs would all use the large hotel dining room for all meals, with no segregated areas. However, given there were two lounges, the senior officer set aside the larger of the two, on the ground floor, for the NCOs, given that there would probably be more of them than there would be commissioned ranks, while the officers would use the smaller lounge situated on the first floor. Again, not knowing the ratio of NCOs compared to officer numbers, Michael separated the sleeping quarters accordingly and, befitting his status, selected a large single room for his own use.

The next task was to compile a list of 'standing orders', which, when completed, ran into three foolscap pages. These were typed out by Pilot Officer Daborn and fixed to suitable boards where they would be on permanent display. A school exercise book was acquired, ruled up as a signing-in log and placed with the displayed orders; each new internee having to sign and date as having read and understood the orders. Finally, having ensured everything had been properly thought out, Michael got the manager to telephone the colonel in Zaragoza and advise him that the internment centre was ready for occupation. The latter was duly impressed by the speed with which the operation had been completed.

Two days later, the first internees arrived; among them was the Halifax crew who had ditched near Alicante. The new arrivals all settled into their new accommodation fairly quickly, although one or two of them did moan about having to conform to the written orders. At the appropriate time, Michael called them all together and briefed them on how he wanted them to conduct themselves; whether they were officers or other ranks, it was a policy he adopted with all new arrivals.

To Michael's surprise, and the joy of the internees, the air *attaché* from the British Embassy in Madrid, Squadron Leader Robert Taylor, arrived one afternoon bearing consignments of books, games, playing cards, and footballs; he also carried with him a large amount of Spanish money. which was passed to Michael with instructions that the latter was to issue a set amount to each man on a weekly basis.

Early on Christmas Day morning, the air *attaché* and his wife, along with a number of other members of the Embassy staff, arrived with enough turkeys and Christmas puddings, together with all the other related trimmings, to give the internees some festive cheer, and there was plenty to go around.

Looking around and seeing how well his efforts had been supported by the men under his jurisdiction, Michael thought it was about time he spoke with the colonel:

> I contacted the colonel and told him I had fulfilled my side of our agreement and would like him to honour his side. He came to Alhama a few days later and spent the best part of the day with us to see if I was running a satisfactory organisation. At the end of the day he declared himself very satisfied with all that he had seen. His only criticism was that he thought the attire of some of the men left a lot to be desired. I told him I agreed but there was no way of getting clothing for them. Before he left he thanked me and said he would shortly arrange for me and my crew to leave, along with a flight lieutenant who was far from well.

At the end of the first week of January, Squadron Leader Taylor, the air *attaché*, arrived with a small bus on to which Michael and his crew loaded their meagre possessions; his sole remaining task now was to hand over to a new senior officer who would be responsible for continuing the smooth running of the 'camp'. Once everyone was on board, the bus pulled away and made the very slow-going journey to Gibraltar via Madrid, where they stopped for five days, before continuing on to Seville, where they stopped for one day. On 15 January 1943, Michael, his crew, and the flight lieutenant stood again on British soil when they crossed the frontier into Gibraltar and alighted from the bus.

Although the flight lieutenant was not named, and no mention was made of his crew travelling with him, it could well be that this airman was Flight Lieutenant Dowse, the Halifax pilot, whom it is known travelled via Gibraltar and arrived back in England on, or around, the same date as Michael and his crew.

Having spent a couple of days relaxing in the British Overseas Territory, the group of RAF airmen boarded MS *Ville D'Oran*, a small passenger ship, for their return to the United Kingdom. Just before boarding the ship, much to his chagrin, Michael was informed that he had been appointed officer in charge of troops for the voyage: 'This annoyed me a lot as I felt I was due some peace which I had not had since we took off from Bourn on 20 November 1942. However, I found the duties were not too onerous'.

The ship docked at Gairloch in Strath Bay, on the coast of the Northwest Highlands of Scotland, where British intelligence officers from MI9 were waiting to meet the airmen. Having disembarked, the RAF group was escorted to London, where they underwent a long and tedious debriefing at the Metropole Hotel in Central London. It is not recorded how long this process took, but when the operatives from MI9 had exhausted all their lines of enquiry, and gathered all the information they could, the former internees were given periods of leave. Michael was given approximately fourteen days leave, until 18 February, on which date he was ordered to report to XV Squadron at RAF Bourn:

> On arrival at Bourn I found the Squadron had been taken over by a new CO who did not know much about my adventures on the trip to Turin, or my subsequent sojourn in Spain, and was not interested enough to ask me any questions about it. My flight had been given to somebody else so I was given 'C' Flight which was a new one being formed.

As he had not flown for some while, Michael undertook several day and night-flying exercises, along with his crew, to familiarise themselves with operating procedures; they commenced operational flying duties on the night of 8 March, with an attack against Nuremberg. The next night, Michael and his crew attacked Munich, both operations being completed without incident. Two nights later, they attacked Stuttgart and later recorded seeing their own bombs burst in a built-up area.

Changeable and inclement weather conditions, together with the administrative duties he had to undertake as a flight commander, prevented Michael from flying operationally again until 10 April, when he flew a sortie to Frankfurt. Although he did not know it at the time, the attack against Frankfurt proved to be the last operational sortie he was to fly with XV Squadron.

On the 14th, the squadron moved to RAF Mildenhall and, although Michael made the move with them, he was only to remain with XV until 2 May, due to the fact he was promoted in the rank of wing commander and given command of No. 75 (New Zealand) Squadron with whom he went on to have further adventures. Later that same year he was the recipient of a Distinguished Flying Cross, which was gazetted on 10 September 1943.

5

The Diary: Sergeant Frederick 'Steve' Stevens

After facing oblivion—no dreams, no images, just total oblivion and silence—his eyelids flickered once or twice and slowly opened. Equally slowly, his eyes began to focus, but he was not seeing clearly. He felt as though he was upright, but he was not standing on anything solid.

With his eyes regaining focus, he glanced down to see the ground a short distance below his dangling feet. Turning his gaze upwards, he perceived that he was hanging by a parachute from a beech tree. As he slowly regained his senses, the sounds of battle began to whirl around in his brain; the staccato rattle of machine gun fire, the crackle and roar of flames fanned by a vortex of rushing wind, the screaming of tortured aero-engines as the aircraft plummeted to earth, and the fight for survival before oblivion. As the recollections came flooding back, Sergeant Frederick 'Steve' Stevens remembered the horror and nightmare of being shot down. What he did not know or realise at that time was that excluding the 'second dickey' pilot, he was the sole survivor of his seven-man crew.

Going back in time approximately three years, Frederick Stevens's RAF story started when he joined the Royal Air Force on 16 February 1940. He was mustered as a clerk, General Duties Branch, given the rank of aircraftman second class and was sent to RAF Manston, Kent, for basic training before being posted to the RAF Records Office at Ruislip.

The young airman was a diligent worker and took his duties seriously. This paid off in the promotion stakes as he was made up to leading aircraftman less than six months later, on 1 August 1940, and received further promotion to the rank of corporal on 15 March 1941. Needless to say, when the Records Office was relocated to Gloucester in 1941, Corporal Stevens went with it.

It was in Gloucester on Saturday, 31 October 1941 that Steve decided to purchase a diary in which to record his daily routine and experiences, although what sort of adventures worth recording he thought would befall him in a clerical office, he did not say. Probably the most exciting entry he recorded in his diary at that time was that with effect from 1 January 1942, he was promoted to the rank of sergeant.

As the days ticked by, Steve began to have thoughts about his future, the war, and what other part he could play in it:

> During 1942, I felt I could be more useful to the war effort. Therefore, without warning my parents, I applied to remuster to aircrew. My application was granted and on 20 September I reported to the Aircrew Selection Board, at Weston-super-Mare, where I was accepted to train as an air gunner.

Training took place at Hereford and Dalcross (Inverness), the latter being where Steve was awarded his air gunners brevet on Friday, 29 January 1943. Steve moved on to Marham, near King's Lynn, where he joined an operational training unit. Although the OTU flew Vickers Wellington bombers, on his second day at the base Steve was surprised to see a Short Stirling bomber. Being the first time he had ever seen the real thing, he felt moved to record the event in his diary. Two weeks later, on Saturday 13 February, Steve left Marham and made his way to 1657 Heavy Conversion Unit, at Stradishall, where he was to renew his acquaintance with the Stirling. It was at HCU that he was initiated into the mysteries of the inner working of the huge aeroplane, not only through various lectures on the aircraft, but by gaining flying experience when the weather permitted.

One week later, Steve was assigned to 'B' Flight and was crewed up with Pilot Officer Jim Stowell, a New Zealander, from Timaru, South Island. The rest of the crew consisted of Sergeants Leslie Pattisson, wireless operator; Jim Banyer, bomb aimer; Ted Kirby, flight engineer; and William Jennings, mid-upper gunner. The navigator, Sergeant Jackson, was to join the crew a few days later.

Being declared ready for operational duties on Tuesday 2 March, the crew received a posting to XV Squadron at RAF Bourn, Cambridgeshire. However, their actual order to move was not received for a further two days.

Even though he was about to undertake operational flying, with all its trials and tribulations, Steve had still not informed his parents that he had volunteered for the more dangerous occupation of aircrew. As far as they were concerned, their son was still ensconced in an office, sifting through paperwork and drinking copious mugs of tea.

Having arrived at Bourn at 4 p.m. on the afternoon of Friday 5 March, Steve and his crew spent the rest of the day settling in. The following day, they all travelled to Oakington where they had been ordered to draw flying clothing from the stores section.

In order that the rookie crew could get to know the area from which they were to operate, they made their first cross-country flight two days after their arrival at Bourn. Flying Stirling BK611, which carried the name *Te Kooti*, after a New Zealand Maori leader, the crew flew north, via King's Lynn to Whitley Bay. Pilot Officer Stowell then turned out over the North Sea in a wide sweeping turn, before re-crossing the coast and overflying the city of Lincoln, with its magnificent aerial views of the Cathedral. BK611 then retraced her flight plan south, landing back at Bourn a couple of hours later.

The following day, Jim Stowell took charge of Stirling Mk I EF345, which the crew took on a night cross-country exercise toward the end of that same day. Nothing of note occurred on that trip, but Steve did record one comment which should have given a little cause for concern, it read, '[It took] a long time finding base'.

Knowing they would soon be undertaking operations sorties, the crew spent every minute they could getting to know their aircraft, inside and out, on the ground and in the air. Finally, their names appeared on the battle order for a mine-laying operation on the night of 11–12 March. The following morning, Steve made an entry in his diary:

> Did air test on M—Mother over the Wash—tested guns—Took off at 19.00 hours to lay mines in enemy waters—Took six mines, saw them float down [on parachutes]. A flak ship opened-fire on another aircraft, apart from that no excitement—Took three hours.

The following night, another mine-laying operation was undertaken, in the Friesian Islands. As with the previous raid, Steve was able, from his rear turret, to watch the mines go down and saw one explode soon after hitting the water.

During mid-March, three attempts were made by XV Squadron to bomb the docks at St Nazaire, situated at the mouth of the estuary of the Loire River, but each time the operation was scrubbed at the last minute due to unfavourable meteorological reports; finally, on 28 March, the attack was carried out. After all the waiting, the crews who participated were rewarded with an entry in the operational record book which read, 'The operation was deemed a success'. Five days later, a follow-up attack on St Nazaire was programmed; originally, nine aircraft were detailed to participate in the attack, but just before the final briefing took place, four of the aircraft listed were scrubbed.

Stirling EF345, with Pilot Officer Jim Stowell at the controls, took off at 7.46 p.m. and set course for the Bay of Biscay. From the very beginning, the pilot realised there was some sort of mechanical problem, the aircraft was sluggish in its response to the controls and was experiencing difficulty maintaining altitude. When out over the sea, off the south coast of England, the pilot ordered Jim Banyer, the bomb aimer, to jettison a 1,000-lb bomb.

Stirling EF345 crossed the French coast at 8,000 feet and had only managed to climb another 1,000 feet by the time the target was reached. Although Jim Stowell was experiencing problems with regards to aircraft control and maintaining altitude, he had no such problems regarding speed, as was evident when the Stirling arrived over the target area ahead of the ETA. Steve made a note in his diary:

> Arrived over target early, at 9,000 feet—the defences opened up. [We] stooged around until the Pathfinder Force (PFF) marker flares were dropped. Going in [to bomb] AA had our height to a tee. We dropped our six 1,000 lb and one 500 lb bombs [at 11.50 p.m.] and scrammed.

The ground defences opened fire and EF345 was buffeted and tossed around as the flak exploded around them, hitting the aircraft several times, but fortunately not damaging any vital parts. The only problem was that Ted Kirby, the flight engineer, felt unwell as the aircraft pitched up and down and was, eventually, airsick. Steve, sitting in the claustrophobic confines of his rear turret, later confided in his diary that he too had felt unwell.

The Stirling flew on and, having left the target area, headed north towards the south coast of England. Apart from having to contend with flying a damaged bomber, Pilot Officer Stowell also had to contend with a navigator of less than required standards, who got confused over the aircraft's actual position. This resulted in the aircraft landing at the grass fighter airfield at Middle Wallop, Hampshire.

The crew had breakfast and lunch at Middle Wallop while the aircraft was patched up and refuelled, before flying it back to Bourn. On landing back at their home base, Sergeant Ted Kirby was immediately grounded and removed from the crew; his place as flight engineer was taken by Sergeant Pete Sharman.

An operation against Kiel was ordered for 4 April. Thirteen aircraft were detailed for the assault, including Stirling bomber BF475, which Pilot Officer Stowell and his crew were to fly, due to their usual mount, EF345, being unserviceable. They took off at 8.30 p.m. and headed for the target, flying in 10/10th cloud which hindered them for the duration of the flight. As BF475 crossed the enemy coast on the way in, two searchlight beams endeavoured to penetrate the cloud in search of the raiders. Flak rose into the night sky in a very haphazard, and almost lazy, manner. The raid was not considered a success, possibly due to the number of decoy fires drawing the bombers away from the real aiming point. Although the flak was more intensive on part of the route out of the target area, it did not create any problems for Jim Stowell; fortunately, neither did the fighters, which was good news for the air gunners, as Steve later wrote in his diary: 'Aircraft—Tommy, turret not up to scratch'.

Above: Five members of the original crew who flew with Plt Off. Jim Stowell are *from left to right*, Sgt Jim Banyer, B/A; Sgt William Jennings, AG; Sgt Ted Kirby, F/E; Sgt Leslie Paterson; and W/op; Sgt Frederick 'Steve' Stevens, AG. (*Author's collection*)

Below: A Horsa glider aircraft being loaded up with equipment at RAF Bourn, in preparation for transporting to XV Squadron's new operating base at RAF Mildenhall. (*Author's collection*)

Above: The runway at RAF Mildenhall, viewed from the cockpit of a XV Squadron Stirling bomber. (*Author's collection*)

Below: Frederick Stevens (standing second left) in Reichswald Forest War Cemetery, accompanied by post-war members of XV Squadron, pays tribute to his fellow crew members who perished on 5 May 1943. The former air gunner stands behind the headstone marking the grave of his pilot, Plt Off. Jim Stowell, RNZAF. (*Author's collection via XV Squadron*)

The following day, during the afternoon, although the war was still on-going, all XV Squadron personnel were called together for the purpose of getting some squadron group photographs. First the members of aircrew were arranged, either sitting or standing lined across the front of a Stirling bomber; the appropriate image having been captured on film, the same procedure was applied for members of ground crew.

Bomber Command ordered an attack against Duisburg on the night of 8 April, for which XV Squadron detailed fifteen aircraft and crews for the operation. Although the names of Pilot Officer Stowell and his crew were on the battle order, and they took off at 9.39 p.m. along with the rest of the squadron, they were destined not to accomplish their task. As Stirling bomber EF345 headed towards the North Sea, the navigator informed the pilot that he had mislaid his navigation charts. Jim Stowell continued his track out to sea, where he jettisoned the bombload before returning to base. The following morning, the pilot had the unenviable task of informing the members of his crew that the navigation charts had been found; they were in the navigator's satchel. As survival depended very much on each man carrying out his specific duties to the best of his ability, Pilot Officer Stowell had no alternative but to replace the navigator.

A raid on Frankfurt on the night of the 10th was the last operational detail XV Squadron made from Bourn prior to transferring to RAF Mildenhall, Suffolk. Unfortunately, one crew was not destined to make the move to the Suffolk located base, a fact Steve recorded in his diary:

> Operations—Frankfurt. Saw nothing on way in. Flak not very heavy near us although plenty of dummy fires—Pathfinder Force late. Wimpy [Vickers Wellington bomber] came up close to us on way back. We [Bomber Command] lost eighteen kites, one from our squadron.

Steve was a little out on his calculations relating to aircraft losses that night. Eight Wellington bombers, five Lancasters, five Stirlings, and three Halifaxes failed to return. He was however correct in that one of the Stirling bombers was from XV Squadron, it was the machine his crew had flown only a week before. Short Stirling BF475, piloted by Sergeant Eric Trezise, was shot down at 4.16 a.m. by a night fighter piloted by *Oberfeldwebel* Reinhard Kollak, of 7 *Gruppe*, *Nachtjagdgeschwader* 4 (7./NJG4); it was the German pilot's seventeenth aerial victory. The bomber crashed at Sainte-Geneviève, north-east of Montcornet, France, with the loss of the whole crew.

During the afternoon of Tuesday 13 April, Steve, along with a number of other spectators, watched the arrival at Bourn of two Whitworth Whitley bombers and two Airspeed Horsa gliders; these aircraft were to be used to transport equipment to RAF Mildenhall. Later that day, remembering that he had his own kit and possessions to pack ready for the move the next morning, Steve made his way back to his billet.

With the move complete, and everyone settled into their new abode and workstations, XV Squadron returned to operational duties on the night of the 16th. The allotted target was Mannheim and a total force of 271 aircraft was to carry out the attack, eighteen of which were detailed by XV Squadron.

Stirling bomber EF345 took off at 9.26 p.m. and climbed to an altitude of 9,000 feet. Pilot Officer Stowell had his usual crew on board, with the exception of Sergeant Jackson, whom he had been forced to replace. Flying as navigator to the crew on this trip was Pilot Officer Phil Murray, whom it was hoped was good at his job, especially as Steve wrote in his diary, 'Crossed French coast at 9,000 feet then dropped [down] to 1,500 feet'.

Approaching the target, Jim Stowell increased height to 12,000 feet in order to make his bombing run. The flak was now bursting with a vengeance and could be heard above the constant drone of the four huge Bristol Hercules engines and the whistling of the bombload, as the latter fell to earth. The aircraft vibrated as a flak shell exploded close to the bomber, shrapnel ricocheting along the fuselage and shattering the astrodome. No one was hurt and the crew breathed a sigh of relief as they escaped the flak barrage, but their troubles were not yet over. In the glow of the moonlight, Steve saw a Ju 88 night fighter stealing up from below the rear starboard quarter of the bomber. He yelled a warning to the pilot, who, on receipt of the instruction 'Port go', began evasive action. The Ju 88 did not follow but was seen to fly over the top of the Stirling and away into the night.

The homeward leg of their journey went without incident or trouble, and the crew landed back at Mildenhall at 3.54 a.m. However, nine minutes after Pilot Officer Stowell landed, Stirling BK657, piloted by Flight Lieutenant Charles Lyons, crashed on the runway, having been badly shot up over the target.

Although no adverse comments were recorded relating to Pilot Officer Murray's navigational skills, when the crew undertook an operational sortie on the 20th, they had a different navigator on board.

Pilot Officer Daniel Spooner was an experienced navigator who had flown on eighteen operational sorties, three of which were aborted for various technical reasons. Daniel Spooner had been posted to XV Squadron during August 1942, as a sergeant, but was granted a commission on 9 December the same year.

The target selected for Spooner's first sortie with Jim Stowell and his crew was the Heinkel Works near Rostock. A total of eighty-six Stirling bombers were assigned for the attack, fifteen of which were detailed by XV Squadron, two of which, unfortunately, failed to take off.

Stirling bomber EF345 took off from Mildenhall at 10.30 p.m. and flew at very low level out over the North Sea. Nearing the French coast, Jim Stowell steadily coaxed the aircraft up to 8,000 feet as he approached the German industrial port, situated 18 miles south of the Baltic coast. The attacking force found the target concealed by a smoke screen, but crews attacked on their ETA positions. Others, seeing the glow of fires burning beneath the smoke, unleashed their bombs loads to add to the conflagration.

Searchlights and flak were much in evidence and as EF345 flew over the target, Steve saw another Stirling coned by searchlights with flak bursting all around it. Having added their bombload to the burning fires below, Jim Stowell dived out of the target area and flew north at low level, over the Danish coast. Several flak ships around the Danish islands opened fire as the Stirling skimmed overhead; Steve returned fire and one of the flak ships immediately ceased firing. Several other flak ships continued to fire at the intruder, but when two searchlights joined the fray Steve depressed his guns and fired, causing one of the searchlights to extinguish its blinding ray.

While all this was going on, Daniel Spooner gave his pilot a new course to fly, one which would be the start of the homeward leg but, as Jim Stowell pulled the aircraft round on to the new heading, there in front of him, directly in the aircraft's flight-path, was a factory chimney. There is no written account of how the pilot avoided the chimney but avoid it he did and took the Stirling out into the dark expanse of the North Sea. The crew landed safely at Mildenhall, tired and weary, having been airborne for eight hours.

A total of eight Stirlings were listed as failed to return, including BF476, piloted by Flight Lieutenant Charles Lyons. Fortunately, although two of his crew were wounded, the pilot and his whole crew survived a crash-landing and were taken prisoners of war.

Inclement weather during the third week of April prevented the undertaking of any operational attacks. However, on the night of the 26th, conditions improved allowing Bomber Command to resume its assault against German cities and towns. On that night, a total of 561 aircraft were sent to bomb Duisburg.

Although an estimated 300 buildings were reportedly destroyed, the raid was not considered a success as the bombing was scattered over a wide area. Searchlights were very active and possibly played a part in affecting the aiming and dropping of the bombloads. Stirling EF345 was caught by the searchlight beams, another item noted by Steve: '[We were] coned in searchlights for six to eight minutes. [We] got everything including the "kitchen sink"—very lucky, counted about sixteen holes in all, some just missing vital spots'.

Sergeant Jennings, the mid-upper gunner, had a lucky escape when a large piece of shrapnel entered his turret, shattering the Perspex and just missing him. Fortunately, both the aircraft and its crew returned to Mildenhall without further misfortune.

On arriving on a squadron as a new, recently declared 'operational ready' pilot, before he was allowed to fly operational sorties with his own crew, the 'new boy' would be required to fly with an experienced crew on at least two operational sorties to ensure he was competent and confident under combat conditions; these flights were known in the RAF as 'second dickey' trips. One such pilot who was about to fly on his first 'second dickey' trip was Sergeant Tom Malcolm who arrived on XV Squadron at the end of April. He was detailed to fly with Pilot Officer Jim Stowell and his crew on an attack against Dortmund, on the night of 4 May.

The day had started like any other day on which operations were being flown, with 'daily inspection' of the aircraft, ensuring it was fit to fly, followed by an air test to further ensure it was airworthy in every respect. Later in the day came the briefing on the forthcoming raid, followed in turn by the pre-op meal of bacon and eggs.

Having taken off at 10.40 p.m., Jim Stowell set course across the North Sea. The flight to the target was uneventful, even though the night was clear and there was a new moon. As Stirling EF345 approached the target area at about 1.20 a.m. on the morning of the 5th, the crew could see the green markers on which they were to bomb quite clearly. Sergeant Jim Banyer from his position in the bomb aimers' compartment in the nose of the Stirling had an excellent view of the shimmering sea of fire ahead and below the aircraft. Every few seconds, the scene was punctured by columns of orange flame and black smoke erupting into the air as more bombs and incendiary devices found their target. Pilot Officer Stowell joined the bomber stream and prepared for his bombing run. Each member of the crew was at his respective station on the aircraft, including Sergeant Banyer, who was directing the pilot on his run-in. Nerves were stretched to the limit as the tension mounted, when suddenly, and with the stark realisation of what was happening, the weaving searchlights locked on to their aircraft. The pilot's immediate response was to push the control column forward, putting the aircraft into a dive in an effort to evade the groping beams. The blinding rays stayed with the Stirling as it dived and twisted from 16,000 feet down to 4,000 feet. Angry black bursts of flak, guided by the searchlights, exploded around the diving aircraft. The controls were momentarily wrenched from the pilot's grasp as EF345 lurched through the air as an 88-mm cannon shell exploded under the wing, setting fire to the port inner engine and wing-root.

With the stricken bomber plunging earthwards, Jim Stowell gave the order to abandon the aircraft. Steve hurriedly clambered out of his turret, retrieved his parachute from its storage rack above the rear escape hatch and clipped it on to his harness. Jettisoning the escape hatch cover and with one hand on the D-ring release handle of his parachute, Steve steadied himself as best he could and prepared to jump. Then there was total oblivion, until Steve regained consciousness in a beech tree, on the outskirts of the village of Anholt, Westphalia, near the German–Dutch border.

Sergeant Frederick Stevens was captured immediately and held in custody by the local *Bürgermeister*, until he was handed over to the authorities; he was to spend the next two years as a prisoner of war.

Unbeknown to Steve, Sergeant Tom Malcolm had evacuated the doomed aircraft via the forward escape hatch and had also floated down on his parachute to land near the Dutch border.

The blazing Stirling crashed at 2 a.m., with the rest of Steve's crew still on board; it penetrated deep into the ground in the common grazing land on the outskirts of Anholt. The remains of the crew were recovered from the wreckage and buried with full military honours in the parish cemetery on 6 May. The following day, a further body was found and buried by the side of the four already interred. Although the grave was marked 'Unknown', the airman was accorded the same respect as his comrades. The sixth member of the crew was, at that time, unaccounted for, but was found later.

Unbelievably, Steve's parents were still not aware that their son had remustered to aircrew; as far as they were concerned, he was still a records clerk. Their feelings can only be imagined when they received a telegram from the Air Ministry informing them that their son was listed as 'Missing' in action.

Forty years later, almost exactly forty years to the day, Steve joined a group of ex-XV Squadron members on a weekend visit to RAF Laarbruch, West Germany, where the then post-war XV Squadron was based. While there, on Sunday, 8 May 1983, along with the rest of the group, Steve attended a memorial service at Reichswald Forest War Cemetery, where many RAF aircrew are buried. After the service, the group were given twenty minutes to have a quick look around before returning to the RAF base for lunch. Steve chose at random a row of headstones to amble slowly between, a small representation of the 3,985 airmen resting there. Suddenly, he stopped and remained motionless, staring at the names on six headstones which had caught his eye. Ex-Sergeant Stevens read the names and then stood with head bowed in silent tribute, for the names were those of his own crew: the names recorded in the pages of his diary.

6

Te Kooti: Sergeant Arthur Edgley

Arthur William Edgley was a country boy born and bred. He entered this world on Easter Sunday, 27 March 1927, in the small Lincolnshire village of Gedney Dawsmere, near Long Sutton and Holbeach. Arthur's parents, Charles and Fan Edgley, had lost their first baby, a daughter, when the child was only six months old, so it was a blessing for them when Arthur was born a year later.

Although an only child, Arthur was not a lonely lad; he had many friends at the local school where, being a quick and intelligent boy, he excelled at all of the lessons. It was also fortuitous that his beloved granny Neave lived near the school and Arthur went to her home every day for his lunch. Arthur's ability at school led him to pass the exams which secured him a place at grammar school, but he chose instead to stay at the Dawsmere school where all his friends were. Apart from this, Arthur did not relish the idea of all the travelling involved getting to and from the grammar school and not getting home to pursue his many outdoor interests until late.

Among his interests, Arthur included being a choirboy at Gedney Dawsmere Church, which gave him a strong Christian grounding; he enjoyed cycling around the countryside with his friends, playing football and cricket. As he grew, he added racing pigeons, ferrets, and a dog to his list of interests, the dog always accompanying him on his wildfowling trips.

The area in which Arthur grew up was one with a close-knit farming community, which also became an integral part of his life; he knew the names of every family and who lived where. At the age of fourteen, Arthur left school and took employment on one of those farms, where he learnt to work with and care for Shire horses; he also learnt to drive a team of these majestic animals. Arthur always held his employer, Mr Denis Clifton, in very high esteem and also spoke highly of him.

With the Holbeach Marsh bombing range located about 1 mile from Dawsmere, and the many and varied RAF planes flying over it, Arthur also got to know many of the airmen based in the locality, it was almost inevitable that when the time came for Arthur to sign up for military service he chose to enlist with the Royal Air Force. However, being in a reserved occupation (agriculture), Arthur had to make many visits to the recruiting office, before he was finally accepted on his fifth attempt.

Having passed a medical in Lincoln, he was then sent to Padgate, near Warrington to be sworn in and receive his service number, following which he was sent home on deferred service. During July 1940, Arthur received instructions to report to Blackpool for kitting out and basic training; three weeks later, he was posted, along with some of his squad, to No. 4 Balloon Centre, at Chigwell, Essex, on the outskirts of East London. Unfortunately, due to Chigwell being under the flight path of the incoming German bombers intent on attacking the London docks, they spent much of their time in air-raid shelters.

From No. 4 Balloon Centre, Arthur was posted to the Ground Defence Section of Chigwell, from which he was to move on fairly quickly. He remustered to the trade of instrument repairer before volunteering, a month later, for flying duties as an air gunner. At his interview for the latter trade, the interviewing officer confirmed he would recommend Arthur for training in this capacity, but the education officer talked Arthur into remustering again for pilot training. Arthur took the latter's advice and was sent to RAF Cardington for an interview with the Aircrew Selection Board. Having been accepted, a newly promoted Aircraftman First Class Edgley made his first flight in a Fairey Battle over the Holbeach Bombing Range.

The postings then began to come thick and fast, first he was sent to the Isle of Man for a ground gunners' course, then back to Chigwell where he was promoted to the rank of leading aircraftman, before going to Aircrew Receiving Centre (ACRC) at St John's Wood, London. From ACRC, Arthur was posted to No. 12 Initial Training Wing at RAF Leuchars, near St Andrews, Fife. On 4 April 1942, LAC Edgley arrived at No. 15 Elementary Flying Training School at Kingstown, Carlisle, where he received instruction in how to fly a Miles Magister, a two-seater aeroplane; by the end of that same month, Arthur was permitted to fly solo.

With all this moving around, it seems incredible that Arthur was able to conduct a meaningful relationship with a young lady named Joan Lawson, to whom he became betrothed. Joan was a local lass from the village of Long Sutton, not that far from Arthur's birthplace. It was due to the fact that the potential pilot had been granted embarkation leave that Arthur got to spend some time with Joan and their respective families before being shipped overseas.

The Atlantic crossing to Canada, which took eight days, was made on board the 14,000-ton SS *Batory*, a pre-war, Polish-registered luxury liner, which was now operating as a troopship. Arthur spent his first few days in Canada based at No. 31 Personnel Depot, at Moncton, New Brunswick.

Travelling via Montreal and Winnipeg, the young pilot-under-training arrived at Moose Jaw, then moved on to No. 34 Elementary Flying Training School at Assiniboia. The flying training was rather haphazard, mainly due to the inclement weather, but also partly due to problems with some of the airfields in the locality. Arthur and his contingent were forced to fly the Tiger Moth aircraft into and out of any airfields that could accommodate them. To add to their problems, Arthur and a few of his contemporaries never really got on with the instructor; a situation which culminated, on 22 June 1942, with the latter removing them from flying training. Two days later, this small group of discontented airmen reported to Trenton, Ontario, where they were given the opportunity to remuster as air gunners.

Nearly three weeks later, on 14 August, Arthur reported for duty at No. 9 Bombing and Gunnery School at Mont-Joli, Quebec, where, between 26 August and 24 September, he completed a total of twenty aerial gunnery flying exercises and passed out third in his course with an exam rate of 83.5 per cent. The next day was one Arthur would not forget: 'On 25 September 1942, I received my air gunner half-wing [flying brevet] and was promoted to Sergeant. Also on this day I left for Moncton with the rest of the course who passed'.

Sergeant Edgley was posted back to No. 31 Personnel Depot for one month, in preparation for embarkation back to the United Kingdom. The homeward voyage was made on the Cunard liner, RMS *Queen Elizabeth*, on this trip the ship only took six days and docked at Gourock, Scotland, on 4 November. The next day, having disembarked from the vessel, Arthur and his contingent were entrained down to No. 7 Personnel Despatch and Reception Centre, Harrogate, where almost immediately after their arrival the contingent was sent on leave. Prior to his departure for home, Arthur was informed that on his return he would be posted to No. 12 Operational Training Unit. No. 12 OTU was based at Chipping Warden, Oxfordshire, with a satellite airfield located at Turweston, Northamptonshire. Not knowing what to expect at Chipping Warden, Arthur was in for a bit of a shock:

> At Chipping Warden there were lots of aircrews who all found themselves together and were told to form them-selves up into crews. I got talking to a bomb aimer whose home was at Holt, Norfolk. We liked each other so decided to crew together. I then asked if any pilot wanted an air gunner and a bomb aimer, to which an Australian pilot responded that he liked the look of us and we shook hands with him. The pilot then spoke with a wireless operator and asked

> him to join the crew, before going off to find an officer navigator. Sometime later he came back and told us our crew was complete.

Apart from himself as rear gunner, Arthur's crew consisted of Sergeant Jack Wilson, RAAF, pilot; Pilot Officer B. Cooper (born in Concepcion, Chile, to English parents), navigator; Sergeant Sidney Maxted, wireless operator/air gunner; and Sergeant Patrick Arnott, bomb aimer.

It was at OTU that newly formed crews started training for operational flying; for Arthur and his crew, that commenced on 31 December 1942. They were introduced to twin-engined Vickers Wellington Mk III aircraft, on which their first flying exercises were 'circuits and bumps'. The training was harder and the flying hours were longer than Arthur had experienced previously; he recorded that one cross-country training exercise lasted six hours and thirty minutes. The route Arthur and his crew had flown was from Turweston across to Blackwater Rock off the coast of Ireland, back over the Irish Sea to Dalbeattie, Scotland, down to Conwy, North Wales, down to Worcester and back to Turweston. Arthur also recorded that during that flight the crew experienced frozen oxygen pipes and he personally endured ice forming on his flying suit.

On completion of their course at OTU, the crew were sent back to Chipping Warden, the parent airfield, from where they were sent on leave. Arthur was able to spend twenty days with his beloved Joan before their time together was abruptly interrupted: 'Whilst on leave, I got a telegram telling me to report to No. 1657 Conversion Unit at RAF Stradishall on 25 March 1943. On arrival [I found] the rest of my crew were already there, so we were still together'.

Arthur also found on his arrival at Stradishall that two additional members of aircrew had been assigned to his crew: Sergeant 'Bud' Seabolt as mid-upper gunner and Sergeant Ronald Pittard as flight engineer. Needless to say, with two additional members having joined the crew, plus the fact they were now going to be flying the four-engined Stirling bomber, further training was essential. Pilot training, cross-country exercises, and air tests (one lasting over three hours) were all recorded in Arthur's logbook. During the same period, Arthur also undertook a short course at No. 1483 Bombing and Gunnery Flight at RAF Marham.

On 30 April, the crew, having satisfactorily completed the course at No. 1657 CU and been deemed ready for operational flying, were posted. RAF Stradishall, the base they were leaving, was to the east of the city of Cambridge, which they had to pass through to reach their new posting west of the city. Arthur could not resist the opportunity of visiting a jewellery shop with the sole intention of purchasing an engagement ring for Joan, his fiancée:

> We were posted to XV Squadron based at Bourn. [However] on arrival at the local railway station our pilot phoned Bourn for transport and was told that XV

> had left some time before and that the Squadron had moved to RAF Mildenhall. We caught a train back to Cambridge, where we changed to a train to Shippea Hill and rang for transport from there. On arrival at Mildenhall we were greeted by Squadron Leader Bill Prune, a large white Bulldog, who we later found out, was the Squadron mascot.

Attached to 'B' Flight, Arthur and his crew made their first flight from Mildenhall, a low-level bombing exercise, on 7 May; the exercise lasted only seventy-five minutes. Over the next ten days, the crew were put on 'standby' for two operational sorties, but both were cancelled at the last moment. The time was however filled with further exercises, including air to sea firing. On one of the latter exercises, having fired off 7,000 rounds of ammunition at sea markers, Arthur and the crew flew back to base via Long Sutton, which gave them the opportunity of flying over Joan Lawson's house. They made three runs over the house and from his position in the rear turret Arthur had an excellent view of Joan and her family running out into the garden waving enthusiastically. A few minutes later, although Joan was hopefully unaware of the fact, one of the Bristol Hercules motors failed and the aircraft had to return to Mildenhall on three engines.

During the early hours of the morning of 14 May, the crew undertook their first operational sortie, a mine-laying trip off the coast of Terschelling, in the West Friesian Islands. Although the squadron had detailed a number of aircraft for an attack against Bochum, two aircraft were detailed for mine-laying. The first aircraft took off from Mildenhall at 12.30 a.m., but Sergeant Jack Wilson, piloting Stirling BK611, LS-U, did not leave the Suffolk airfield until 1.25 a.m. All went well with the sortie, but Arthur had cause to remember the occasion: 'We had five mines in total. Everything went as planned. We flew there and back at an altitude of 700 feet and landed at 04.40 hours. We were fired at, on the outskirts of Norwich, by our own forces'.

Short Stirling Mk I bomber BK611 had been taken on charge by XV Squadron on Christmas Eve 1942; its first operation being undertaken on 14 January 1943, with Sergeant Irvine Renner, at the controls. Sergeant Renner, a New Zealander, named the aircraft *Te Kooti* after a famous Maori leader who, apart from being a ruthless fighter, also did some good for his countrymen. Although Renner was the usual pilot of BK611, a number of other pilots were to fly the bomber, including Wing Commander Stewart Menaul.

After two weeks of flying various exercises and air tests, the names of Arthur Edgley and his crew appeared on the battle order for an attack against Dortmund, on the night of 23 May. A total of 826 aircraft were dispatched by Bomber Command, of which fifteen were detailed by XV Squadron; one of the latter aircraft returned early due to unserviceable bomb doors and circuit failure. Sergeant Wilson lifted Stirling bomber BF533 off Mildenhall's runway at 11.30 p.m., and climbed to join the bomber stream. The crew dropped their bombload on the markers at 1.47 a.m., from an altitude of 14,000 feet. All went well and they returned safely to Mildenhall where, after landing, Sergeant Wilson received the news he had been granted a commission in the rank of pilot officer.

There was time for a quick celebration among the crew that night, before they returned to operations on the following night, when 759 assorted bombers were dispatched for a raid on Düsseldorf, for which XV Squadron detailed eighteen Stirling bombers. On checking the battle order during the day, Arthur saw the crew's names listed together with the fact they would be flying BK611, *Te Kooti*, again.

In preparation for the attack, the crew took BK611 up on an air test and found everything to be in good order. Then they waited. At 11.56 p.m. that night, they took off and climbed out. Over the sea, Arthur tested his guns, being sure not to panic the crew of a Stirling bomber flying on their starboard side. On the last leg of the flight to Düsseldorf, flying at 12,300 feet, Arthur rotated his turret back and forth, looking for night fighters, he became aware of a number of large black objects close to and level with the Stirling. It suddenly dawned on him these objects were flak shells, but before he could utter a warning, the starboard engines took hits, exploding on impact, putting both of them out of action.

The mid-upper gunner had a perfect view from his turret and reported that the starboard outer engine had lost its propeller and was on fire, while the starboard inner engine had lost both its propeller and cowling.

Although Pilot Officer Wilson had instructed the crew to prepare to bail out, Sergeant Seabolt, in the mid-upper turret, asked if he could jump immediately. The pilot confirmed the request and, without hesitation, approximately 5 miles south-west of the target, the mid-upper gunner was gone. Realising the situation was grave, together with the fact he was experiencing difficulty holding the aircraft in level flight, Jack Wilson gave the order for the crew to jump; Arthur saw no reason why he should stay where he was:

> My turret was out of action as it was powered by the starboard inner engine. I unplugged my oxygen pipe, intercom and electrically powered flying suit, turned the turret with the hand control, centralised and locked it, so I could climb out. I clipped on my parachute and pulled on the rear gunner's escape hatch lever. As the hatch cover eased opened, the slipstream caught it and wrenched it away.

As Arthur began to lower himself through the escape hatch, the slipstream caught his legs and thrashed the lower half of his body from side to side with terrific force. Feeling uneasy about the situation, Arthur clung on for dear life and gradually fought his way back into the fuselage. Given the aircraft was, unbelievably, still flying on a somewhat level attitude, he reasoned that the pilot might be able to ditch the aircraft. Arthur returned to his turret, reconnected his intercom and explained what had just happened. Arthur raised the question as to whether he would be more useful in the mid-upper turret, to which the pilot responded in the affirmative. Unfortunately, entering the mid-upper turret proved a problem for Arthur and the only solution for was for him to remove his parachute.

Having gained access, Arthur inspected the guns and found everything to be in order, except he did notice the aircraft was flying slightly nose down—ignoring that fact he resumed the role of an air gunner:

> I started searching for fighters and rotated the turret to starboard. It was then I could see what a mess the starboard engines were, resembling a scrapheap. Rotating back, I noticed that the port wing was slightly low and that the rudder was hard over. Not once had the skipper shown any sign of panic. I called over the intercom and asked Jack Wilson what our altitude was, to which he replied '9,000 feet' and then added that he thought we might make it to the coast. [A while later] I asked again what the altitude was and this time he replied, '5,000 feet'. Sergeant Maxted, the wireless operator, was still on board and started throwing all excess equipment overboard. Pilot Officer Wilson asked me to help the latter.

As Pilot Officer Cooper, the navigator, advised those still on the aircraft that they had just crossed the German–Dutch border, Arthur felt the need to ask the same question a third time. The answer came back that they were down to 3,500 feet and had better make their way forward and bail out from there. Arthur climbed down from the turret and went forward.

> I got to the front and saw the skipper and bomb aimer struggling to hold the aircraft level. I went down the steps to the front escape hatch but, to my dismay, the handle broke off as I turned it. I made signs for the others to go back, holding up the handle, which would have been difficult to see in the darkness. As I passed the [flying] instruments I saw the altitude was now 1,500 feet. I showed the broken handle to the pilot and bomb aimer and pointed back down the aircraft, they both immediately understood the situation. I got to the rear escape hatch opened it and beckoned for the navigator to go; he disappeared quickly into the night. I then bent down to go next, but saw the flight engineer standing there, so I let him go first. Unfortunately, Ronald Pittard must have jumped when we were only about 30 feet above the ground because, as I got down go out through the hatch, we struck the ground. There was a renting, tearing sound as the aircraft turned over and slid sideways a number of times before coming to rest.

As the aircraft struck the ground, Arthur had put his arms around his head, curled forward and hoped for the best. After the horrific sound of tearing, twisting metal, there was a strange silence, but Arthur became aware of a fire burning and ammunition exploding. He carefully stood up, found he could walk and called out to see if anyone else was around. To his delight, Sidney Maxted, the wireless operator, replied. The latter stated his leg hurt but, like Arthur, he too could walk.

Relieving themselves of the flying clothing and parachutes, which they threw into the fire, the two airmen set about searching for the pilot and bomb aimer, but the wreckage was strewn over a wide area. Giving up their search, they then decided to make good their escape.

Stirling BK611, *Te Kooti*, the veteran of twenty-nine operational sorties, had crashed on the south side of the Horst–Venlo/Sevenum–Grubbenvorst crossroads, approximately 8 km north-west of Venlo. Getting their bearings from the Venlo–Helmond railway line, which they crossed, Arthur and Sidney Maxted started walking in a south-westerly direction towards Meijel.

Chancing their luck by knocking on doors of isolated Dutch houses or entering farmyards, they were able to gather varying amounts of food, milk, and cigarettes. In one village, a Dutchman invited the evaders into his home, where he allowed them to sleep, while the lady of the house dried their clothing and boots. As they left the house approximately eight hours later, Arthur was handed a note, written in English, which read, 'Sorry we cannot help you more. Try to make your way into Belgium. Keep off the roads as the Germans know the 'Pilots' have escaped and police are patrolling the roads'.

Having arrived in Meijel at 6.30 a.m. on the morning of 27 May, Arthur and Sidney approached two houses where they asked for help but in each case their request was rejected. The latter house was occupied by a school teacher, who taught English and who, in a polite manner, asked them to go away as he could not help them. However, at 5 p.m. that same day, the school teacher arrived at a house where the two airmen had been given sanctuary; he was bearing gifts in the form of civilian suits and footwear and apologised for the fact he sent them away. It transpired that he thought the two Englishmen were Germans posing as RAF evaders. The schoolmaster returned later in the evening with a map and, following an agreed plan, met them on the outskirts of the village, away from prying eyes and escorted them across the moorland where he then pointed them in the direction of the Belgium border. Thanking the Dutchman for all his help, and now using Polaris as their guiding star, the airmen set off on the next part of their journey.

The evader's luck held, as Dutch farmers continued to help them, although some were more apprehensive than others. However, while still on Dutch soil, Arthur and Sidney were to receive some unexpected help from a group of Belgians:

> We knew we could not be far from the Dutch/Belgium border. After walking for about an hour, we met some Belgium smugglers [who dealt] in corn, so we linked up with them. We came to a railway line running from Weert to Eindhoven, which we had just crossed when a train flashed by. Next we came to a road, which ran at right angles to the railway line, where the smugglers went one way and we went the other. We then found a haystack and were both soon asleep.

Arthur and Sidney woke up around 5.30 a.m. on the morning of 29 May, somewhat damp from the morning dew. From their resting place, they could see a church spire in the town of Budel, which they decided to keep on their left as they continued their journey.

As they got to the border, the two airmen were stopped by an official who asked to see their papers. Arthur thought their time was up, but amazingly the official let them continue. They had only gone a further few paces when they saw a man wearing a black uniform talking to a civilian. Having watched the uniformed figure approach the evaders and search them, the civilian left without saying a word, but left alone, the uniformed officer informed the pair he had to search them otherwise he could be reported to his superior. Arthur took the chance and explained who he and Sidney were before asking for help to cross the border, which was achieved without further ado.

Once on Belgian soil, the pair continued chancing their luck by stopping at various farmhouses, where they were rewarded with acts of kindness with regard to food, clothes and directions. One English-speaking farmer actually escorted the duo through Hamont-Achel to Neerpelt, where they parted company with their guide. Arthur and Sidney found a safe pasture, where they had a rest, a wash and a shave and then walked on to Lommel, where they spent the night sleeping at another farm.

It seemed to Arthur and Sidney that the generosity and courage of the Dutch people knew no bounds, as the next morning, the two evaders followed a farmer to the local railway station, where he bought them both a ticket for the train to Antwerp. On the way to Lommel station, Arthur and Sidney saw many Germans, but on arrival at Antwerp, they were to see many more.

Not knowing Antwerp and getting lost, the airmen had just sat down in the main square to consider their situation when they were approached by a local person who engaged them in conversation. After a short while, Arthur took yet another chance, explained who they were and asked for help. The stranger took them to two taverns, the first where they talked, smoked and drank beer and the second where they were fed and met a number of other local people. They were then taken to a lady who ran a second-hand shop and were fitted-out with new clothing. It was in the second tavern that they met a chap named Jim Cornelis, who took them to his home, where they spent the next nine days.

Above: Posing for a photograph outside a Nissen hut are (*left to right*), Sgt Arthur Edgley, R/G; Plt Off. B. Cooper, Nav; Sgt Jack Wilson, pilot; Sgt Patrick Arnott, B/A; and Sgt Sidney Maxted, W/op. (*Courtesy of Dianne Chester, née Edgley*)

Below: Sergeant Bobby Gault sits astride the port inner engine of Stirling bomber BK611, *Te Kooti*. The character and name can be seen under the cockpit window. (*Author's collection*)

Above left: Artwork painted on the fuselage of Stirling bomber BK611, *Te Kooti*, depicts the aircraft bombing various targets in Germany and occupied France, smashing the swastika with flames engulfing German cities and shipping. (*Courtesy of Dianne Chester, née Edgley*)

Above right: Sergeant Arthur Edgley's prisoner of war identity photograph, complete with POW number and camp identification: IVB. (*Courtesy of Dianne Chester, née Edgley*)

Below: Sergeant Arthur Edgley and Miss Joan Lawson photographed in 1942. Arthur and Joan were to share fifty-eight years together in a very happy marriage. (*Courtesy of Dianne Chester, née Edgley*)

Arthur and Sidney resumed their journey at 6.30 p.m. on the evening of 9 June, when they left Jim Cornelis's house and headed for Brussels. Having previously been given instructions on what to do and whom to meet, the evaders arrived at the home of M. Calame-Rosset with whom they were to stay for fifteen days, before being passed to the care of a Salvation Army Captain. Two days later, on 26 June, the airmen were moved to the home of Mime Maes, where they stayed for five days before being relocated again.

At 3.30 p.m. on the afternoon of 1 July, Arthur and Sidney were taken by car to a location referred to only as the 'Captain's'; the latter it was noted spoke English but with an American accent:

> At the 'Captain's' we met other members of the RAF who had been shot down, and more RAF aircrews arrived during the week we were there. We left Brussels at 7.00 a.m. on the morning of 8 July and boarded a train for Paris. In the group [with us] was Frank Hugo, a bomb aimer, from 7 Squadron, Bill Coles, who flew with Frank, Jack Smith, DFM, and Larry Maloney, RCAF, an American. Accompanying us were two Belgian nationals, one of whom was a lady doctor. At the Belgium—French border, all the passengers got out of the train to be searched, but our group were left in the carriage. The Germans had walked through the train, looked at us, but never spoke. They must have known who we were.

The group arrived in Paris that evening and were taken to a small hotel where they were to spend the night, but things were not to work out the way they had all hoped:

> At 7.00 a.m. on 9 July I arose from my bed, feeling quite confident that before many more days I should be in England again, Sidney thought likewise. We both got dressed and prepared for the journey to Bordeaux. We got together in the hotel [lobby] and were told we were going to the railway station heading for Spain. When everything had been arranged, we were asked to each write a letter thanking those people who had helped us. The letters were (supposedly) passed back to these same people who thought that we were free, so they kept helping aircrew and sent them down the same line, but this was not the case. Our guide arrived with a few last minute instructions, and all seemed well. The railway station was not far away, although none of us ever saw it.

Having walked through two empty streets, their guide handed the group over to another person, informing them that this person would be their new escort. As a group, they all thanked the departing guide and greeted the former's replacement.

The group were standing on a long, straight, tree-lined, street, with wide pavements and several streets off each side. Having walked about 200 yards, the guide told them to keep close together. As the group complied with the instruction, approximately eight armed men in civilian clothes leapt out of one of the side turnings and ordered them to raise their hands up into the air. With pistols and machine guns aimed at them, the group quickly complied with the order.

Arthur was pushed against the wall of a house and handcuffed to a Frenchman who happened to be passing the group at the time of the arrest. They were all marched off down the side turning to a waiting bus, which they were bundled on to and driven away.

Twenty minutes later, the bus drove through huge iron gates into the compound of a large building surrounded by high walls. Inside the building, they were, individually, interrogated by the Gestapo, then thrown into a box cell 9 feet high, with a floor area of 3 feet square, with a wooden bench on which to sit. Arthur had no idea what happened to the poor Frenchman he had been handcuffed to.

Around lunchtime, a soldier brought Arthur a bowl of potato soup but, although he felt hungry, after a couple of spoonfuls, he placed the bowl on the floor. That same afternoon, Arthur was placed in a proper cell, minus his braces, shoelaces, cigarettes, and matches; it was then that he realised he was in a real prison. He looked around his new abode and saw a filthy mattress and two dirty blankets, but no pillow. He made up a bed, but when he got into it found he could not sleep.

The Germans played mind games with the prisoners, first taking away their possessions, then returning them a short while later, and interchanging their accommodation between time in the box cells and then the larger cells; finally, they were moved to the top floor of the building, to a cell 12 feet long by 9 feet wide. This cell, which had a toilet with a water tap over the bowl and one folding bed, was to accommodate four of them—Bill Cole, Frank Hugo, Larry Malaney, and Arthur—for a period of six weeks. Their food ration was just as bad, comprising a small bowl of soup and three very thin slices of bread (sometimes with jam but usually meat paste or cheese). Every two weeks, they received one Red Cross food parcel, which was to be shared between them.

The Germans continued to play mind games, with one officer telling them to gather up their possessions as they were going to be shot as spies, then laughing at their response and telling them he was only joking. Things began to add up in the prisoner's minds: the treatment they had to endure, the mind games, and the food rations told them they were in the most notorious prison in France, 'Fresnes'.

Having been told a week earlier that they may soon be moving, on Saturday 21 August, a total of thirteen members of RAF aircrew left Fresnes Prison and started the journey to *Durchgangslager der Luftwaffe* (more commonly known among British aircrew as a Dulag Luft), a Luftwaffe interrogation facility at

Oberursel, north-west of Frankfurt. Although tension was still running high among the prisoners, they were very relieved to know they were being escorted by Luftwaffe guards, who were more sympathetic to the prisoners' plight.

On entering Dulag Luft, each prisoner was given forty French cigarettes, and some English food and drink, all courtesy of the Red Cross. During his week-long stay at the centre, Arthur got to play football, received some new clothes, and was allowed to write a letter home.

At 5 p.m. on the 30th, eighty-eight POWs including Arthur, left the interrogation centre and were marched to the railway station, where they were divided into two equally sized groups and herded into two cattle wagons; the latter, in reality, only had enough space for half the number of men each truck was carrying. During the journey, the train stopped in order that the prisoners could relieve themselves, but there was little or no privacy.

On 1 September, the train arrived at its destination, POW Camp, *Stalag* IV B., situated to the north-east of Mühlberg; the town was located on the right bank of the river Elbe, approximately 80 km north-west of Dresden. On arrival at IV B, the prisoners were searched, relieved of their Red Cross parcels, ordered to take a shower and then vaccinated. The final indignity was to have their heads shaved before being photographed holding their allotted POW numbers, resembling civilian convicts. Arthur never forgot the appalling conditions inside the camp:

> The camp was separated into compounds, each divided by a double row of barbed wire, originally to keep the numerous nationalities apart. The wooden barrack huts were large and dirty, each housed approximately 400 men. The Germans never supplied any brooms, brushes or cleaning materials; the only brushes we had were bundles of twigs tied together. Each hut had a room for washing but, for some reason, we never got water until late in the day, and then there was only one tap. Sanitary conditions in the barracks were medieval, as were the outside latrines, which were designed to seat forty people, about two feet apart, in four rooms of ten, with absolutely no privacy. The bathhouse for the camp was quite a modern building, brick built, with hot and cold showers and a very effective delousing unit; it was a shame we were only allowed to use these facilities once every three weeks. On the positive side, there were football and rugby pitches and volleyball courts.

For those not into sport, or who wanted another form of distraction, there was a range of educational lectures or forms of entertainment on offer, all supplied by the prisoners themselves. Arthur participated in some of them:

> British prisoners were entertained by a number of lectures, with subjects ranging from big game hunting to the cost of dry cleaning. The camp had a number of bands and we often had, in good weather, outdoor band concerts.

Arthur enjoyed playing cards, naming Bridge as his favourite game. Arthur and his friend Ralph Elliott, a former rear gunner on Stirling bombers, with No. 214 Squadron, played together as partners; they became quite proficient at the game and used the cigarettes they received from home, or in their Red Cross parcels, as currency.

Over a period of approximately fifteen months, Arthur found that discipline was not as strict or severe as he expected it to be; that is not to say the prisoners did not suffer hardship or punishment but he also came to the conclusion that among all the different nationalities in *Stalag* IV B, the British were outwardly the most favoured. For the latter, at least, their day started at 6.30 a.m. with roll call (or *Appell* as the Germans called it), from then on until 8 p.m. (the second and last roll call of the day), time was their own.

During the time Arthur was in *Stalag* IV B, many things happened. He learned that he had been promoted to the rank of flight sergeant, it was backed-dated but he did not know by how long. There were some escape attempts which failed due to the fact the Germans discovered the tunnels. Sometimes, a group of fellow members of RAF aircrew would arrive at the camp, some of whom Arthur knew. There was one chap he did remember:

> When a new contingent came through the gates at *Stalag* IV B. we lined up to see if we knew any of them. Late in 1944 one such party came in and I saw Taff Davies, a bomb aimer. Taff looked very downcast, so I called out 'Cheer up Taff', on seeing me his face lit up. I later told him I had been in the camp about fifteen months and was there with Sidney Maxted, or as we knew him 'Maxie'. After Taff had settled in, we used to get together and have long talks about the past and what had happened in England since May 1943.

The prisoners knew that it was only a matter of time before the war ended, but come New Year 1945, they got evidence of that fact on a regular basis. In February, they witnessed the bombing of Dresden, when approximately 800 British bombers attacked at night, followed by over 300 American bombers attacking the next morning. The latter were escorted by numerous Mustang fighters, who were ordered to strafe road traffic.

As the Allies advanced deeper into Germany, the roving American fighters, according to Arthur, seemed to get more 'trigger happy':

> On 21 March three Mustangs machine-gunned the camp putting holes through barrack blocks 47A, 47B and 49B; they also toppled one of the [small hand-operated] searchlights off one of the German watchtowers. American aircraft appeared over the camp on a daily basis, machine-gunning anything that moved. On one particular day, a Mustang opened fire at one of our wood

collecting parties, killing or wounding a total of eleven casualties, which included Russian, British and Germans. American Flying Fortresses bombed rail centres all around us.

One morning, towards the end of April, the prisoners arose from what little sleep they had had, due to the constant barrages of gunfire, to find the Germans had deserted the camp, leaving the prisoners to fend for themselves. However, the latter were not alone, for when they looked around, they saw, in Arthur's words, 'hundreds of Russian Cossacks' on the south side of the camp. Although the senior British officer had ordered all British prisoners to remain within the confines of the camp, most of them, including Arthur, were already scouring the countryside for food:

> [Some] Russians were killing two large bullocks and gave me and two of my colleagues a large hulk of beef, which we took back to camp. What a feed we all had but the rich food gave us diarrhoea and some of the chaps were really ill; we had been nearly starved for three months. We then went out to the local village and found what food we could there in the way of porridge, tinned and powder milk, flour and bottled fruits.

At the end of April, the Russians took the British airmen to Riesa, approximately 15 miles south of Mühlberg, where they crossed the Elbe and were billeted in a large brick-built house. Although seemingly under the protection of Russian forces, the English airmen still had to fend for themselves when it came to finding food; the responsibility fell on Arthur when it came to livestock, due to his coming from an agricultural and rural background.

Having heard about VE Day on the radio, and with nothing happening, one or two of the men, including Arthur, were getting restless:

> We stayed several days at Riesa, but nothing seemed to be happen [*sic.*], so three of us decided to try and reach the American lines. Percy Brett, a Stirling pilot who operated from Witchford, Eric Weare, a navigator from No. 156 Squadron at Warboys and me gave the Russians the slip one morning about 7.30 a.m. When the guard couldn't see us we made a bolt for it. That night, about 8.00 p.m., we came to a German village and stopped beside a pond and were thinking about where we might sleep when an elderly German gentleman approached us. When we informed him we were former British POWs, he took us into his home. Both he and his daughter slept on the floor, having given up their beds for us. We actually spent the night in real beds!

The next morning, after breakfast, the trio set off again, heading west, and reached Wurzen by midday. As they neared the river Mulde, they encountered some Russians who challenge them but, by saying they were Americans they were allowed to continue on their way.

On reaching the river, the trio could see the bridges were down but, looking across to the other bank they could see uniforms, American uniforms, and there were several of them. Assisted by the American soldiers, Arthur, Percy Brett, and Eric Weare crossed the river by clambering over the wrecked railway bridge and set foot on American-occupied territory. They were free at last.

After the war, Arthur learned that the 'Captain' was in fact Prosper-Valere de Zitter, who had been born in Passchendaele in 1893. Having spent six years in a Belgian prison, he went to Canada, where he learned to speak English, albeit with a North American accent. On returning to Belgium just before the outbreak of war, he became an agent in the pay of the Gestapo in 1940. Arthur also learned that the whole escape line was a set-up, with all its 'helpers' receiving payment for each fugitive caught. At the end of the war, justice prevailed when de Zitter and his co-conspirator mistress faced a Belgian firing squad.

7

The Permanent Reminder: Pilot Officer Graham 'Mick' Cullen

The hanger assembly area at No. 11 Operational Training Unit, RAF Westcott, near Aylesbury was full of flying personnel. Some wore pilot's wings on their tunics; others wore the half wing brevets of navigators, wireless operators, bomb aimers, or air gunners. To the discerning eye, there were also one or two slight variations in the shades of blue of the uniforms some of the airmen were wearing, along with shoulder flashes, signifying whether they were members of the Royal Air Force, Royal Canadian Air Force, Royal Australian Air Force, or Royal New Zealand Air Force.

The purpose of the gathering was for these men who were, in the main, total strangers to each other, to form themselves, voluntarily, into groups ready to train together as operational aircrew. It was normally the pilots who took the initiative and spoke to other members of aircrew, deciding instantly whether the navigator, bomb aimer, wireless operator, or air gunner he was talking to was the sort of chap he wanted on his crew. In the heat of battle, a wrong choice at this stage could cost him and his crew their lives.

One pilot had an advantage over the rest; he had already completed a tour of operations and wore the ribbon of the Distinguished Flying Medal beneath his pilot's wings. On completion of a period of instructing in Canada, usually referred to as a rest period, Robert Megginson had returned to England, received a promotion to the rank of flight lieutenant, along with a posting to Westcott, Buckinghamshire, in preparation for a second tour of operational duties.

As he meandered among the assembled throng, Flight Lieutenant Megginson cast his experienced eyes at the faces he passed, trying to assess the character of each man. In the first instance, he was looking for a wireless operator, and saw a slight, handsome man wearing the appropriate brevet, whom he engaged in conversation. The pilot immediately noticed that the sergeant was obviously from the Antipodes, the clue being his shoulder flash; he also noticed that the young man, a New Zealander, was a confident but not a brash individual. The sergeant gave his name as Graham Cullen, adding that he was known to all as Mick. When invited to join Megginson's crew, Mick Cullen did not hesitate to answer in the affirmative.

Flight Lieutenant Megginson adopted the same procedure with regard to selecting the remainder of his crew, which consisted of Pilot Officer H. 'Bunny' Burrows, navigator; Pilot Officer Andy Hayden, bomb aimer; and Pilot Officer Desmond 'Mitch' Mitchell, rear gunner. Sergeant Peter Woollard and Sergeant 'Geordie' Soulsby joined the crew as mid-upper gunner and flight engineer respectively, at 1657 Conversion Unit.

From the outset, they trained hard. Robert Megginson knew the value of a good team and therefore did not let up, even when they were posted to the conversion unit at RAF Stradishall for training on four-engined Stirling bombers Megginson continued the pressure, as Mick recalled:

> As a crew we were highly trained, probably more so than other crews and, therefore, hopefully stood a better chance of survival. Our skipper insisted that we practise all aspects of crash drill, ditching procedure and the very important one of fighter control. Whenever the chance arose we would be in the air with fighters from the nearest airfield, practising fighter affiliation. The fighters were fitted with camera guns, and the nature of the exercise was to prevent the 'attacker' from getting a bead on our bomber, thus preventing the fighter from 'firing' his camera guns. This was achieved by the gunners watching the attacking fighter and relaying instructions to the pilot as to which direction to break and when. Although the procedure was great fun, it was of course more important to our survival, too many crews were lost for lack of knowing what to do at the right time.

On completion of their conversion course, the crew were posted, on 17 May 1943, to XV Squadron at RAF Mildenhall, where they were allotted Stirling bomber BK818, LS-O as their own aircraft. Although all Stirling bombers are identical in construction, Flight Lieutenant Megginson, with his usual thoroughness, instructed his crew to 'get to know' their aircraft; also being an experienced pilot, with knowledge of a combat environment, Robert Megginson did not fly the usual 'second dickey' flight, which was required of all new, untested in battle, pilots.

Four days after their arrival on the squadron, on 21 May, the crew found their names on the battle order for operations that night. Along with six other aircraft, Megginson and his crew would be taking BK818 on a mine-laying operation in the Frisian Islands. The attack was almost textbook-like, with all crews being recorded as having dropped their mines as ordered, in the correct locations, and all returning safely to base without incident.

In the RAF, all mine-laying operations were given the codeword 'Gardening', with the mines themselves being known as vegetables. The sea lanes into which the mines were dropped, or 'sown', were divided into specific areas, each area being given its own name; the Friesian Islands area, which was often visited by XV Squadron crews, was known as 'Nectarines'.

On the night of the 23rd–24th, Bomber Command detailed a total of 826 aircraft to attack Dortmund. The squadron dispatched fifteen Stirling bombers, two of which returned early. Mixed loads of high-explosive and incendiary bombs were dropped on the city, causing a large amount of damage to both industrial and residential areas. Robert Megginson, piloting Stirling BK818, took off at 11.16 p.m. on the 23rd, bombed at 1.31 a.m. on the morning of the 24th, and landed back at Mildenhall at 3.35 a.m.

Although there were a number of pubs and hostelries in and around the Mildenhall area, the most popular one at the time was the Bird in Hand Hotel, situated adjacent to the perimeter fence, at one end of the village of Beck Row. Most crews like to get away from the airfield during their off-duty periods, but with its proximity to the air base, the 'Bird' became a much-visited haunt for thirsty airmen. Mick and the crew became regulars at the 'Bird', not because of the quality of the ale, but because of one of the barmaids. Brenda Jaggard was a young, slim, blonde, local girl who lived in the village, which was within easy walking distance of the hotel. Brenda originally worked as a waitress in the hotel's dining room but, one night when Mick and the crew visited the establishment, Brenda was behind the bar. There was an instant attraction and soon a friendship blossomed between the two of them. Brenda's boss, George Ashley, the proprietor, noticed the budding romance and, as a result, got to know Mick and his crew very well. In due time, he afforded them certain privileges, such as allowing them credit when they wanted to dine at the 'Bird' but found they were short of funds.

Operations on the night of 25–26 May did not bode well for either Bomber Command or XV Squadron. A total of 759 aircraft were detailed for an attack against Düsseldorf, which would prove to be a failure due to two layers of cloud over the designated bombing area. As a result of the cloud, plus the added problem that German forces were using decoy marker flares and fires, the Pathfinders experienced problems marking the actual target.

This same attack was also to prove a problem for XV Squadron, who detailed eighteen aircraft for the raid. In the first instance, one failed to take off, then two returned early, one with engine trouble and the other experienced intercom failure, and two failed to return from the operation. A further two aircraft returned with battle damage, the first being Stirling EF339, LS-Y, piloted by Sergeant Reginald Allen, which was attacked by a night fighter. Unfortunately, seventeen days later, on 12 June, Reginald Allen was to be killed in action when his aircraft was again attacked by a night fighter, piloted by Major Kurt Holler, of III *Gruppe Nachtjagdgeschwader* 4 (III./NJG4). Reginald Allen's body was washed ashore near Ameland on 1 July 1943; he was buried in Ameland (Nes) Cemetery, in the rank of pilot officer. The second aircraft to receive battle damage on the Düsseldorf raid was Stirling BK818. Flight Lieutenant Megginson had delivered his attack running the gauntlet of searchlights, with flak shells bursting all around BK818. Some of the hot fragments of exploding metal were close enough for the Stirling to sustain damage to the airframe. Over the next few days, the aircraft's stalwart ground crew set about repairing the damage, most of which seemed to be in the area around the tailplane and involved severed hydraulics and flak holes. Mick Cullen remembered the 'erks' (as members of aircraft ground crew were known) with affection:

> Our ground crew were first class chaps. We spent many hours of our 'standby' time out at dispersal talking and clowning around with them. Having seen us off on a mission, one of them would always be at out dispersal point to welcome us back. We, as a crew, had great faith in their ability to keep our aircraft airworthy.

The mechanics, fitters and instrument 'bashers' all did a grand job and had BK818 airworthy in time for a raid against Wuppertal on the night of 29–30 May.

> Raids over the Ruhr area, I think, were the worst. The towns in the valley were so close together they just passed you from one group of defences to the next. The bombers could therefore be under continuous enemy fire. The situation was aggravated by the searchlights; once in their cone it was very difficult to evade them, for as you flew out of range of one set, the next battery would take over. The real danger was the blue master beam, for once this locked onto an aircraft the other beams homed in on it to form a cone. Andy Hayden, our bomb aimer, would lie in the nose of the Stirling and inform Megginson of the position of the master beam. If and when it approached our aircraft the skipper would pull back on the control column for a steep climb then roll over the beam and away. I remember one occasion when Megginson carried out this manoeuvre and held back on the control column a fraction too long and all four engines cut out. The experience was amazing, one moment the noise of four throbbing, roaring Bristol Hercules engines, followed by a second or two of silence, as the aircraft stalled and tail-slid into a dive. As the Stirling went down the engines, with a shattering crescendo of noise, roared back into life.

The attack on Wuppertal was declared an outstanding success, with the town left in ruins. The textile producing and light engineering areas of Barmen were devastated. Many other factories, along with numerous public buildings, were also severely damaged.

During the first two weeks of June 1943, XV Squadron undertook an extensive training programme, which did not include Mick and the crew as they had been granted a period of well-earned leave. Given that he lived many thousands of miles away, Mick could not go home and see his family; the crew and Brenda were his family now and, as his friendship with Brenda grew, he was to spend much of his off-duty time at her home. On returning to RAF Mildenhall, Robert Megginson was informed that, in his absence, he had been promoted to the rank of acting squadron leader, with effect from 18 June.

The rest of June saw the crew participating in raids on Krefeld, Mülheim, Wuppertal and Gelsenkirchen. Cologne was raided twice, first on the 28th–29th and again on 3–4 July. Acting Squadron Leader Megginson and his crew were detailed for the attack on the latter night, and were assigned to fly Stirling bomber BK805. They took off from Mildenhall at 11.25 p.m. and followed the bomber stream out over the east coast and across the North Sea. The route was clear, with good visibility, and fires were later seen burning on the east side of the River Rhine.

The bombing run was made at an altitude of 11,000 feet, with the bombload being released at 1.32 a.m. A couple of minutes later, as Megginson was about to turn the aircraft on to a heading for home, the port outer engine burst into flame having been hit by flak. Unfortunately, the starboard inner engine chose that moment to over-heat and, when feathered, caused the front and mid-upper turrets to go unserviceable due to lack of power. Using all his knowledge and experience, Robert Megginson nursed the ailing bomber back across the sea and landed the aircraft at the fighter airfield at Manston, Kent, at 4.34 a.m.

Between the dates of 5 July and 11 August, XV Squadron carried out a number of mining operations in both the estuary of the Gironde River and the eastern Friesian Islands. The squadron also participated in what was later to be known as the 'Battle of Hamburg', when Bomber Command aircraft turned their attention to the German city at the end of July, where the bombing culminated with a firestorm.

On the night of 12–13 August, the bomber crews turned their attention to northern Italy, having received orders to attack Milan and Turin. Nine aircraft were detailed by XV Squadron for the raid on the latter target. Mick remembered those trips:

> Trips to Italy were regarded as the best of the lot, very little flak and not too much interference from fighters. These raids were usually carried out during a full moon period and the magnificent sight of the snow-covered Alps had to be seen to be believed. On one occasion, as the Stirling droned its way to the target flying about 1,000 feet above the mountains, the crew marvelled at the brilliance of the moonlight reflecting its silver rays on the snow-covered backcloth.

> Suddenly, a pyrotechnic scene erupted ahead of us as the green and red marker flares cascaded down marking the destruction of a Pathfinder aircraft. As we watched in awe we clearly saw the mushrooming canopies of the parachutes as some of the crew floated down. I must admit that even our sorrow and concern for the crew could not override the beauty of the scene.

Mick and Brenda's friendship had blossomed and they were by now engaged and spent as much time as possible together. One night, accompanied by other members of the crew and their respective partners, the betrothed couple went to a dance held on the base. At the end of the evening, the revellers made their way, in the blackout, back to the Bird in Hand Hotel. Not having a key to gain access, it was decided that as Brenda was the smallest person in the group, standing just under 5 feet tall, she should climb through a ground floor window of the hotel and open the front door for them. Having found a window that was slightly open, the aperture was quickly and quietly made large enough for Brenda to squeeze through, but she was unceremoniously pushed through by overeager, willing hands; as she crashed to the floor, a startled sleepy male voice came gruffly across the darkened room, demanding to know who was there.

Unfortunately, in the darkness of the blackout, the group had not reached the hotel as they had thought but had only got as far as the officers' mess, which was adjacent to the hotel. Needless to say, Brenda made a hurried retreat.

Four nights after its previous attack, on the night of 16–17 August, Turin was to receive further attention from Bomber Command, when a total of 154 aircraft, from both 3 Group and 8 Group, undertook another raid on the city. Fourteen aircraft were detailed by XV Squadron, three of which failed to reach the target. Robert Megginson and his crew were accompanied on the operation by Air Commodore Herbert Kirkpatrick, DFC, Senior Air Staff Officer, Headquarters 3 Group, who went along for the experience. This trip was in total contrast to the one made four days earlier:

> Crossing the South of France, we began to experience trouble with the engines which had started to heat up. Whilst climbing to gain more height to cross the Alps, one of the engines deteriorated to the extent that it seized up completely. It was impossible to maintain height so we meander our way through the mountains, watching carefully in the light of the full moon for the peaks that towered above us. Having safely negotiated the Alps we finally arrived over the target area, which in our case was a small factory. However, due to low cloud we could not locate the building and so attacked the main target. Owing to our engine problems we bombed at a lower level than the other crews. We unloaded our cargo and left the area as quickly as possible. The skipper debated with the

Above: Pilot Officer Robert Megginson, DFM, photographed at RAF Wyton, during XV Squadron's Blenheim period, with Flt Lt William Morris. Both pilots would later be the recipients of a DFC. (*Author's collection*)

Below: Members of ground crew give an indication of the size of Stirling bomber BK818, the usual aircraft flown by Sqn Ldr Megginson. (*Author's collection*)

Above: Squadron Leader Megginson and his crew. *Standing left to right*: Plt Off. Desmond Mitchell; Fg Off. Andy Hayden; Flt Lt Robert Megginson, DFC, DFM; Sgt 'Geordie' Soulsby; and Sgt Peter Woollard. *Seated left to right*: Plt Off. 'Bunny' Burrows and Sgt Graham 'Mick' Cullen, RNZAF. (*Author's collection*)

Right: Sergeant Mick Cullen photographed in full flying kit at his workstation on Stirling bomber BK818. (*Author's collection*)

A formal portrait photograph of Mick Cullen, taken following his being appointed to a commission in the rank of pilot officer. Note the Royal New Zealand Air Force shoulder flash. (*Author's collection*)

rest of the crew as to whether we should carry on and land in North Africa for repairs, but it was decided to try and get our VIP passenger back to Mildenhall. Once again we successfully negotiated the valleys through the Alps, but this caused a strain on the already overheated engines. As we crossed out over France, a second engine had to be stopped. We were now in an emergency situation. We decided to forget Mildenhall and land at the first available airfield, which turned out to be Tangmere on the south coast. Unfortunately, fog had closed the bomber bases in East Anglia and all aircraft were diverted to fighter airfields along the same coastline. As we were preparing to land an aircraft with a strange call-sign came on the air requesting priority for an emergency landing, saying he only had two motors going. The runway was cleared and a rather old and battered Wellington bomber with, of course, only two engines going, touched down. Our situation was now critical and as Megginson put BK818 on the runway another engine seized completely. An inspection the following day revealed that two of the engines had completely melted the pistons to the block. We had a couple of days' unexpected holiday while Mildenhall flew down two new engines together with our ground crew to fit them. We then all returned to base aboard BK818. I was looking forward to getting back to Mildenhall, but my welcome was a very cold one. Being young and not very thoughtful I had, in the excitement of the situation, neglected to notify Brenda that I was alright.

Although it was not realised at the time, this raid on Turin would be the last attack made on any Italian city.

Sunday 22 August was Brenda's birthday and Mick, not being detailed for ops that night, decided to go with his fiancée to the Bird in Hand for a drink or two. If the young couple were hoping to spend the evening together on their own, it was not to be, as the rest of the crew opted to join them. After closing time, Brenda invited the crew back to her parent's home, where the latter were always welcome, possibly as one of the crew could play the piano in a very efficient manner.

Pilot Officer Desmond Mitchell, the rear gunner, had been trained at the Royal Academy of Music, where one of his closest friends was another student by the name of Neville Marriner, who many years later was to become founder and conductor of the Academy of St Martin in the Fields; he was to be knighted in 1985.

That night, Mitch sat at the piano and played all the popular songs of the day, which Brenda and the others all sang along to. The evening concluded with much laughter and merriment. Mick and Brenda said their 'Goodnights' in private, not realising that by contrast, the next night was to bring with it much sadness.

During the summer months, due to the long hours of daylight, Bomber Command did not direct any operations against Berlin. However, that was to change on 23 August, when the first attack of the new campaign was detailed. That morning, the names of Robert Megginson and his crew were listed on the battle order for the attack that night, along with twelve other crews and their respective aircraft. Another name, added to Megginson's crew list, was that of Sergeant Joseph Milner, RCAF, who had recently been posted to XV Squadron. Milner, a Canadian from Ontario, was undertaking his first 'second dickey' trip before flying with his own crew.

Squadron Leader Megginson turned the Stirling on to the runway at RAF Mildenhall and, on receipt of the green Aldis lamp signal, pushed forward the throttles and lifted BK818 off the tarmac at 8.40 p.m. The Stirling lumbered into the air and headed for the east coast at Cromer, the designated crossing point for the bomber stream. The night was clear with excellent visibility; it was obvious to the bomber crews that, even at this early stage in the operation, enemy night fighters would be active. Mick always remembered that night with great sorrow:

> Having reached the turning point thirty miles south of Berlin, our navigator, Pilot Officer Bunny Burrows gave Megginson the new course. We carried out our bombing run without any problems and when Andy Hayden called 'bombs gone' Megginson turned onto a course for home. It was at this point we were attacked by night fighter, which fired aggressively before losing us. The skipper called for a

> damage report, and one by one the crew responded from their respective stations that all was well; all except for Pilot Officer Mitchell. There being no reply, the pilot instructed me to investigate. I made my way down the fuselage towards the rear turret, feeling slightly apprehensive. The turret was jammed but with the aid of an axe I managed to break open the doors. The night fighter had turned the turret into a twisted mass of tangled steel and shattered Perspex and there, slumped over the gun butts lay Mitch. I gently eased him back and found that he had been killed by a solitary bullet through his left eye. I informed the skipper of the situation and then proceeded to remove Mitch's body from the turret. I struggled for a few minutes and then called Andy Hayden on the intercom to come down and assist me, and between us we managed to extricate Mitchell's lifeless body from the wreckage. Although the guns were useless, Megginson ordered me to occupy the shattered turret to watch for night fighters on the homeward journey. With no heating it was a cold, uncomfortable and unenviable trip. Following our return to Mildenhall, the crew were given a few days' leave, during which time we all travelled to Rugby to attend Mitch's funeral.

Pilot Officer Desmond Mitchell had a girlfriend, to whom he intended proposing. In a letter he wrote to her, shortly before he was killed, he made mention of the fact he always flew with a photograph of her, wedged between the gun butts, in his turret; did he perhaps glance down at that photograph at the wrong moment?

By coincidence, there was at that time on the squadron a rear gunner without a crew. Sergeant Andy Fell had been grounded due to illness, but his crew continued to fly operations and had failed to return. It was therefore agreed, by all concerned, that Andy Fell would complete his tour of operations as Robert Megginson's rear gunner.

Sadly, Joseph Milner, who had flown his first 'second dickey' trip with Megginson's crew eight days earlier, was killed in action on the night of 31 August–1 September, while participating in another attack on Berlin with his own crew; he was buried in the Berlin 1939–1945 War Cemetery in the rank of warrant officer first class.

Cause for celebration returned to Megginson's crew when Sergeant Geordie Soulsby got married. Mick Cullen remembered the wedding with amusement:

> The wedding was a quiet affair with a reception held at his mother's house. All the crew, with the exception of Andy Hayden attended. After the formal proceedings and toasts the guests went up to one of the bedrooms to view the wedding gifts. One, nameless, member of the crew suddenly held up a large chamber pot he had found, presumably under the bed. Much laughter and joking ensued, including the suggestion that it should be filled with beer. Geordie said he would willingly pay for the beer if the others carried the chamber pot to the local pub. Without

> further ado the ceramic pot was ceremoniously conveyed with military escort to the nearest pub. The landlord was instructed to fill the receptacle with ale, prior to it being passed round. Bearing in mind the colour of the ale, one or two people were hesitant in drinking from the vessel.

On the night of 8 September, Mick and the crew returned to operational flying. Their names appeared on the battle order for an attack against Boulogne. Piloting Stirling EE974, Robert Megginson took off from Mildenhall at 9 p.m. Flying with the crew was another new pilot, Sergeant George Clarke, undertaking his first 'second dickey' trip.

There was no cloud cover over the target and the crew reported seeing their bombs bursting 14,000 feet below. Surprisingly, given the clear weather conditions, there were no reports of enemy fighters. The flight home was also uneventful and the crew landed at Mildenhall at 11.10 p.m. the same night. This particular raid is the only recorded occasion that Robert Megginson and his crew bombed a French target.

On 25 September 1943, Air Vice-Marshal Harrison, Officer Commanding 3 Group, signed a recommendation for the award of a Distinguished Flying Cross to Squadron Leader Megginson, DFM, who had by this time completed a total of fifty-one operational sorties.

A cause for further celebration came on 12 October when Mick Cullen was granted a commission in the rank of pilot officer. Mick often lamented about what happened to his new cap that night:

> Whenever one of the crew was commissioned a celebration was called for. This involved an initiation ceremony whereby the new cap was escorted to the Bird in Hand and on its arrival was duly filled with beer. It was then passed around for each member of the crew to drink from.

During November 1943, XV Squadron commenced training in preparation for the squadron's conversion to Avro Lancaster bombers, as a result of which very few operational sorties were undertaken. However, on the night of the 19th, Megginson and his crew flew their last bombing mission; they were detailed, along with eleven other crews for an attack against Leverkusen, north of Cologne. The raid was somewhat shambolic, with both marker flares and bombs being widely dispersed. Although Megginson released his bombs from an altitude of 17,000 feet at 7.18 p.m., he later reported at the debriefing that the green target indicators could be seen, but no red target indicators were evident.

On completion of their tour, the crew that had trained hard, played hard and shared each other's joys and sorrows was split up. Squadron Leader Megginson was posted to No. 1653 Conversion Unit, at RAF Chedburgh,

Suffolk; Pilot Officer Andy Hayden was posted to No. 12 Operational Training Unit at Chipping Warden, Oxfordshire; Flying Officer Bunny Burrows stayed at Mildenhall having been posted to No. 622 Squadron, with whom he flew a further nine operational sorties; and Pilot Officer Mick Cullen was posted to No. 17 Operational Training Unit at Silverstone, Northamptonshire.

On 7 August 1944, Mick crewed up with Brenda on a permanent basis when they married at St John's Church, Beck Row. The Air Force Padre officiated at the wedding which was attended by over 100 guests. The local schoolmaster's wife made a three-tier wedding cake, with ingredients secured from various sources. One tier of the cake was sent to Mick's family in New Zealand. Ration coupons were donated and gathered together to provide food at the reception. Everybody gave willingly and all joined in the preparations for the big day.

Eventually, Pilot Officer Graham Cullen was posted back to his native New Zealand and, naturally, took Brenda with him, a loving and permanent reminder of his time at RAF Mildenhall.

8

The Biter Bitten: Sergeant Douglas 'Doug' Fry

In 1938, at the time of the Munich Crisis, Douglas Robert Fry was a fourteen-year-old schoolboy. Following a lengthy chat about the possible situation that was arising, it was agreed between Douglas and his mother that his name would not be put forward for evacuation. As it turned out, the political situation calmed down, and evacuation was not necessary, but the calm was not to last, the inevitable had only been delayed. Hundreds of young people, like their respective parents, wanted to 'do their bit' when the time came. With this thought in mind, they joined various organisations such as the Queen's Cadets (which was an army cadet force), the Territorial Army, the Sea Scouts, or Sea Cadets. Having acquired an interest in the development and progress of military aircraft, Doug opted to join the Air Defence Cadet Corp (ADCC). Remembering those days, he recalled:

> I was in the 9F/Islington Squadron and we were affiliated to 54 Fighter Squadron, based at Hornchurch, Essex. A flight lieutenant would sometimes come and give us a talk, as did people from Handley Page, the aircraft manufacturers.

When war was officially declared, the Air Ministry took over the ADCC and it officially became known as the Air Training Corp (ATC). Young Douglas attended two summer camps with the ATC, both at RAF Halton, near Wendover, Buckinghamshire, where he gained his first experience of flying, albeit in a de Havilland Dragon Rapide biplane.

On leaving school in May 1939, at the age of fifteen, Doug secured a job in the City of London, a short distance away from his home in Islington. When the Blitz on London started towards the end of 1940, it was, in more ways than one, close to home. Doug recalled:

> Hardly a morning went by when I didn't have to walk to work, usually the long way round to avoid blown down trolley-bus wires, craters in the roads and pavements, fires and unexploded bombs. Once I saw five feet of wing-tip from a Dornier Do 17 [German bomber] lying in the road in Shoreditch. I must confess to being scared in the Blitz with a feeling of helplessness, and had thoughts of being on the delivering end instead of the receiving end.

As he turned eighteen years of age, his chance came: Doug joined the Royal Air Force Volunteer Reserve as a direct entry air gunner, having obtained a certificate of service from the ATC.

His training went smoothly and followed the normal course, first being sent to St John's Wood Receiving Centre, which was situated in Lord's Cricket Ground, then on to Initial Training Wing at Bridlington; Air Gunnery School at Dalcross, Inverness; and No. 12 Operational Training Unit at Chipping Warden, where he was invited to join a crew being formed by a pilot named George Judd. Pilot Officer George Judd's crew, apart from Douglas Fry as mid-upper gunner, consisted of Pilot Officer Ken Banks, rear gunner; Sergeant Dennis Brown, navigator; Sergeant William Wells, wireless operator; and Sergeant Sydney Long, bomb aimer. Sergeant L. 'Dick' Richards would join the crew as flight engineer at No. 1651 Conversion Unit, where the final part of their formal training would be undertaken: learning how to fly the four-engined Stirling heavy bombers. On completion of their training, and being declared ready for operational flying duties, Pilot Officer Judd and his crew reported for duty at RAF Mildenhall, Suffolk, on Tuesday, 15 June 1943.

Every new pilot who joined a bomber squadron, before operating with his own crew, was required to fly one or two 'second dickey' trips, which were mandatory and consisted of the inexperienced pilot flying with an operationally experienced crew to ensure the former could withstand the pressures of operational flying as captain of his own aircraft and crew. Needless to say that while the new pilot was being initiated into the pressures of war, his crew remained on the ground and were in effect 'spare', a situation that could have dire consequences for a 'spare' member of aircrew.

> I was sitting in the crew room one morning, chatting with another mid-upper gunner, when the gunnery leader entered and asked for a mid-upper gunner to fly with Flying Officer Hawkins' crew. It transpired that the latter were on the battle order for that night and their mid-upper had not reported back from leave. I volunteered to join the crew but was not allowed into the pre-raid briefing, so I hung around with my flying kit at the ready. When Flying Officer Hawkins re-appeared he informed me I was not needed as his own mid-upper gunner had reported back to base. The errant air gunner had apparently cut across the airfield direct from his billet, without going through the formal procedure of

> reporting in at the guardroom first. The allotted target that night was Mulheim and Flying Officer Hawkins and his crew failed to make it back, they were all killed. How lucky can you get?

George Judd completed his two 'second dickey' trips and was declared fully operational.

Their first sortie as a crew occurred on the night of 22–23 June when, accompanied by two other aircraft piloted by Squadron Leader Martin and Sergeant Grundy, they carried out a mine-laying operation in the East Friesians. Between that date and 3 July, Doug and the crew flew on five raids, including two against Cologne. With five completed operations recorded in their respective logbooks, these 'veterans' were given six days leave. Naturally, Doug went home to see his family in north London.

While Doug was enjoying the wartime comforts of home, Air Chief Marshal Sir Arthur Harris, the Commander-in-Chief, Bomber Command, was putting the final touches to his plans for a major operation. It was on the morning of Thursday 22 July that he decided to put his plan into action and launch Operation Gomorrah, the Battle of Hamburg, which was to commence two nights later. Doug and his crew returned to Mildenhall to find their names on the battle order for the first of these raids on the night of 24–25 July.

Mildenhall airfield, like the majority of other airfields under Bomber Commands control, was a hive of activity on the morning of the 24th. At the Suffolk base, Stirling bomber EF427, Pilot Officer George Judd's designated aircraft, was being prepared for the forthcoming attack that night. Likewise, at seventeen other dispersal areas around the airfield the ground crews worked feverishly, pumping gallons of high-octane aviation fuel into each aircraft, while instrument fitters checked the various dials and controls in the cockpit, and armourers winched a 2,000-lb bomb, six 4-lb canisters, and seven canisters of 30-lb incendiary devices into the bomb bay of every aircraft. To add to their demanding workload, the 'erks' (as the ground crew members were affectionately known) were ordered to load a specified quantity of paper-wrapped bundles on board each Stirling bomber. As these bundles were to be deposited close to the flare chutes, many 'erks' thought propaganda leaflets were to be dropped over Hamburg along with the bombloads.

These bundles were in fact a new form of weapon, so simple in design the ground crews did not realise the significance of the bundles of paper; the latter had even been given a codename: 'Window'. 'Window' was in fact strips of aluminium foil, each of which was cut to half a wavelength of the German radar. The foil, when floating down to earth, acted as a resonating dipole aerial and radiated more of the radar pulse than an aircraft, thus giving a stronger echo on the German radar screens.

En route to the target, as the bombers reached the north German coast, the bundles were cut open and the aluminium strips were pushed down the flare chute and out of the aircraft. Within a very short space of time, the sky was full of foil strips fluttering and snaking gently down on the night air. Confusion began to reign in the darkened German radar control rooms as one controller after another announced that their particular screen had developed a fault, each reporting the same problem—a 'snowstorm' of blips was giving the impression that a vast armada of aircraft was heading for Hamburg, but the German controllers knew this could not possibly be true. In reality, only 791 aircraft of Bomber Command were heading for the German port, and such was the success of this new innovation that the enemy defences only claimed twelve RAF bombers that night, eleven of them falling to the guns of the Luftwaffe night fighters.

The scenario played out during the attack was much the same on each bomber, with the wireless operator and flight engineer pushing the bundles of 'Window' out of the aircraft every two minutes. The scene on Pilot Officer Judd's aircraft was no different, but while Sergeant Wells cut open the bundles and pushed them down the flare chute, the two air gunners, Ken Banks and Doug Fry, kept scanning the sky for enemy fighters. Doug remembers the Hamburg raids:

> Between 24 and 29 July, we operated against Hamburg on three nights [Operation Gomorrah] and Essen, all of them highly successful raids. The only trouble my crew met was when we were coned over Hamburg on the second raid of the series. Luckily the flak came nowhere near us to do any damage, so we were able to bomb, withdraw and get back to base safely.

However, had it not been for the keen ear of Sergeant Wells, the wireless operator, the crew's next trip to Hamburg could have had a different ending:

> On the way back from our third Hamburg raid, we did have a brush with a Junkers Ju 88 night fighter, but we were alerted to the possibility of attack by Bill Wells our wireless operator, who had tuned into the German radio frequency and let us all hear their chatter through our intercom. We were over the North Sea and flying a somewhat parallel course to the Dutch coast, but were several miles out from it at the time. Thus Ken Banks, the rear gunner, and I were not too surprised when a fighter-flare burst above and slightly astern of us. Incredibly, the German pilot flew past the flare at roughly our height, but slightly to starboard and was also well illuminated. I was somewhat unsighted by the fin and rudder of our Stirling, so could not get a bead on the Ju 88. I suggested, over the intercom, to Ken that he 'open up' to let the German know we were awake. Ken fired off a long burst, and although I could see the tracer falling short—the range was

> about 700–800 yards—it had the desired effect. The fighter sheered-off without firing a shot. The flare disappeared into the mist below, thus returning us to the safety of the night.

Doug and his crew had been flying operationally almost continuously over the past week, so it came as some surprise to him, when wandering into the crew room on the morning of 30 July, to see the crew's names on the battle order for an operation that night. Although not voiced, they had all hoped to either spend the evening in the Bird in Hand Hotel adjacent to the perimeter fence of the airfield or go dancing in Cambridge, but Bomber Command had other ideas as to how the crew would spend their evening:

> Briefing was scheduled for eight-o-clock that night, and when we arrived [in the briefing room] we found arc-lamps had been set up and there was an RAF Film Unit crew preparing to film the briefing. We then recalled that a few weeks previously 'Butch' Harris [Air Chief Marshal Sir Arthur Harris] had visited the Squadron and had informed us that Winston Churchill wanted a film made about the work of Bomber Command and that it should be called *The Biter Bit*. It seemed that they were now making this film. In fact later, whilst we were waiting for the crew bus to take us out to our 'kite', and standing around chatting trying to control our nerves, I noticed a cameraman busily filming us. Subsequently, my mother saw the film at her local cinema; incidentally, whilst I was still posted as 'missing' in action. The Ministry of Information gave her some 'stills' from the film showing yours truly in close-up.

The target that night was an attack against Remscheid, south of Wuppertal, on the edge of the Ruhr, for which a total of 273 aircraft had been detailed, which included twelve Stirling bombers from XV Squadron.

A crescendo of noise rose into the night air and reverberated across the airfield as forty-eight Bristol Hercules engines powered up, enabling the crews to ensure that engines, turrets, flight instruments, and communicating systems all worked properly. One by one, on receipt of a torch flash signal from the ground crew chief, the bombers began to taxi out towards the runway. One final check before turning into the wind at the end of the runway and then they were away. The first aircraft to take off was piloted by Pilot Officer Goldwin Gabel, RCAF, who left the ground at 10.35 p.m.; seven minutes later, Pilot Officer George Judd took off, piloting Stirling EF427. In the bomb bay of the aircraft was a full load of 4-lb and 30-lb incendiary bombs, which were to be dropped during the second wave of the attack.

After the bombers had crossed the enemy coast, the crews began to see a few searchlights lazily sweeping back and forth across the sky. Occasionally, a few desultory flak bursts were also seen, but neither constituted a problem for the bombers at that moment in time. On reaching a point near Cologne, the bombers altered course, putting them on the final leg before lining-up for their bombing run. Riding high in the mid-upper turret on the back of the Stirling, it was not long before Doug Fry saw the target:

> I saw the glow of the target dead ahead, and the usual hell of bursting shells, [I also saw] searchlights and photo-flashes going off. We were now preparing for the imminent bombing run and Syd Long, our bomb aimer, was already in position in the nose of the aircraft. We, the gunners, were desperately trying to look into every corner of the sky at once. Syd's quiet, calm voice informed the pilot that the bombs doors were open, a call the skipper acknowledged with a simple 'OK'. By this time we were into the outer defences of the town and although the barrage of flak was not all that heavy, the searchlights were probing and the target was already well alight.

Suddenly, as Doug was searching to the starboard side of the aircraft, a blue master beam flickered across the mainplane wingtip and 'locked' on to EF427. Doug recalled the event.

> I kept up a running commentary as to the position and number of other beams which were trying to cone us, as we pressed on with our bombing run. The flak began to get our range. 'Bombs gone—let's get out of here' I heard Syd shout. The skipper replied, 'Let's get our picture first', which meant another ten seconds of straight and level flying. A fatal ten seconds, because we were now being hit [by flak] quite a lot. I then heard a different sort of sound over and above the noise of the engines and bursting shells. I glanced down and saw the flickering light of flames, and as I was not doing much good in the turret by this time, I decided to get down and see if I could do something about the fire which was well underway and appeared to have started in the priming boxes on the port side. The flames had already burned through the bulkhead and were consuming my 'K' type dinghy, which was hanging thereon. As I was stepping down from my turret, with one foot still on the ladder, there was a shell burst astern, and I felt what seemed to be a hefty kick in the stomach. I doubled up and fell to the floor, very close to the flames, and then there was an almighty explosion up in the nose of the aircraft, a direct hit.

Following the explosion, the Stirling immediately went into a near-vertical dive as the pilot lost control of the aircraft. Such was the force of the dive that in a moment of negative gravity, the mid-upper gunner found himself floating, but even in his dazed condition he knew it was not a dream:

> At that moment I resigned myself to death, because how could we possibly pull out of such a dive? However, our skipper, who must have been badly wounded

> by that flak burst, did pull the Stirling out with what must have been a super human effort and thus gave me a chance of survival. I fell to the floor once again, only half-conscious and whilst lying there, vaguely saw Dick Richards, our flight engineer, go past. Richards bailed out of the rear escape hatch which had previously been opened by the rear gunner, who also made good his escape. Although I felt pretty ropey, I decided that I now had a chance to get out, but when I went to get my 'chute from the rack it had gone, presumably breaking free when we went into the violent dive. Just when I was thinking 'Well, this is it', I saw the 'chute which had slid along the floor and had come to rest at a small step which was part of the bulkhead.

Having no choice but to crawl past the flames, Douglas retrieved his parachute and clipped it on to his harness. The wounded airman removed his flying helmet and slowly made his way to the rear escape hatch where, having dangled his legs through the open hatch and giving no thought to the aircraft's altitude, he tumbled out of the stricken machine.

> I had no idea what altitude we were when I jumped. As we had lost a lot of height since we were first hit, we may have been only about fifty feet up for all I knew. However, I never gave this aspect a thought, I just went. My 'chute opened perfectly and I saw poor A—Apple falling away, nose down, with flames streaming from her, and unhappily four members of the crew still on board, dead or wounded. I think we must have been at about 5,000 feet when I jumped. As I drifted down I saw what I thought was a vast lake, by virtue of the way it shimmered and moved, and so I inflated my 'Mae West' life-jacket. What I took to be water was in fact a field of wheat or some other crop undulating on the night breeze.

It was a clear starlit night, and even though there was no moon, Douglas watched as the ground rapidly came up to meet him. As he drifted forwards, he noticed a small wall directly in his path and lifted his legs up so as to avoid striking it with his feet. He landed in what turned out to be the back garden of a small house, which gave Doug some cause for concern.

> I immediately released my harness and took off my life jacket, as my first thought was to be on my way and try to escape. However, I had been wounded and was not feeling quite myself and thus, firstly, I failed to retrieve and hide my parachute which was draped over the wall, and secondly, I'm damned if I could find a way out of the garden. At this point, I collapsed and lapsed into semi-consciousness, soon to be aroused by the sound of the all clear siren, followed by somebody calling, 'Halloo, halloo' from the shadows at the other end of the garden.

As Doug's vision returned, he saw a man in uniform, who he took to be a soldier on leave, coming out of the house. The uniformed figure helped the wounded airman to his feet and with the assistance of two other men, who had also appeared on the scene, carried Doug into the house. On entering the property, a lady shook her fist at Doug in a threatening manner, before pointing to a chair into which he was lowered. The room soon filled up with villagers, all of whom looked very pale and apprehensive. Some of them lifted his clothing and exposed the wound, which had been created by a chunk of shrapnel which left a jagged hole about an inch in diameter, as it penetrated his stomach; the biter had been bitten.

The two men who had assisted in carrying Douglas into the house produced a stretcher on which the latter was conveyed to the local doctor's house. Here the wound, which was on the right side of the body, close to the liver, was cleaned and dressed prior to Doug being given an injection. He was then physically carried out and placed on the back seat of a car, which sped off into the night.

During that journey, Doug drifted in and out of consciousness; he was not even aware of the arrival of daylight until he was lifted out of the vehicle and glimpsed sunlight through his half-closed eyes. The air gunner was carried up a flight of stairs and into a hallway where, as he receded back into oblivion, he was asked if he wanted a cigarette.

Stirling Mk III bomber EF427 photographed at Rochester, Kent, prior to being delivered to XV Squadron at RAF Mildenhall. (*Author's collection via Doug Fry*)

Right: Nineteen-year-old Doug Fry, photographed at air gunnery school, Dalcross, Inverness, Scotland, while under training. (*Author's collection via Doug Fry*)

Below: A cartoon sketched by Doug Fry during his training period; he was to find out the reality of air warfare soon after drawing the image. (*Author's collection via Doug Fry*)

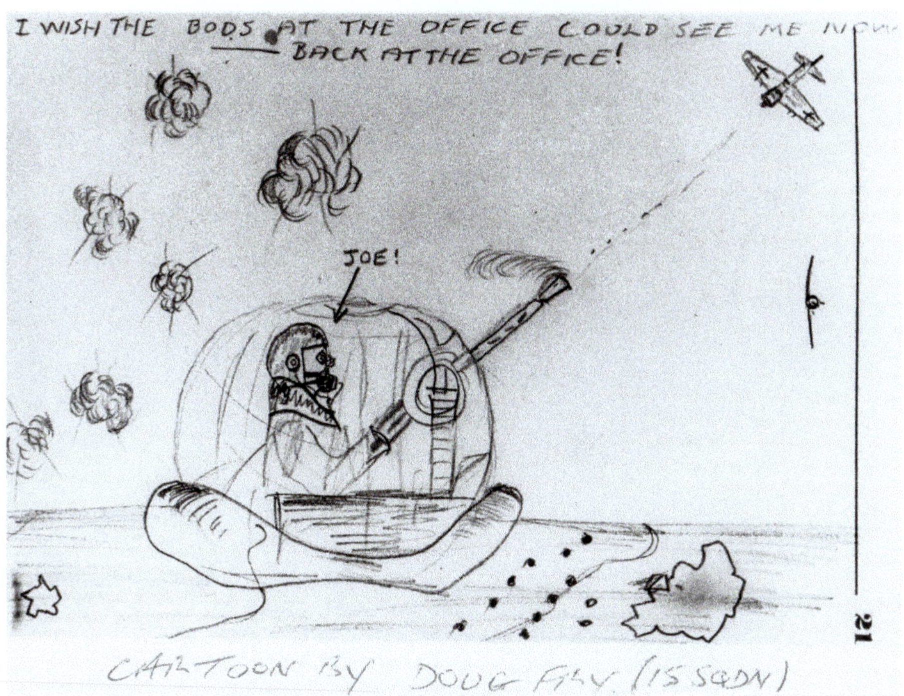

Above: A still from the film *The Biter Bit*, showing members of aircrew relaxing in the crew room prior to an operational sortie. Pilot Officer George Judd, Doug Fry's pilot, is second from left in the background. (*Author's collection via Doug Fry*)

Below: A second still from the film *The Biter Bit* with (*left to right*) George Judd and Doug Fry, while the crews waited for take-off on the night of 30 July 1943. (*Author's collection via Doug Fry*)

The movement of the stretcher on which he lay being carried to a waiting ambulance, seemed to bring Doug back to reality. It was as the stretcher was slid into the lower tier of the back of the vehicle, that Doug recognised a voice emanating from the upper bunk; it was that of Ken Banks, the Canadian born rear gunner, who had also been wounded.

Douglas remembered little of his journey, other than seeing the tops of bomb-damaged buildings through the half-open window of the ambulance. Oblivion was his companion for most of the trip. On regaining consciousness, he found he was being undressed by strangers in a brightly lit room:

> I was lying on some sort of table, and in what seemed to me to be the far distance but was only a few feet away, was another person also lying on a table. It was in fact our rear gunner who later told me that when they undressed me, I looked as though I was made of marble and well on the way to becoming a corpse. Somebody in a white coat bent over me and by way of sign-language, asked me if I had false teeth. I shook my head. A pad then came down over my nose and mouth and I was gone again.

Doug's condition was a cause of concern to many for several days, including some of the other patients. When he did 'come to' three or four days later, he found he was on a saline drip entered into his back passage, with a bottle hanging from a wooden pole fixed to one corner of the bed. Although he had never been aware of it, Doug had also been wounded on his right hand, which he found was supported by a wire frame.

As he recovered and took note of what was happening, Doug learned that he was in a small camp approximately 3 km from Düsseldorf, with a number of other flyers, who had also been shot down and were recovering from their respective wounds. Amazingly, Doug still remembered who they were:

> There was Pete Saunders, a Halifax pilot, shot down over Wuppertal, who sustained a broken leg and facial injuries when he was blown out of the starboard side of the cockpit as the port wing exploded. There was a Canadian who had lost a foot when he crashed through the roof of a monastery in Holland, and an American, Luke Wilson, who had his left elbow shattered by flak. There was 'Chuck' Johnston, another American, who had half-slipped out of his parachute harness and landed upside down, head first. He had a split pelvis and facial injuries. There was also, of course, Ken Banks and myself.

One night, Pete Saunders, whose bed was under a window, reported a reddish glow emanating from above. As he continued to watch, he saw a red sky marker drifting out of 10/10th cloud. The patients had not heard any aircraft flying over, so assumed the pathfinders had dropped a marker. They were concerned as to whether it was a spoof raid or a turning indicator for an attack on the Ruhr. Slowly the throbbing drone of aero-engines could be heard, growing louder as the invaders were almost overhead. Then bombs began to fall and all the patients who could, including Doug, 'hit the deck' dragging their bed-clothes with them: 'I learned that "Cookies", 4,000-lb and 8,000-lb bombs, made a horrible tumbling, rushing noise as they fell. Some bombs and incendiaries fell fairly close, but we suspected these were undershoots'.

The raid, which occurred on the night of 22–23 August, was against the I. G. Farben factory at Leverkusen. The attack, which was not a success due to the thick cloud, was undertaken by a force of 426 bombers and lasted for approximately forty minutes.

Once the prisoners of war were deemed fit to travel, they were moved on. One morning Doug, Ken Banks and the one-footed Canadian were taken to Dulag Luft, the transit and interrogation centre for shot-down aircrew, located at Frankfurt. The three prisoners, escorted by two German soldiers armed with rifles, first took their charges on a public transport bus to Düsseldorf, where the group caught a train to Cologne. The necessity to change trains at Cologne Station gave Doug the opportunity, while waiting on the platform, to see the damage inflicted by Bomber Command during recent raids on the city, bearing in mind the fact that Doug had participated in two raids himself.

Arriving at Frankfurt in the evening, just as it was getting dark, the armed escort took their charges to a large room over the station where, to Doug's astonishment, there was a number of other RAF airmen, all recently shot down, including a badly burned fighter pilot whose head and hands were heavily bandaged.

The following morning, the whole group were herded out into the street where they boarded a public service tram. The local German travellers took the opportunity to hurl abuse at the English fliers as the tram rattled through the bomb-damaged streets, but the latter were too tired and hungry to care as they had not eaten for two days.

On a signal from the guards, the bedraggled group of airmen alighted from the tram and were divided into two groups. The first group consisted of those detailed to go straight to Dulag Luft for interrogation, while the second group were taken to the Hohemark Sanatorium, Doug was directed towards the latter group.

On arrival at the sanatorium, the prisoners were given a bath (their first in weeks), issued with long white nightshirts, and told to get into bed. Doug's bed was in a room of four, which also boasted a hand wash basin; a short while later, a doctor arrived to check the men's injuries. When he got to Doug, he inspected the wound, saw it was healing quite nicely, and then changed the dressing.

A few days later, Doug was ordered to get out of bed and was escorted down a corridor to a room where a Luftwaffe officer was sitting behind a small table. It was a short-lived meeting:

> I felt a bit of a twit prancing along in my nightshirt, but sat down and waited for the inevitable questioning to begin. The officer merely asked me to fill in the so-called Red Cross form. However, we all knew about these forms, so just filled in my name, rank and number and then put on a blank uninterested look. The interrogating officer tried to persuade me to complete all the other details such as squadron number and other pertinent information, but I refused. He then left and I was returned to my room.

A short time later, Doug had another 'interview', with a different Luftwaffe officer, and knew this is when the real interrogation would start. The officer started by telling Doug that he, the officer, knew and liked England having been educated there, at Oxford. He then produced a large file.

> This file contained details and information relating to XV Squadron, there was even a picture of the Squadron badge on the inside cover of the file. The top page listed all my crew and against four of the names were marked small crosses. He told me they were dead and I told him that I already suspected they had been killed, thus letting him know that he was not telling me anything I did not already know. Presumably, he was trying to lead me to believe that they knew all and that there was no point in keeping anything from them. They merely wanted to confirm certain facts. I was asked which runways at Mildenhall we used when we took off, where and when we crossed the coast and what sort and colour of markers were used. I was also asked the circumstances of our being shot down. After pretending to rack my brains, I humbly confessed that as I had been somewhat badly wounded and it was several weeks ago, I could remember nothing of what happened and that as a gunner, I had no idea of what colour the markers were. In short, I played dumb and uninterested and although I suspect he knew what my game was, he calmly gathered up his file, said, 'Goodbye', and cleared off.

A few weeks later, a number of the prisoners were taken to a holding camp to await transfer to a permanent camp. They were photographed, each with their respective prisoner of war numbers around their necks and fingerprinted. When the tally of prisoners had grown sufficient in numbers, they were herded into cattle trucks for a five-day journey to Heydekrug on the Memel Peninsula.

Occasionally, as the train steamed northwards towards its destination, some of the men would peer out through cracks, knot holes and apertures in the sides of the timber cattle trucks, in the hope of identifying some location or other. One day, an air of excitement began to spread through the wagon. Doug, like those who could manage the task, pressed one eye against the nearest hole in the wood to see the cause of the excitement. To Doug's utter amazement, he saw, sitting there looking somewhat majestic in a field, an apparently intact American Army Air Force B-17 Flying Fortress bomber. For a while at least, it gave the men incarcerated in the cattle wagon something new to talk about.

Eventually, the train arrived at its destination where, in the sidings, the prisoners detrained, formed up in a long line, and marched to their new home, *Stalag* Luft VI. On arrival in the outer compound of the camp, the men were stripped and searched before going through into 'K' Lager. This was a new compound that consisted of two large blocks, which were divided into twelve barrack rooms, with six rooms to a block. There were approximately thirty two-tier bunks in each room and Doug settled himself into a lower bunk at the far end of one of the rooms, away from the door and, hopefully, away from any winter draughts that were blowing through, especially when the door was opened.

Some of the prisoners, Doug included, had nothing in the way of clothing, other than the tattered clothes he stood up in. Fortunately, the new 'Kriegies' (as they were known) were kitted out from the stores according to their immediate needs. Doug received a pair of boots, a greatcoat, and some underwear, all of which were RAF issue and provided by the Red Cross. The food situation was another matter:

> We received one-eighth of a loaf of bread a day each, this was about five slices cut very thinly, although it became quite an art cutting bread as thin as possible in order to get the maximum number of slices. At this particular time, 1943, Red Cross parcels were in good supply so at Luft VI we received a regular once a week issue of one food parcel each.

This first intake of prisoners had arrived at the camp during the first week of October, but they were quickly followed a couple of weeks later by another intake comprising of 700 prisoners who had, until recently, been resident at *Stalag* Luft I at Barth, on the Baltic coast. Among the latter number was 'Dick' Richards, the flight engineer on Doug's crew. Expressing surprise at seeing Douglas alive and well, the former apologised to Doug for not helping him. Seeing Doug lying face down on the floor of the aircraft, with flames flickering towards the prostrate figure, Dick thought Doug was past all help.

Having settled into their new surroundings, the prisoners put their various talents to good use. An empty hut became a theatre and recreation room, with a stage, seating, and lighting. Others, including Doug, turned their talents to 'Goon-baiting':

> Occasionally, if the ground was dusty, we would quietly fall-in behind a guard as he was leaving the compound after roll-call and pour dirt down his rifle barrel,

> sometimes a cigarette end was substituted; they were just the right calibre for the old German rifles which were always slung so that the barrels pointed skywards. It was just a bit of fun.

One night, Doug lay in his bunk listening to the rain pounding against the side of the wooden hut. As he laid there, he became aware of another sound, a familiar one, and then realised it was the uneven drone of aircraft engines. A group of Kriegies had soon gathered around one of the hut windows and by peering through the top of the external shutters (which were closed against the window), they were able to see landing lights reflected on the clouds. The aeroplane circled a couple of times before veering off. There then followed the high-pitched scream of tortured engines before the inevitable earth-shattering sound of an explosion. A discussion among the prisoners led to the conclusion that the crew of the aircraft, which was in trouble, had mistaken the camp perimeter lights for an airfield. Assuming from the sound of the engines that the aircraft was a German one, the Kriegies let out a loud cheer. During the morning roll call, the camp commandant thanked the prisoners for cheering when the Luftwaffe crew bailed out, the German officer did not understand they had two reasons for cheering: 'We cheered merely because the Luftwaffe had lost another aircraft and, as we thought, a crew. After all, they were our enemies!'

The severe winter gave way to spring and gave the men in *Stalag* Luft VI a new hope for the future. That hope came in June, when they heard the news on their secret radio, known to all as the 'camp canary', that the Allies had landed in Normandy. A state of jubilation ran around the camp, along with the cry 'It's only a matter of time'. Speculation about the future was rife, and many thought they would be home for Christmas.

Unfortunately for the Kriegies, with the Russians advancing on Estonia and Latvia, the Germans decided to evacuate the camp. The inmates were divided into two groups, the first being sent by rail to another camp, while the second group were entrained to Memel, where they board a German merchant ship. Doug Fry never forgot the conditions on that ship:

> We were battened down in the hold, where one dim bulb provided light. Toilet facilities consisted of a bucket lowered down on a rope. As I was one of the last into the hold there was no room left for me to stand on the decking, so I found myself a spot on a strake, a small girder, about twelve inches wide, three feet long and about four feet above the deck. I spent three days and nights squatting on my little shelf.

The ship eventually docked at the port of Świnoujście, where the prisoners were relieved of their footwear on disembarking, before being herded into the now familiar cattle wagons. Suddenly, the air was filled with the wailing of air raid sirens, followed a few minutes later by the heavy drone of many Wright Cyclone engines, as a formation of B-17 Flying Fortresses of the 1st Bomb Division, American 8th Air Army Air Corps flew overhead. Immediately, a smokescreen erupted as the German cruiser *Prinz Eugen*, berthed nearby, opened fire with her ack-ack guns. The B-17s, who were subsequently to lose three of their number, continued on to their allotted target at Peenemunde.

Having endured a short train journey, the prisoners arrived at Stargard, approximately 35 miles on the Polish side of the border of what later became East Germany. The prisoners, having been reunited with their footwear, marched off to Gross Tychow, the location of *Stalag* Luft IV, their next home. Doug remembers his arrival at Luft IV:

> When we arrived at the camp, on 20 July 1944, we saw the first group to leave milling around outside the camp. We noticed that some of the men were wounded and some were in a state of shock. We soon learned that these prisoners had been manacled together and forced to run up and down the road at bayonet point. Several of the men had been bayoneted during this episode, some more than once. Some short while later, we learned that an attempt had been made on Hitler's life that same day.

Conditions in the camp were very poor and the accommodation was severely cramped. Food was scarce and all thoughts and hopes of being home for Christmas began to fade. As time progressed, some of the conditions improved, the prisoners were moved into a new compound where a pump provided cold water, and coal-fired boilers provided heat. Doug volunteered to look after the boiler for his hut and thereby managed a few extra perks for himself, like being first with the hot water for shaving and washing clothes. He also managed to get involved in a bartering system. The start of 1945 was not a good one, with a scarcity of both bread and potatoes, and to add to the prisoners' concerns, Red Cross parcels were in short supply.

With the Russians still advancing, the Germans decided to move the men yet again. On the morning of 6 February 1945, the Kriegies were awakened and ordered to parade outside the huts. It was just 6 a.m., a blizzard was raging, and they were forced to stand in the freezing snow for over two hours. Eventually, the order to move off was received. As they passed through the camp gates, each man received two Red Cross food parcels; they were informed these were the last of the supply.

The human column marched doggedly on during the day, resting for five minutes at a time, only when they were told they could. The roads were covered with deep snow and the going was hard, it was difficult for the men to walk and keep their balance, and many of them took a tumble. At night, they occasionally had the luxury of sleeping in a barn; if not, it was out in the open countryside.

At Świnoujście, they crossed the estuary by using a bridge and a ferry boat, and then continued their march until they came to a farm where they were rested for a couple of days.

The days passed, the snow melted and was replaced by seemingly constant rain, but the column kept moving, on towards the Elbe. Having crossed the Elbe, the prisoners passed through a town in which there were a vast number of wounded German soldiers, who watched in silence as the column moved on, through the streets and out towards open countryside. Accompanied by the distant drone of aircraft engines, which did not really bother them, the prisoners began to cross an area of open ground, which was edged by small wooded areas. The drone of the engines increased in volume to a throbbing beat as a large formation of B-17 bombers, escorted by a squadron of Mustang fighters passed directly overhead. Reaching the centre of the open ground, some of the prisoners cast their eyes upwards and saw movement on the underside of the bomber fuselages; the B-17s were opening their bomb bay doors. Almost immediately, dark cylindrical shapes, some trailing smoke, began to fall from the formation leader's aircraft. The other aircraft in the formation followed their leader's example and unleashed their deadly loads. The ground shook as bombs exploded either on buildings in the town or on the outer edges of the open space, causing the prisoners and their guards to scatter towards the small wooded areas available for cover.

With no returned fire from the ground, the fighter escort leader hauled his aircraft over in a banking turn and dived towards the ground, with the rest of the escort following him. Flashes of light emanated from the leading edges of the Mustangs wings, as the fighters made their first strafing run at tree-top height. Although cold, hungry, and tired, and helping the stragglers among them, the prisoners found the strength to reach the safety of the trees; it was an experience neither they nor Doug would ever forget:

> When the lead bomb aimer dropped his load in which there were bombs trailing smoke, the others in the formation dropped their bombs. There was no opposition from the German defences whatsoever but, seeing the smoke bombs go down, the German commandant in charge of us Kriegies started shouting, 'New weapon, new weapon', thinking the smoke was trailing from shot-down aircraft. As there were no German fighters or flak in evidence, he was under the impression a new weapon was responsible for what he thought were crashing aircraft. He was, of course, sadly disappointed.

Having survived the aerial onslaught, the prisoners kept walking. During the march, the Luftwaffe guards handed over their charges to the *Wehrmacht*, who immediately bundled the prisoners into the all too familiar wooden cattle wagons.

Although the Kriegies did not know it at the time, the train was detailed to take them to Hannover, where they were to be incarcerated in a camp at Fallingbostel. On arrival at the compound, as each man passed through the camp gates, he was given a Red Cross food parcel. Food was still in very short supply, the Germans providing the prisoners with only one bowl of turnip soup a day, but it was more akin to greasy water with one or two bits of turnip floating in it.

Owing to the rapid advance of the British 2nd Army towards Hannover, the Germans decided to move the Kriegies to another location, even though they had only been at Fallingbostel for about two weeks. It was April 1945 and it was obvious that the German guards' morale was, by this time, somewhat lower than that of the prisoners. The latter knew that the prospect of liberation was not far off, and the guards knew it too. With that thought in mind, some of the guards began befriending the prisoners, talking to them and showing them photographs of their respective families, but Doug Fry and the others were only too well aware of the German soldiers' motives.

Early one morning, the prisoners were given a sign of hope that literally came out of the sky. As the column was tramping across a field two Spitfires appeared and while one kept top cover at about 1,000 feet, the other one executed several tight turns over the column at about 200 feet. Straightening out to rejoin his wingman, the pilot waggled the aircraft's wings in recognition and encouragement before flying off. The men, Doug included, stood and cheered, waving like mad, while the German guards dived to the ground in terror.

At the end of that day's march, having experienced a boost to their morale, the men slept soundly in a barn. The next morning dawned bright and sunny and, as always, the prisoners were up early. As they were assembling outside the barn the tranquillity was shattered by the roar of Merlin engines. Looking up, they saw two Spitfires racing toward them at tree-top height. Suddenly, fire spat forth from the fighters' wings as the two aircraft opened fire at something behind the barn. Spent cannon and machine gun shells rained down among the men, as they were ejected from the guns. The noise of battle increased as ground defences the other side of the barn retaliated. The Spitfires came around again, following the same course. The same scenario was re-enacted, this time accompanied by the deep-throated roar of another aircraft taking off. The prisoners turned toward the noise and were amazed to see a German Fw 190 fighter climbing steeply into the air, engulfed in flames. They continued to watch as it banked sharply on to one wingtip, stalled, and spun into the ground, killing its pilot as it exploded on impact. Their duty done, the two Spitfires climbed away unharmed having attacked a German airfield situated immediately behind the barn in which Doug Fry and his comrades had spent the night.

The march continued. On the evening of the next day, the column came to a farm which had two barns, both timber-framed with brick infill and thatched roofs. The floors were concrete with the usual covering of straw. The event that happened later that night was unforgettable:

> At about one o'clock in the morning, I was woken by the sound of an aircraft engine followed by a loud explosion. At first I thought the aircraft had crashed, but then I heard it flying away. As I listened I realised it was coming back and, looking through an opening in the wall I saw the flash of guns and streams of tracer coming straight for the opening. I turned my face to the floor as all hell broke loose. Cannon shells exploded in and around the barn. The thatched roof caught fire and bits of burning debris dropped to the floor, where it immediately set light to the straw. I felt a dull thud on my back and knew I had been hit, although it turned out to be a small cut, probably from a shell splinter. I was lucky because the chaps either side of me were killed. One was an American and the other was a friend, Reg Brown, who had been a prisoner for about four years. Four others were injured, two seriously, one of whom later died. I knew I was not badly hurt but could feel blood trickling down my back, and as I knew my body and clothes were somewhat dirty, I thought I should at least have my 'scratch' cleaned-up.

The wounded, including Doug, were taken in a horse-drawn cart in search of a place where they could be attended too, which was achieved when they arrived at a small camp at Schwerin. They were immediately placed in the camp sick bay, where they were treated and cleaned up by some of the inmates.

Unfortunately, the camp, like the barns, was situated very close to a German airfield which, due to the constant attention it received from Hawker Tempest fighters each morning, Doug believed housed many Luftwaffe fighters, including Focke-Wulf Fw 190s and Messerschmitt Bf 109s. However, the Tempest pilots did not always have things their own way:

> On one occasion I saw a Tempest go down in flames, after being caught in intensive light flak. The pilot managed to bail out, but the Germans still continued to fire at him. Now and again, a 20-mm shell would hit the deck in the compound and explode, so it was not too healthy for us to be out watching the action.

The aircraft to which Doug referred was probably Hawker Tempest V EJ599, piloted by Flying Officer Stanley Thomas Worbey of 3 Squadron. This aircraft failed to return from an attack against Schwerin airfield on 30 April 1945. The pilot was killed and has no known grave.

Two days later, on 2 May, a day before Doug's twenty-first birthday, an early-rising Kriegie excitedly rushed into the hut shouting that the guards had gone and that there were some broken rifles lying on the ground outside the wire. This news took about an hour or more for the truth to sink in, and then only when assisted by the sight of a Jeep, with a 0.5-inch Browning machine gun mounted on the back, crewed by two American soldiers who were driving past.

It was not long before the Americans arrived with ample supplies of food and drink, more than these men had seen for a number of years. Unfortunately, some had forgotten that over a period of time their stomachs had shrunk, and that they could not eat all they could see.

Due to the number of refugees and fleeing German servicemen, the roads around Schwerin became blocked, causing confusion and frustration. It was about a week later that the ex-prisoners of war were taken to Lüneburg, where they were accommodated in the comparative luxury of the former German barracks in preparation for the repatriation to England.

There was plenty of food, including white bread, plus they had the opportunity of a shower, with plenty of hot water, whenever they felt like it.

Unfortunately, although everybody now just wanted to get home, the able-bodied men had to wait until the sick and wounded men had been given priority and loaded on to the waiting Douglas Dakota aircraft, but the former had no objections to this ruling. In the event, arrangements were made for the ex-Kriegies to fly home from Lübeck airfield, to which they were transported in British Army trucks. At Lübeck, the ex-prisoners were divided into groups of twenty-four men, ready for the flights home, something else Doug never forgot:

> We met the crew of a Lancaster in which we were to fly home. As the mid-upper gunner of the crew had nipped-off home for a quick '48' [hour pass], the skipper allowed me to ride home in my old position—the mid-upper turret. Thus events had come full circle. I had flown out to Germany in the mid-upper turret of a Stirling bomber of XV Squadron, and eventually returned in the mid-upper turret of a Lancaster.

9

The Darkness of Pain: Flight Sergeant Gilbert 'Gil' Marsh

Gilbert Marsh, known to everyone as Gil, was born on 23 January 1922 in Liverpool. He was the younger of two brothers who were both destined to become pilots in the Royal Air Force during the Second World War. While Gil became a Stirling bomber pilot flying bombing operations over Europe, his elder brother William, confusingly known as Bill, became a fighter pilot, flying Hawker Hurricane fighter-bomber aircraft over the desert during the North African campaign.

For Gil, his journey to the skies over Europe began when he volunteered for service with the Royal Air Force Volunteer Reserve, in January 1941. Having signed on the dotted line, he was sent home with instructions to await his call-up papers. Six months later, he received notification that he was to report to the Aircrew Receiving Centre at Regent's Park, London, on 14 July, where he was billeted for two weeks before being posted to Torquay, Devon, for basic training with No. 5 Initial Training Wing. Having marched back and forth along the promenade, swinging those arms higher each time until the whole squad did it in unison, and endured the rigours of physical training every morning in the same location, for six weeks, on 2 August, Gil received a posting to West Kirby transit camp.

West Kirby was, in one sense, an ideal posting for Gil, as it was only 12–15 miles from his home in Liverpool. Unfortunately, it was also the location from where he would commence his journey to Africa for overseas flying training.

The troopship SS *Empress of Russia* sailed from Liverpool on 25 September and headed for South Africa, arriving at Durban at the end of October. After spending a week at the Clarewood Transit Camp in Durban, Gil was transferred to an initial training wing at Bulawayo, before moving on to No. 26 Elementary Flying Training School, at Guinea Fowl, where he arrived on 31 January 1942. Training commenced immediately with Gil, according to his logbook, making his first air experience flight in Tiger Moth T6128, on the day of his arrival, with Sergeant Chamberlain, an instructor, at the controls. Flying almost every day with Sergeant Chamberlain, Gil learned the basic techniques of flying, how to handle the aircraft and getting used to the machines various responses. On 13 February, after a fifty-five-minute dual flight with Sergeant Chamberlain, Gil was sent off on his first solo flight: a short 'hop' lasting only ten minutes.

Between the dates 29 March and 10 September, Gil, who had risen in rank from aircraftman second class to leading aircraftman, flew North American Harvard aircraft—a very powerful, single-engined machine, which was in use for training with No. 22 Service Flying Training School. During this same period, in August, he spent a week living under canvas, at the Kabanga Operational Training Unit emergency landing ground.

On returning to England at the end of October, wearing the rank of sergeant, Gil was posted, on 17 November, to No. 14 (Pilots) Advanced Flying Unit, based at Ossington, north-east of Nottingham, where he converted to twin-engined aircraft and flew Airspeed Oxfords. Having completed the course at No. 14 (P) AFU Gil was posted to No. 26 Operational Training Unit, at Wing, Buckinghamshire, on 2 February 1943. All previous training had been learning how to fly and control aeroplanes, diving, climbing and recovering from spins etc. At the operational training unit, Gil would learn not only how to fly and use an aircraft as a weapon of war, but also how to command a crew; yet first, he had to form a crew.

The aircraft Gil would be training on at No. 26 OTU were Vickers Wellington bombers, which required a five-man crew. Using the time-honoured method of roaming around a large room or hanger, looking for and talking to prospective crew members, Gil was able to put together a crew of his liking. Apart from himself as pilot, there was Pilot Officer A. Richards, navigator; Sergeant George Wright, wireless operator; Sergeant Arthur Hynam, rear gunner; and Sergeant John 'Jack' Bailey from Saskatoon, Canada, bomb aimer. As a crew, they flew and trained together and got to know each other both in the air and on the ground during off-duty periods, which was to stand them in good stead later in their operational career.

Following a week's leave at the end of May, the crew reassembled on 3 June and reported to 'B' Flight, No. 1651 Heavy Conversion Unit, based at Waterbeach. It was at Waterbeach that Sergeant Jimmy Meaburn, flight engineer and Sergeant W. Smith, mid-upper gunner joined the crew. It was now, with a full crew complement, that the final part of their training took place, not only learning to work together, but also to learn the intricacies of the Short Stirling four-engined bomber, the machine in which they would go to war. Fourteen days after their arrival at Waterbeach, on 17 June, Gil Marsh and the crew flew their first solo on Stirling bomber BK622; the flight lasted one hour and forty minutes. Although they did not know it at the time, the aircraft serial number would have a significant bearing on the crew's future operational flying. Having satisfactorily completed the course at HCU, the crew were declared combat ready and posted to XV Squadron, based at RAF Mildenhall, on 30 June.

On arrival at the Suffolk base, Sergeant Marsh and his crew were attached to 'C' Flight, commanded by Squadron Leader John Martin. The latter, a powerfully built man who had been a farmer before the war, had himself only been posted to the squadron, from No. 1651 HCU, ten days before Gil and his crew.

As all new pilots had to do, three days after his arrival at Mildenhall, Gil Marsh flew a 'second dickey' flight with Flight Lieutenant Francis Norris, a very experienced pilot from New Zealand. The operation was an attack against Cologne, giving Gil an insight as to what he could expect on a bombing raid; his crew had yet to find out. Later, following the debriefing, Gil made the first operational entry in his logbook; it read: 'Fighters and searchlights very active—Flak medium to heavy'.

The crew were initiated into war operations on an easier mission, when they flew a 'Gardening' or mine-laying sortie on the night of 5 July. Piloting Stirling bomber EF351, Gil lifted the aircraft off the runway at midnight and set course for the Friesian Islands. They planted their mines at 1.56 a.m. from a height of just 2,000 feet. Gil later recorded in his logbook: 'Quiet trip—No troubles at all'.

The crew's second mine-laying operation, on 8 July, in the Bay of Biscay, had to be abandoned shortly after take-off due to hydraulics failure in the rear turret. A total of 1,500 gallons of fuel had to be jettisoned before Gil was allowed to land, but he did so with three mines still on board.

Practice bombing and fighter affiliation exercises were carried out over the next few days, flying on BK816, LS-X. Although this Stirling was officially known as X—X-ray, when it became their regular aircraft, the crew were to rename her: *Madame X*.

On 13 July, the crew took BK816 over Germany for the first time when they participated in a raid against Aachen. The flak was light and the searchlights few, which was probably due to the very active presence of night fighters. Although the aircraft was attacked over the target area, she sustained no damage. Likewise, BK816 was also fired upon by flak ships as she flew over the enemy coast on the homeward journey. Bringing into practice his earlier training, Gil manoeuvred the Stirling away from the danger area and concentrated on flying across the expanse of the North Sea, while the gunners kept watch for any marauding night fighters. The only problem Gil and his crew encountered on this operation was as they crossed the east coast of England, near Lowestoft, when they were suddenly subjected to the blinding glare of searchlights, the dazzle of which all but destroyed their night vision. Bringing his piloting skills to the fore again, Gil managed to evade the searchlights and landed at Mildenhall without further trouble.

When not scheduled for operational flying duties, it was important for the crew to keep honing their respective skills; this is what they did until the night of 24 July, when they were detailed for an attack against Hamburg. The raid was significant for two reasons, not only was it the start of a ten-day campaign against the city during which the RAF made four heavy night raids. The American 8th Army Air Force undertook two daylight raids; it was also the first occasion on which the RAF used 'Window', the anti-radar strips of aluminium foil used to confuse the enemy radar.

At 8.30 a.m. that Saturday morning, Air Officer Commanding 3 Group, Bomber Command, Air Vice-Marshal Harrison had issued a directive ordering a maximum strength attack and XV Squadron responded with a full complement of eighteen aircraft and crews, including Gil and his crew.

Carrying a 2,000-lb bomb, six canisters of 4-lb and seven canisters of 30-lb incendiary bombs, plus a fuel load to get them to Hamburg and back, BK816 lumbered into the air. Pilot Officer Richards, the navigator, logged the take-off time as 10 p.m.; he also gave his pilot a course on which to fly. Somewhere, out in the darkness the Pathfinder Force led the way. Arriving ahead of the main force, the Pathfinders marked the city with their target indicators, which were dropped at exactly 12.57 a.m. Stirling bomber BK816 arrived over the target sixteen minutes after the target indicators floated down. Things were beginning to hot up. The probing beams of the searchlights scanned the sky, while prowling night fighters hunted for prey.

Committed to his bombing run, Gil Marsh kept BK816 steady at 13,000 feet, taking care to adhere to the instructions issued by Jack Bailey, the bomb aimer. At 1.13 a.m., Sergeant Bailey pressed the 'tit' and the bombload cascaded down into the shimmering sea of flame below. Free of its heavy load, the aircraft lurched upwards, causing Gil to get a tighter grip on the control yoke, while turning the aircraft on to a new heading provided by Pilot Officer Richards.

Having been the first XV Squadron crew to bomb Hamburg that night, they landed back at Mildenhall at 4.20 a.m. and were, presumably, the first crew into debriefing and therefore the first crew to reach their respective beds.

The following night, the crew, along with their beloved aircraft, did it all over again, but on this occasion, they bombed Essen, where they acted out the same drama and felt the same tensions as they had the previous night.

On the morning of 10 August 1943, without any formal ceremony, the personnel, transport, and equipment (along with seven Stirling bombers, all of which constituted 'C' Flight, XV Squadron) were moved across the airfield at RAF Mildenhall, where it became 'A' Flight, No. 622 Squadron. The news

Above: *Left to right*: Sergeant Gil Marsh, pilot, with Sergeant Arthur Hynam, rear gunner, at RAF Mildenhall. (*Author's collection*)

Below: *Left to right*: Sergeant Jack Bailey, RCAF, bomb aimer, with Sergeant George Wright, wireless operator. Jack Bailey was later to be awarded a Conspicuous Gallantry Medal and granted a commission. (*Author's collection*)

Above: An image of Stirling BK816 from a painting which hung in Gil Marsh's home for many years. (*Author's collection*)

Left: The ground crew who helped keep Stirling BK816 airworthy included John Pratt (fifth from right), Tony Godfrey (fourth from right), Sgt 'Tubby' Hiscock (second from right) and Corporal Billington (first right). (*Author's collection*)

Left to right: George Wright, former wireless operator; Tony Godfrey, former member of ground crew; and Gil Marsh, former pilot, share a private drink together before attending a XV Squadron reunion at RAF Mildenhall. (*Author's collection*)

of this act did not come as a total surprise, as some of the personnel had been transferred during the previous few days. The only noticeable change was that in becoming a squadron in its own right, the code letters on all seven aircraft had to be altered; instead of LS, signifying XV Squadron, they were amended to GI, to signify 622 Squadron. Was the serial BK622 on the Stirling the crew had flown at No. 1651 Conversion Unit some sort of prophecy?

Squadron Leader John Martin assumed temporary command of the squadron until Wing Commander G. H. N. Gibson, DFC, arrived on 20 August to assume full command. During this same period, Gil Marsh was promoted to the rank of flight sergeant.

With all personnel of the new squadron being operationally experienced from their service with XV Squadron, they were not allowed a settling-in period but were detailed for a mission that night. The designated target was Nuremberg and although all seven aircraft took off, two returned early. Apart from being 'shadowed' across the target area by an enemy night fighter; as far as Gil and his crew were concerned, it was 'a quiet trip'.

No. 622 Squadron participated in two operations against Turin on the nights of 12 and 16 August respectively, and Flight Sergeant Marsh and his crew flew on both operations. Piloting *Madame X* on both occasions, Gil flew a night-flying test prior to both raids, in order to ensure the 'the old girl' was up to standard. As with the last operation, 'Lady Luck' continued to support

Gil, allowing him to record in his logbook regarding the 12th, 'Good prang—light flak over France—very accurate'. Similarly, following the attack on the 16th, the entry read, 'Target partly obscured by cloud—Exceptionally quiet trip—landed at Hurn'. Unfortunately, due to adverse weather conditions on the return leg of the latter operation, all 622 Squadron aircraft were diverted to the Bournemouth airfield, but returned to RAF Mildenhall the following day.

Given the distance and flying time to Berlin, the long summer days and shorts nights had precluded the German capital from being attacked by Bomber Command since 29–30 March 1943; however, that was about to change.

RAF Mildenhall, along with a number of other Bomber Command airfields, was a hive of activity on the morning of 23 August, which grew in intensity as the day wore on. That morning, an order had been issued by headquarters for a maximum effort against Berlin, the first such attack of the coming winter and both XV Squadron, who detailed thirteen aircraft, and 622 Squadron, who detailed seven aircraft, were to participate in the operation; in all, a total of 727 aircraft were dispatched that night.

Engine fitters, flight mechanics, instrument 'bashers', armourers, and refuelling bowser crews crawled in, over and around each aircraft, ensuring everything was in order for the coming attack. While some ladies of the Women's Auxiliary Air Force cleaned the Perspex on the canopies and turrets, others drove the tractors and trolleys, carrying various types of bombs, out to each individual aircraft.

With the briefings completed and the weathermen predicting that the night sky over Berlin would be clear with good visibility, a condition of which the bomber crews knew the German night fighters would take full advantage, they were set to go. As the day gave way to early evening, the crews began to make their way out to their respective aircraft. Some cycled, but the majority hitched a ride on the trucks driven by the WAAFs, the latter giving the members of aircrew the chance of a last-minute bit of banter with an attractive young driver.

As they approached Stirling BK816, GI-X, the crew saw *Madame X* silhouetted against the setting sun. The beauty of the image belied what was waiting for them in the night sky over Germany.

Having been informed it was time to go, the seven crew members climbed the four-rung metal ladder in to the fuselage and made their way to their respective stations. There was one change in their number that night, which Gil Marsh remembered:

> Our normal mid-upper gunner, Sergeant Smith, who had some form of physical complaint, had been stood down by the medical officer, and Flight Lieutenant Leslie Berry, who had recently arrived to take over as Gunnery Leader of

> No. 622, on learning that Sergeant Smith was in station sick quarters said to me, 'That's o.k. I'll come with you tonight as mid-upper'. I don't know if he subsequently regretted that decision.

Flight Lieutenant Leslie Berry was posted to No. 622 Squadron the day before this imminent attack on Berlin, to assume the duties of gunnery leader. Ten months later, on 1 June 1944, he was blown out of his turret, when the aircraft in which he was flying exploded in the air, following a night fighter attack, which left him the sole survivor of that crew. He parachuted to safety, evaded capture, and was awarded a Distinguished Flying Cross.

The seven Stirling aircraft of 622 Squadron stood at their dispersal areas. The peace of the evening was broken only by the occasional call of an 'erk' shouting to a colleague, or the chirping of a few birds as they settled down at the end of the day. A cough, a splutter, and a cloud of blue exhaust smoke rose as the first propeller came to life, turning slowly at first and then gathering speed as the three other engines raced to catch it up. The peace of the Suffolk airfield was shattered by the roar of twenty-eight Bristol Hercules engines as the squadron's aircraft came to life one by one, but it was not to end there; the fact XV Squadron had detailed thirteen aircraft for the attack meant that on the other side of the airfield another fifty-two engines joined the cacophony of noise that evening. Although a test flight had been carried out during the day, using the power supplied by these engines, every member of Gil's crew checked his instruments or controls one last time prior to take-off.

Using the outer engines for manoeuvring, the bombers taxied out one by one, snaking around the taxi track and lining up for take-off. When his turn came, Gil swung the aircraft on to the runway, powered up each engine and, on receipt of the green Aldis signal from the control caravan, opened the throttles, and released the brakes. With the aircraft's tendency to swing to starboard on its take-off run, Gil and Jimmy Meaburn (the flight engineer) held on to the throttles to counteract any such movement. Armed and loaded for war, each Stirling trundled along the runway gathering speed as it did so and slowly lifted into the air.

The intended route to and from Berlin was out over the east coast at Cromer, crossing the North Sea and Zuiderzee at 8,000 feet, and then holding course to a location approximately 30 miles south of Berlin. At the latter, a turn was to be made for the run in, bombing, and run out of the target area. The course was to be maintained until reaching the Baltic, in the area of the Kattegat, and then turn across southern Denmark, followed by a run home back across the North Sea. Gil Marsh never forgot that flight out:

> The weather was clear, but [strangely] there was no activity of any kind during the outward journey. No fighters, no flak, no searchlights; a most eerie sensation

> which created a feeling that doom was looking over one's shoulder. Then, as we arrived at the turning point south of Berlin, the Pathfinders dropped their marker flares for the first wave of Lancasters; we Stirlings were usually fourth wave, or mid-field. At that moment, masses of searchlights forming a circle probably ten miles or so in diameter come on, with all beams directed vertically, like bars of a huge circus cage. The whole sky over Berlin was as light as day and fighters were observed at higher altitudes flitting about like moths.

Activity was now increasing with the fighters swooping down to attack the intruders and a number of bombers being logged as they fell in meteorite-like balls of orange and red flame. 'Window' fluttered down to confuse the enemy radar, adding to the drama. Later statistics revealed that a total of fifty-six aircraft (comprising Halifaxes, Lancasters, and Stirlings) failed to return from the attack.

Fires on the ground began to increase in intensity, as the master bomber instructed the bomber crews to bomb on the green markers just dropped by the Pathfinders. Smoke rose to a height of between 10,000 feet and 12,000 feet.

Gil Marsh held *Madame X* steady on course at 12,000 feet, following Jack Bailey's instructions as the latter guided his pilot over the target. Sergeant Bailey having called, 'Bombs gone', Gil leaned forward and flicked the switch, situated to the right of the throttle levers, in order to close the bomb bay doors. At 12.07 p.m., as the bomb doors were closing, a Junkers Ju 88 night fighter crept out of the darkness and attacked BK816, opening fire at a range of approximately 500 yards. Flight Lieutenant Berry in the mid-upper turret and Sgt Hynam in the rear turret quickly responded and returned fire. The Stirling, with its bomb doors still partially open, took violent, but sluggish, evasive action. Gil had responded to the rear gunner's call:

> Once the rear gunner had sighted and reported the enemy fighter I waited for the instruction 'Port go' in order to start evasive action. When the instruction came I pulled back on the control column and hauled the aircraft over to port. As we went down and then up and over to the starboard side, a hosepipe of different colour tracer shot in through the canopy above our heads; this was followed by cannon shells slamming into the port cockpit side from slightly above.

Sergeant George Wright, who was the wireless operator, gave another aspect of the action:

> We were attacked three times in all. The hydraulics to the rear turret were severed during the final attack thus putting it out of action, but not before the enemy aircraft started to fall away. It was later claimed as a probable.

As a result of the attack, the bomber sustained damage to the tailplane, the port elevator was shot away, and the port outer engine was hit and had to be feathered. Continuing the story, George added a few more details:

> During the attack a cannon shell appeared to hit the edge of the armour plate on the pilot's seat and explode. Gil Marsh was hit by shrapnel in some six places around the groin and leg, cutting the sciatic nerve. The aircraft fell rapidly as the pilot slumped over the controls. Jack Bailey was still in the bomb aimer's compartment and took a bang to the head as the aircraft went down, and was temporarily stunned.

Not only did the Stirling sustain serious damage, so did the pilot as Gil himself recalled:

> I remember a big bang, my hands covered in green luminous phosphorous and a seemingly 14-lb sledgehammer hit me with full force. The encounter with the enemy aircraft had left me in a considerable state of discomfort, as the sciatic nerve had been severed at the top of my right leg and a large hole made through my shattered right hip. I was instantly overwhelmed by the spreading blankness of shock, which started at my feet and rose upwards ending in oblivion when it reached the brain.

With the pilot unconscious in his seat, George Wright and Dick Richards had a struggle to get the aircraft out of its dive. With a superhuman effort, working together in chaotic circumstances, they succeeded in their endeavours and the aircraft levelled just in time; only 1,500–2,000 feet above the ground.

Regaining consciousness, and in his weakened state, Gil summoned all his strength and managed to get the bomber back up to an altitude of 4,000 feet but owing to the state of the flying controls and surfaces, *Madame X* refused to climb any higher.

> I called Jack Bailey for assistance, but he had been rendered unconscious by hitting his head. I therefore asked Dick Richards, the navigator to occupy the second pilot's seat and eventually we managed to get [the aircraft] back on course for the Baltic, still at 4,000 feet.

Jimmy Meaburn called up on the intercom and issued a warning that the port outer engine oil pressure had gone and was overheating; to avoid a fire risk the engine was shut down. Sometime later, through necessity and after a discussion with the flight engineer, it was decided to risk restarting the engine in an effort to increase altitude. However, due to the necessarily rich mixture setting required for restarting the engine, the motor threw out sheets of red and orange flame which, due to the aircraft's relatively low altitude, was clearly visible from the ground. With the latter thought in mind, the engine was quickly shut down again.

During this period, Jack Bailey had recovered from his bang on the head and climbed up into the cockpit, fortuitously, just in time. It was obvious that Gil's strength was sapping rapidly and he would be of little further use in the pilot's seat. Between them, Dick Richards and George Wright careful manhandled the badly wounded pilot out of his seat and laid him on the floor, propped up against the side of the fuselage; they did not want to risk further injury by trying to get Gil further down the fuselage on to one of the beds. As they undertook this delicate operation, Jack Bailey squeezed himself into the vacated seat and took control of the aircraft.

During the flight back, Pilot Officer Richards, who had recovered the first aid box, over a period of time administered shots of morphine to the wounded pilot. Unfortunately, this action made the latter so thirsty that he drank all the coffee on board. Gil continued to pass in and out of consciousness, but he did remember approaching the Danish coast:

> As we approached the coast of Denmark from the Kattegat, the flak ships below opened fire. At 4,000 feet we would be an easy target for the ack-ack guns so I ordered Jack Bailey to turn away and go further north before crossing the Danish coast. This obviously met with some success, for having receded back into the darkness of pain I came-to to find we were flying over the North Sea.

A discussion ensued among the crew as to the possibility of ditching or baling out, both ideas being decided against, except in case of dire necessity, due to the injuries sustained by the pilot.

George Wright obtained a first-class fix 420 miles out from base, followed by two others *en route*. BK816 crossed the North Sea in daylight and was fortunately not attacked by prowling Luftwaffe day fighters.

Regaining consciousness from another bout of oblivion, Gil realised the aircraft was crossing the east coast of England, which gave rise to another crew discussion. The crew debated whether they should try and put down at the first available airfield or try for Mildenhall. It was agreed that the BK816 had got them this far they should try for home base. Problem solved, Gil once more receded into unconsciousness, only to re-emerge as the Stirling was on finals for Mildenhall, fortuitously allowing him to assist with the landing procedure:

> As the aircraft descended in a steep nose down attitude, I was able to see past Jack Bailey's left shoulder and noticed the glide-path indicators were red. I told him to increase power and maintain height until they showed green.

Being low on fuel, Sergeant Bailey had received instructions to go straight into land; everything had been cleared in case the undercarriage malfunctioned. All escape hatches were jettisoned and the crew decided no one should leave the aircraft until the captain had been safely removed. Jack Bailey was talked down by control and made a very good landing. It was later discovered that there were only 70 gallons of fuel left in the tanks.

Gil remembered nothing of the actual landing, only vague memories of being bumped about on a stretcher as he was being manoeuvred down the fuselage and placed in the waiting ambulance. Although he survived the ordeal, Gil never flew operationally again.

Jack Bailey had been on a pilot's course in Canada but, having 'cracked-up' a Cessna, was remustered as a bomb aimer. He had never before landed a four-engined aircraft. For his gallant effort, Sergeant Bailey received the immediate award of a Conspicuous Gallantry Medal, the highest decoration awarded to a member of 622 Squadron. On 21 September 1943, Sergeant John C. Bailey, CGM, was commissioned and posted to RCAF 'R' Depot, Warrington, prior to returning to Canada for pilot training.

Flight Sergeant Gil Marsh spent a month in the RAF Hospital at Littleport, Ely, before being transferred to Wingfield Morris Orthopaedic Hospital, Oxford, where he remained until the beginning of April 1944. On the 2nd of that same month, Gil was sent to No. 2 Aircrew Convalescent Depot for NCOs at Wirral, Cheshire, eventually returning to RAF Mildenhall, on 3 June 1944, wearing a calliper on his right leg and walking with the aid of two sticks, but the latter were quickly dispensed with. Although he never returned to operational flying, Gil had the satisfaction of training others to fly through his capacity as link trainer instructor. As for Stirling Mk III bomber, serial BK816, coded LS-X and GI-X, *Madame X* was repaired and back in the air on operations three days after the attack.

Such was the pain and trauma of that night for Gil Marsh that the story remained locked away in his mind for a period of forty years; not even his family were aware of the events that unfolded in the darkened sky over Berlin on the night of 23–24 August 1943. It was following a chance meeting with the author, at a XV Squadron Reunion at RAF Mildenhall in early 1983, that Gil decided to relate the story for the first time and consented to its inclusion in the original publication of *Bomber Squadron: Men Who Flew with XV*.

10

A Squadron of One: Flight Lieutenant Oliver Brooks, DFC

At approximately 4 a.m. on the morning of 23 April 1944, a lone Lancaster bomber flying at an altitude of approximately 500 feet over the sea struggled to maintain height as it crossed the Suffolk coastline. To any observer on land or sea, it was obvious that the pilot was experiencing a great deal of difficulty handling the bomber. Fire had ravaged the port inner engine, rendering it inoperative, the starboard outer engine, although working, was giving very little power and the wing flaps were jammed down at a 10-degree angle. To add to the situation, the pilot was not able to close the bomb doors, nor could he lower the undercarriage.

Baling out of the aircraft was not an option for the crew. A fire inside the fuselage had damaged three parachutes, many of the controls were unserviceable, and four of the crew had been injured, two of them fatally.

As he crossed over the coastline, the pilot, twenty-one-year-old Pilot Officer Oliver Brooks, could see his objective dead ahead: the emergency landing ground at RAF Woodbridge. He was tired, his arms and legs ached, and his body was bathed in perspiration from the arduous return flight. He had struggled with the crippled aircraft all the way back from Düsseldorf but being aware of the plight of his crew, he was determined to bring them home; he offered up a silent prayer that the aircraft would make it over these last few miles.

Fighting to keep the stricken bomber in line with the 3,000-yard-long runway, Oliver had to contend with yet another problem: he was unable to close the throttles and the Lancaster was sinking toward the concrete runway at an indicated airspeed of 120 mph. The ground controller had been warned that the aircraft approaching the airfield was in distress and that the emergency services would be needed.

Once the aircraft had slithered to a halt, following what could only be described as an exceptional landing in the circumstances, the fire and ambulance crews extricated the aircrew from the wrecked Lancaster quickly and efficiently. Pilot Officer Oliver Brooks had got them home. It was not a bad effort for someone who did not want to be a pilot.

Oliver Brooks was born in Petersfield, Hampshire in December 1922, where he was raised and educated. He left school at the age of seventeen and took employment as a temporary civil servant with the Royal Naval Armament Depot at Corsham, near Bath.

At that time, Oliver was interested in sport, particularly boxing, and when the war began, he considering joining the Royal Air Force as a physical training instructor but was advised to rethink his options:

> I did not think I was a suitable candidate for flying duties as I thought my eyesight would let me down, but I was recommended to try for aircrew which I did and was accepted. I was not one of those people with a passionate desire to fly, but like most young men at that time, I did want to be in action.

Following the same route as many young men before him, Oliver first reported to the Aircrew Selection Board at Weston-super-Mare, Somerset, which he passed in July 1941. Six weeks later, on 1 September, he found himself reporting to the Aircrew Receiving Centre at Lord's Cricket Ground, located at St John's Wood, North London. Being healthy and enjoying sport, Oliver had no problem when he reported to No. 10 Initial Training Wing at Scarborough; the early morning physical training exercises, 'square-bashing', and marching held no terrors for him.

On 16 December, having satisfied his instructors, Aircraftman Brooks was promoted to the rank of leading aircraftman and posted to 'C' Flight, No. 11 Elementary Flying Training School, based at Perth, Scotland. It was here that he experienced his first flight and learned the rudiments of flying, in a de Havilland DH.82 Tiger Moth.

A posting to Personnel Despatch Centre, at Heaton Chapel, Manchester, on 6 January 1942, confirmed that LAC Brooks was embarking overseas for further training. He arrived at No. 31 Personnel Despatch Centre, Moncton, Canada, on 13 February 1942. Thirteen days later, on the 26th, he arrived at Turner Field, Georgia, before reaching his final destination at Darr Aero Tech Field, also in Georgia, on 29 March. Here, in the strange peace of the south-eastern state, Oliver honed his skills flying a varied assortment of American training aircraft, before progressing to the twin-engined Beechcraft AT-10. Further progress in flying took place at Cochran Field and Moody Field, both also in Georgia. By early October, LAC Brooks had satisfactorily completed his course and, in a ceremony held at Moody Field, Oliver, along with the rest of the cadets, received his 'wings'.

> At 09.30 a.m. on the morning of 9 October, I actually got my 'wings'. They were presented at a ceremony held in the Base Chapel, along with a diploma, by the Commandant, Colonel Fred Nelson, Army Air Corp. I was also promoted to the rank of sergeant.

Sergeant Oliver Brooks returned to No. 31 Personnel Despatch Centre at Moncton, in preparation for embarkation back to the United Kingdom. On arrival at the latter, Oliver was posted to No. 7 Personnel Reception Centre in Harrogate, Yorkshire for approximately two weeks before being posted on 5 January 1943 to No. 6 (Pilot) Advanced Flying Unit, based at Little Rissington, Gloucestershire.

By the third week of April 1943, Oliver had completed his course at (P)AFU and was posted to No. 12 Operational Training Unit at Edge Hill, a satellite airfield to Chipping Warden, which was equipped with Vickers Wellington bombers. It was at OTU that Oliver formed his first crew, consisting of Pilot Officer Thomas, navigator; Sergeant McPhel, bomb aimer; Sergeant Thompson, wireless op/air gunner; and Sergeant Clay, rear gunner. The elementary part of the flying programme was undertaken at Edge Hill, following which they progressed to the parent station for the final part of the training. The crew flew together on eight training exercises before Oliver had a boxing accident and sustained a fractured hand. As a result of the injury, which occurred at the end of May 1943, Oliver was temporarily grounded and his crew was broken up.

> At the end of May I took part in a 'Wings for Victory' boxing tournament and fractured my hand. I reckon that [incident] may well have saved my life. Crews were being fed into 3 Group which at the time was operating with Stirling bombers, and the 'chop' rate was very high; only about one in five or six crews were getting through their tours. I have no idea what happened to my original crew, I can only assume they got another pilot. Anyway, I went back after my hand had healed, and virtually started again with another crew who, for some reason, had lost their pilot.

Oliver's new crew, which was formed in early July, consisted of Sergeants Ken Pincott, navigator; Les Pollard, wireless operator; Robert Gerrard, bomb aimer; and Harry Marr, rear gunner. When the crew were posted to No. 1651 Conversion Unit at Waterbeach, during the second week of September, they were joined by Sergeants Ron Wilson and 'Chick' Chandler, who completed the crew as mid-upper gunner and flight engineer respectively. After four weeks at the Cambridgeshire training base and with a total of 485 hours and forty-five minutes flying time recorded in his logbook, Oliver was declared combat ready and posted, along with his crew, to XV Squadron, based at RAF Mildenhall in the neighbouring county of Suffolk.

On arrival at Mildenhall, on 1 October, they were instructed to report to 'B' Flight, commanded by Squadron Leader Robert Megginson, DFC, DFM, a quiet, reserved man, but a bomber pilot with vast experience who was nearing the end of his second tour of operations.

For Oliver and his crew, their introduction into operational flying was a quiet one: a mine-laying sortie in the Bay of Biscay with no interference from either enemy fighters or flak. They experienced much the same circumstances on their second operation four nights later, when they dropped mines in the Gironde River. However, things were slightly different on the night of 18 November when the crew took off for an attack on Mannheim, their first venture over German territory. Following an ordinary take-off, they were forced to abandon the sortie when the starboard outer engine lost power due to a fractured oil pipe.

Four nights after the aborted raid, on the 22nd–23rd, the names of Sergeant Brooks and his crew were recorded on the battle order for an attack against Berlin. Although the operation was to be undertaken by the largest force Bomber Command had dispatched to the German capital to date, Oliver and his crew were to be the only representatives from XV; they were in fact a squadron of one:

> On 22 November there was a big raid on Berlin. My crew were the only representatives of XV Squadron to participate. The reason for this was that the Squadron had been out the night before and were, on their return, diverted to another airfield and could not get back to Mildenhall in time the following day. My aircraft was deemed unserviceable, but a replacement was made ready, whilst I was being briefed, alone, as to target, timings, weather conditions and routes.

Berlin was completely obscured by cloud which kept most of the German night fighters on the ground, although the ack-ack defences put up a fair barrage of flak.

Conscious they were over enemy territory for the first time (the aborted Mannheim trip did not count in their tally), the crew carried out their respective duties with zeal and assiduity. The two gunners traversed their respective turrets back and forth, scanning the darkness for any night fighter that penetrated the banks of cloud looking to increase his 'kill' tally, while Oliver held Stirling bomber EF177, steady on its bombing run, at 16,000 feet. Sergeant Gerrard the bomb aimer, directed his pilot to the estimated aiming point and, when the 1,000-lb bomb and ten canisters of incendiaries had tumbled clear of the bomb bay, called 'Bombs gone'.

The bombing run completed, the pilot received a course from the navigator, turned the aircraft on to the appropriate bearing, and headed for home. Sergeant Harry Marr, sitting in the rear turret, watched the shimmering red glow of the burning city, reflected in the cloud below, receding into the darkness as the bomber flew westward.

As he landed back at Mildenhall, Oliver was unaware of two facts, the first being that this was to be the last sortie undertaken by XV Squadron operating Stirling bombers and, secondly, it was the last operation he would fly wearing the rank tapes of sergeant; Oliver was granted a commission in the rank of pilot officer on Wednesday 24 November.

During December 1943 and the early part of January 1944, XV Squadron stood down while it converted to Lancaster bombers that, for Oliver at least, took place at RAF Lakenheath. Some of the Mildenhall crews undertook their conversion at RAF Feltwell, which was to become the home of No. 3 Lancaster Finishing School.

For the battle-experienced crews, it was like being back at flying training school, practising circuits and bumps, loaded climbs, cross-country exercises, air-to-air firing, and practice bombing exercises on local ranges. Oliver completed the course and was deemed ready for operations with the new aircraft by the third week of January 1944.

The crew's first operation using the new aircraft, in this case, Lancaster ED628, LS-O, occurred on the night of 20–21 January, when they were detailed for another attack on Berlin. As with the previous trip, the target was blanketed by cloud and although Oliver later reported the flak as less severe, the night fighters were vectored early on to the bomber stream and managed to shoot down a total of thirty-five aircraft.

Over the next few weeks, apart from getting used to flying a different type of aircraft, Oliver and the crew also had to get used to a new wireless operator flying with them. During the conversion period, Sgt Les Pollard's name had ceased to appear as a member of the crew and had been replaced with that of Sergeant Robert Barnes, who, according to the operational record book, flew his first operation with Oliver on 20 February.

Robert Barnes was flying with them on the night of 24–25 March, when the crew were detailed to return to Berlin on a raid which was to become known as 'the night of the strong winds', an occasion never forgotten by Oliver:

> We were routed in to the north, via Denmark. The winds were stronger than forecast and were judged to be about 130 miles per hour. The main [bomber] stream was spread out miles to the south of the proposed track.

The target indicators, when dropped, were blown to the south-west area of the city, which took the brunt of the attack as the crews aimed, as instructed at the briefing, at those markers. The glow of the fires below and the exploding flak shells from the German ground defences, all reflected on the patchy clouds, adding to the intensity of the attack; unfortunately, the ground defences accounted for the loss of approximately fifty bombers, while night fighters accounted for a further twenty-three aircraft. It was a night Ken Pincott, the navigator, would not forget either:

> The winds were considerably stronger than the forecast and reached 130mph. In order to use the computers in use at the time, to calculate the triangle of velocities, all speeds (i.e.) true airspeeds and wind velocities, had to be halved to solve the problems. The computer scales were not calibrated high enough to cope with the kind of speeds being found. The resultant answer was then doubled to give the correct solution, thus enabling accurate navigation to stay on track and arrive on target at zero hour.

Strangely, over the intervening years since that raid, there was one event that occurred on this particular operation that Oliver forgot about, but was confirmed by Chick Chandler, the flight engineer. Having carried out their allotted task, Oliver turned the Lancaster on to a course for home, away from the target and back into the darkness of the night. Looking out from the cockpit Oliver and Chick could see nothing; they were, seemingly, flying alone. Without any warning came the deafening noise of the canopy 'exploding'. Oliver ducked as pieces of shattered Perspex flew into the cockpit, followed by the twisted, bloody, lifeless form of a large bird. The unfortunate creature had flown into the path of the Lancaster and been blown through the canopy, depositing its feathers and parts of its anatomy around the cockpit. Although Oliver could not recall this episode, Chick Chandler did: 'I remember the incident very well, as I was the one who had to clear up the mess and dispose of the remains'.

The city of Nuremberg was the focus of Bomber Command's attention on the night of Thursday 30 March. A total of 795 aircraft (comprising 572 Lancasters, 214 Halifaxes, and nine Mosquitoes) were detailed for the attack. Taking off from their respective bases in East Anglia, the aerial armada crossed the coastline over Suffolk and Norfolk and set course, on a south-easterly heading, for Nuremberg. Out over the North Sea, the gunners kept watch for any German intruder aircraft, while the flight engineer made adjustments to the fuel systems and engine settings, the navigator plotted the time and distance to his next change of course, and the wireless operator retuned the wavelength settings on his radio equipment; the pilot, meanwhile, stared out into the night, watching for any aircraft that came too close to his own aircraft, while regularly checking his various flying instruments.

The bomber stream crossed the enemy-occupied coast over Knokke, Belgium, where light flak rose into the sky but was somewhat short of the bombers altitude. Turning on to an easterly heading over Charleroi, the bombers then flew a long straight course to the German frontier, before turning south for a run in to the target.

Unfortunately, recent history was to repeat itself when it was discovered that the information supplied relating to wind speeds and direction, given by the meteorological officer at the briefing, was again incorrect. As a result of this error, the bombers had been blown to the north of their intended track. However, this was only the start of Bomber Command's problems, as the German fighters, who had been ordered to circle the fighter radio beacon Ida to the south of the Ruhr, discovered the bomber stream, and immediately swung into action.

Oliver had taken off from Mildenhall at 10.19 p.m. piloting Lancaster LL827 and had followed the specified route. Up until this point, the flight had been uneventful then he was given cause to remember it:

> That night [the RAF] lost 95 aircraft. The German fighter defences appeared well organised and seemed to know our route. They saw the bombers quite easily due to the light of a half moon reflecting on a thin layer of cloud. As we approached the target the rear gunner reported a twin-engined fighter out on our rear port quarter, high. The enemy aircraft turned in towards us and dived, passing underneath us.

From his station next to the pilot, Chick Chandler, the flight engineer, who had seen the fighter emerge from under the starboard side of the bomber, alerted the gunners over the intercom as to the enemy's position. On hearing this, Harry Marr rotated his turret to the starboard quarter and elevated his guns as the night fighter, which he identified as a Junkers Ju 88, executed a climbing turn into the same piece of sky. The enemy aircraft closed in and opened up with cannon fire, the beauty of the illuminated stars of light leaving the fighter's nose, belied their deadly intent. Oliver immediately dropped the bomber's right wing and threw his aircraft into a corkscrew manoeuvre to starboard, but some of those deadly stars danced along the mainplane of the Lancaster:

> We were hit in number three tank on the port side. That was the small capacity (114 gallons) tank outboard of the outer engine. It was a brand new tank and had not been filled; if it had the results could have been disastrous. The enemy aircraft made just the one attack and disappeared, no doubt to seek other targets.

Harry Marr had opened fire when the Ju 88 turned in towards the Lancaster but stopped when it broke away. Ron Wilson's view of the aggressor was initially obscured by one of the Lancasters tail fins, but he saw it as it broke away and fired off a burst of fifty rounds before the fighter disappeared from view. Ken Pincott, the navigator, remembered that night for another reason:

> I remember the Nuremberg raid because of the large number of aircraft being shot down. I was advised by the skipper to stop recording them, because I had logged over fifty such positions before we reached the target.

With regard to operations, April was a relatively quiet month for XV Squadron. An attack against the marshalling yards at Laon was undertaken on the night of the 10th, while a raid on Cologne was detailed on the 20th.

On Saturday 22 April, Oliver received the news that he had been promoted in the rank of acting flight lieutenant; that same night, the newly promoted officer was detailed for a major attack on Düsseldorf. A total of 596 aircraft were dispatched on the raid, which included 323 Lancaster bombers, 254 Halifax bombers, and nineteen Mosquitoes. Among the former category was Lancaster Mk III ND763, LS-W, piloted by Oliver, who had taken off from Mildenhall at 10.49 p.m. Flying with the crew was Flight Lieutenant John Fabian, DFC, the XV Squadron navigation leader, who as 'Y' operator would have responsibility for operating the H2S 'blind navigation' radar system.

The aircraft undulated gently on the night air as it flew over enemy territory, with Acting Flight Lieutenant Brooks occasionally glancing down at his instruments throughout the flight. As they neared the target, he saw shafts of light penetrating the darkness as searchlight beams began to sweep the sky. Red indicator flares announced the Pathfinders had located the target.

From his position in the bomb aimer's compartment, Robert Gerrard had a clear view of the target through the nose blister and guided his pilot towards the marker flares now burning brightly on the ground. At this point, Flight Sergeant Robert Barnes, the wireless operator, left his station, as Oliver recalled:

> On the run in to the target Barnes would make his way down the fuselage. It was his job to ensure the photo-flash we were carrying was released at the same time as the bombload. Sometimes it would hang up, so Barnes would have to ensure it went down by giving it a push.

At approximately 1.16 a.m., Gerrard pressed the 'tit' and the bombs began to tumble out of the bomb bay but before he could call 'Bombs gone', there was a terrific explosion underneath the aircraft and in a split second, Robert Gerrard lay dying. A heavy calibre flak shell had exploded in the mouth of the bomb bay and the blast reverberated upwards and into the belly of the aircraft, twisting metal and shattering the bomb aimer's compartment. Gerrard, who was to have been married two weeks later, only lived for another two or three minutes. Unfortunately, Robert Barnes was also caught in the blast which, as Oliver related, almost severed one of the wireless operator's legs:

> Barnes was ensuring the photo-flash didn't hang up when the flak shell exploded, severely injuring him. Despite his terrible wounds he crawled a short distant along the fuselage floor crying for help.

Above left: Flight Lieutenant Oliver Brooks at the controls of a Lancaster bomber. (*Author's collection*)

Above right: Oliver Brooks photographed with his original crew. *Left to right*: Ken Pincott, Nav; Harry Marr, A/G; Oliver Brooks, pilot; Chick Chandler, F/E; Ron Wilson, A/G (concealed); Les Pollard, W/op; and Allen Gerrard, B/A. Les Pollard was replaced by Robert Barnes. (*Author's collection*)

Below: The navigational map used by Ken Pincott became blood-spattered when he received wounds following the detonation of a flak shell on the night of 22–23 April 1944. (*Author's collection*)

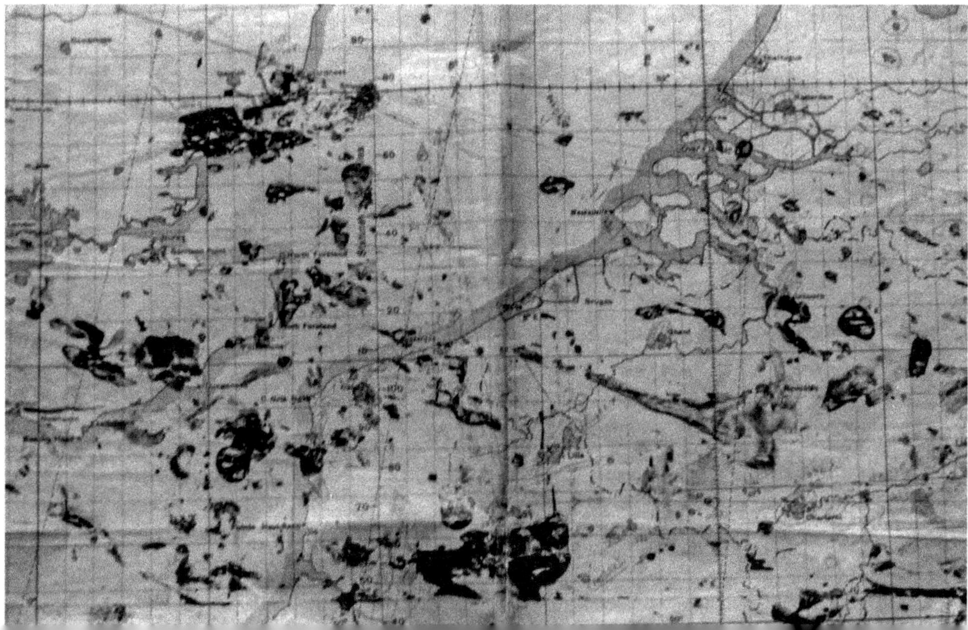

Above: An in-flight photograph of the Lancaster cockpit, as viewed from the flight engineer's station. The aircraft is thought to be Avro Lancaster PB115. (*Author's collection*)

Below: Taken from the cockpit of Lancaster PB115, this photograph shows XV Squadron aircraft participating in a daylight attack on V-1 flying bomb sites at Domleger, on 21 June 1944. This sortie was the final one of Flt Lt Brooks's operational tour of duty. (*Author's collection*)

Obviously in pain and losing a lot of blood, every jolt and bump of the aircraft made its presence felt in his shattered lower body. Help was on the way, but there was little that could be done to save the wireless operator's life. Sergeant Chick Chandler, the flight engineer, was trying to clamber his way through the shattered aircraft checking on damage and casualties, when he found the seriously wounded crew member. In response to Chick's call for help, Ron Wilson climbed down from his turret to assist, as John Fabian, the navigation leader, made his way aft to offer assistance.

Sergeant Chandler also reported that Sergeant Wilson, the mid-upper gunner, had sustained a cut ear caused by a fragment of shrapnel, while Ken Pincott, the navigator, whose hand had been hit by flak, suffered a badly cut finger, blood from which soaked into the navigational log and map.

At the same time as the flak shell exploded, a burst of cannon fire raked the port wing. Undetected, a Messerschmitt Bf 109 'Wild Boar' night fighter had crept in from astern and opened fire at a range of approximately 800 yards, the shells hitting one of the port engines, setting it ablaze. Unfortunately, the turrets were operated by hydraulics powered by this engine, thus putting them both out of action. Although the turrets could not be rotated, it was agreed that Harry Marr should remain in his turret and fire the guns manually to warn off any approaching night fighters.

It was as Ron Wilson was climbing down from his turret that another problem occurred, when a shower of sparks from a short in the electrical circuit ignited and started a fire. Having disconnected his intercom when vacating the turret, Ron was unable to alert his pilot, which in one sense was just as well, as Oliver was in the cockpit battling with the controls of his aircraft, which was rapidly losing height; he had already issued a warning for the crew to be prepared to bail out.

Sergeant Wilson set about trying to extinguish the fire on his own, which he eventually managed to do, but not before the flames had consumed three of the crews' parachutes. Wilson then turned his attention to assisting John Fabian, who was attending to the wounded wireless operator. Between them, Wilson and Fabian cut away Barnes clothing and injected him with morphine, but it was all to no avail. In the undignified surroundings of a battle-damaged Lancaster, lying in a pool of blood oozing from his wounds, Flight Sergeant Robert Barnes succumbed to his injuries and paid the supreme sacrifice.

Lancaster ND763 had been flying at an altitude of 22,000 feet when the bombload was released, but had rapidly lost height following the explosion and night fighter attack. Having battled with the controls in a near vertical dive, Oliver managed to regain control, but not before the aircraft had fallen 15,000 feet. Regaining control at 7,000 feet, the pilot called for a battle damage report; but that was not all he called, for as Ken Pincott recalled:

> Usually on the run in to the target, I would leave my navigation table and stand looking out of the astrodome, another pair of eyes searching for fighters. When we were hit the aircraft went into a dive from 22,000 feet and I was thrown to the floor. I found it very difficult to regain my foothold because the floor was very slippery, being awash with various fluids. Just as I managed to regain a foothold, the aircraft dropped again. Thinking that I did not want to die, having been married for only a fortnight, I was about to find my parachute and get out. I thought I was the only one still alive, then I heard the skipper's voice calling out for a crew check, followed by the comment, 'For Christ sake, navigator, give me a course for home'.

Sadly, due to the dinghy having been shot away, and as the three parachutes had been damaged by fire, the pilot could not consider ditching the aircraft in the sea. Then, as Oliver relates, there was Sergeant Chandler to consider:

> Chick Chandler had a bloody lucky escape. He was leaning slightly forward in his seat when the flak shell exploded. A lump of shrapnel came through the side of the fuselage and sliced through the back strap of his parachute harness. Had he been sitting three inches further back it would have taken a chunk out of his back.

Being the quiet, calm, and collective type of person he was, Oliver assessed the situation he and the crew now found themselves in, bringing his qualities of leadership to the fore. Although he had regained control of the severely damaged aircraft, he still experienced problems maintaining altitude. Even with the latter in mind, he reasoned their best chance was to try to reach one of the emergency landing grounds on the east coast of England. Ken Pincott added some thoughts to this decision:

> Having discovered that the aircraft was flying at approximately 90 mph ground speed, I calculated we should head for Woodbridge, with an ETA of around 03.38 hours. Once over the North Sea, I tried to operate the wireless, sending out SOS transmissions together with expected ditching positions, in case we should go down in the sea.

Having patched up the minor injuries sustained by Wilson and Pincott, with the latter endeavouring to act as wireless operator, John Fabian took over the responsibility of navigation.

The atmosphere on board the Lancaster was highly-charged. The crew were all aware that the aircraft was an easy target for flak and fighters, plus it was still losing altitude; as ND763 crossed the French coast, the altimeter was barely registering 3,000 feet. Then, their worst fears happened—they were coned by searchlights. The intense illumination of the multi-million candle power beams turned night into day. Time stopped; the fear level rose leading to dry throats, thumping heartbeats and constrictions in the chest for probably more than one member of the crew. They waited for what seemed an eternity. As there was no flak, that could only mean a fighter attack. Then, as quickly as the blinding lights had appeared, they were gone. Total blackness followed the strain of nothing but blinding light. Prayers were said, but all in silence, in the mind of each crew member. Daring not to speak, for that moment at least, the crew carried on with their respective flying duties.

Together, Brooks and Chandler flew the aircraft, with the pilot fighting the controls and checking the altimeter every few minutes, while the flight engineer kept up a commentary on the fuel situation and the state of the engines. Unbeknown to Ken Pincott, due to the aircraft's low altitude, his continuous SOS transmissions were not being received.

In an effort to lighten the aircraft, Oliver ordered all unnecessary equipment, including the guns and ammunition, to be jettisoned—a task undertaken by Fabian and Wilson. Slowly and unnoticeably, ND673 began to gain some altitude, enough to get the aircraft over the English coast at 500 feet. Ahead of him, Oliver could see the most welcoming sight of his life, the threshold of the long bitumen-and-sand-covered emergency runway at Woodbridge. He knew he only had one chance at this landing; it was not going to be easy and he had to get it right. He was hampered by the fact the elevator and rudder trims were both unserviceable, he could not lower the undercarriage or close the bomb doors. Furthermore, the crew could not take up their usual crash positions and had to remain at their respective workstations.

With the throttles jammed open, and the airspeed indicator registering 120 mph, Oliver brought the Lancaster into Woodbridge. He held the nose high and let the aircraft sink slowly until he felt contact with the ground. At 3.55 a.m., the emergency services swung into action and raced across the airfield, following the Lancaster as it slid along on its belly. The propellers twisted, buckled, screamed, and tore gouges in the ground, throwing dirt and debris into the air.

As the dust settled, the bodies of Barnes and Gerrard were removed from the aircraft, while the surviving crew members were taken to the station sick bay for attention and check-ups. In the meantime, Lancaster ND673 was unceremoniously dragged from the runway by the crash crews.

Flight Lieutenant Brooks, Flight Lieutenant Fabian, Flight Sergeant Pincott, and Sergeant Chandler were not given time to ponder on the recent experience, as Oliver remembered:

> The next night our names appeared on the battle order for a raid against Karlsruhe. The OC, Wing Commander Watkins, flew as my bomb aimer to see how we got on. As Ron Wilson was still in the sick bay, Sergeant W. Walker flew as mid-upper gunner, whilst Sergeant J. Murphy flew as wireless operator.

Piloting Lancaster LL827, LS-O, Oliver took off from Mildenhall at 9.56 p.m. and headed for Germany. Unfortunately, the strong winds had returned and the bombers were blown north of their allotted track. Although the target markers were well concentrated, they too were casualties of the wind and were blown off the actual aiming point. Cloudy conditions and icing also hampered the attacking force. During the run-up to the target, a night fighter announced its presence behind LL827, by opening-up with a burst of cannon fire. Fortunately for the Lancaster and its crew, the enemy pilot's aim was not that good and missed its target. Oliver threw the bomber into a corkscrew manoeuvre as the fighter curved around for another attack. The enemy's gun spat forth another burst of cannon fire at the Lancaster, but this too missed its intended victim. Just as Oliver was having thoughts about events two nights ago, the aggressor disappeared into the darkness never to be seen again. Having confirmed his crew were all right and that there was no damage to LL827, Oliver returned to the job in hand, and completed his bombing run without further hindrance. Although his aircraft was coned twice by searchlights on the outskirts of the target area, he managed to evade them by taking evasive action on both occasions.

Although the first week of May was quiet for Oliver, he flew only training exercises; he was made aware of some exciting news. Flight Lieutenant Brooks was notified that he was to be awarded a Distinguished Flying Cross. It was also announced that Flight Lieutenant John Fabian was to receive a Bar to his DFC, while Flight Sergeant Ken Pincott was to be awarded a Distinguished Flying Medal.

Having flown an operation with two 'spare' crew members and the Officer Commanding XV Squadron, together with the fact Chick Chandler had been posted to No. 622 Squadron, it became necessary for Oliver to rebuild his crew, in order to complete his own tour of operations. This was achieved when he took over part of an existing crew who had lost their own pilot, after the latter failed to return from a sortie he flew with a 'rookie' crew; Ken Pincott continued to fly as Oliver's navigator.

During the month of May, this new team bombed targets in both Germany and France, the latter including railway yards and coastal gun emplacements. These raids were in preparation for the forthcoming invasion which took place during the early hours of the morning of 6 June 1944.

For Oliver and his crew, their part in this historic moment began when they took off from Mildenhall at 3.34 a.m. that morning; their target was gun emplacements at Ouistreham, on the coast, to the north-east of Caen. There, Flying Officer Evan Jones, the bomb aimer, unleashed the eleven 1,000-lb and three 500-lb bombs they were carrying in the bomb bay, after a timed run by instruments, on to the red target indicators. That same night Oliver and his crew were back over the invasion area, having taken off at 11.35

p.m., for another attack against Lisieux, to bomb road junctions and railway communications behind the beachhead battle area.

Oliver flew his last operation on 21 June, when the squadron detailed twelve Lancasters to bomb V-1 flying bomb sites at Domléger-Longvillers, France. The crew found the target covered by 10/10th cloud and could not see the target indicators, so it came as no surprise when the raid was called off.

On his return to Mildenhall, Oliver was recorded as tour expired and sent on leave for a well-earned rest. However, his leave was to be interrupted:

> I had been on leave about a week when I received a telegram ordering me to report back immediately to Mildenhall. The King, accompanied by Queen Elizabeth and Princess Elizabeth, was visiting the station where an investiture was to be held on 5 July.

With the officers, NCOs, and airmen of XV Squadron drawn up in ranks in a hanger, Flight Lieutenant Brooks stood motionless his eyes level with the cap of the man who stood before him, the man in whose name he fought: His Majesty King George VI. It was one of the proudest moments of Oliver's life, as the King pinned the award of a Distinguished Flying Cross on his chest. Flight Sergeant Ken Pincott also experienced the same feelings and emotions:

> Just like Oliver, I too received a telegram ordering me to return to Mildenhall, where I discovered that an investiture had been arranged. I remember that twenty-nine officers and one NCO were to be invested, so I stood alone in the middle of that vast hanger, the last to be presented to HM King George VI.

For a man who had no great ambition to fly, Oliver Brooks' record was an impressive one. Following a period of instructing at No. 1651 Conversion Unit, he finished the war serving with No. 156 Pathfinder Squadron. Oliver remained in the RAF after the war, becoming a squadron leader and having flown seventeen different types of aircraft including helicopters, before transferring to the less exciting duties with the Fighter Control Branch; his logbook, up to mid-July 1949, recorded a total of 2,180 flying hours, along with innumerable postings. Squadron Leader Oliver Brooks retired from RAF service in 1972.

11

The Born Survivor: Flight Lieutenant Len Miller, DFC

Len Miller, or 'Dusty' as he was inevitably to become known, was born on 7 September 1922, in London's East End, where he subsequently grew up. The depressive years of the 1920s were not the best in which to be brought up, but young Len was to learn many valuable lessons that would stand him in good stead in the years to come. As a youngster, he was left very much on his own; his mother had a job, which kept the family going, while his father was out continually looking for work.

Len was happy spending time on his own. He developed a love of the outdoor life and learned how to make camps to which he would retreat, especially after having scrounged food by fair means or foul, skills which, again, he would find useful in later life. His father's determination to find work paid off when he was offered a job in the London Docks. A regular income brought the welcome benefit of more food on the family table, but Len's skills of scrounging and foraging would never leave him.

As he grew, Len developed an interest in making paper aeroplanes, which quickly progressed to making wooden ones. He also set his mind on being a pilot when he grew up. However, Len's ambition seemed to fall at the first hurdle when his father secured him a job in the docks, with the intent that his son should train as a marine engineer apprentice.

By the age of sixteen Len was grown up, his general attitude to life, at that time, was based on survival and looking after himself, which paid off when he started work: 'The dockers I worked with were a bunch of very nice people to be with, but if you got in their way they would give you a "thick" ear'.

One had to be alert when working in the docks, and also be aware of what was going on around them. In those days, freight and cargo were lifted in and out of ships holds by cranes, with very large rope nets slung beneath them. Sometimes, due to the irregular shape or weight of a load, the nets would break and the cargo came crashing down. Daydreaming or a pensive mood could come to a sudden and abrupt end. Len was taught well and learned fast.

> I was taught all aspects of marine engineering, foundry work and machine brass finishing, with a view that I could take this knowledge to sea. However, I still hankered after aeroplanes and had other ideas, and when war was declared in 1939 I was more or less ready to sign-up. At the appropriate time, I volunteered to join the RAF, but was returned to 'civvy' street when they realised that, as a marine engineer apprentice, I was in a reserved occupation. I was wiser when I made another attempt to join up. On that occasion I said I was a plumber's mate and was accepted. By the time the deception was realised I was in Canada.

The ex-apprentice was instructed to report to the Aircrew Reception Centre at Lord's Cricket Ground on 11 August 1941. Having been accepted for aircrew training, Len was posted to No. 10 Initial Training Wing at Scarborough, Yorkshire, where he spent approximately two months learning to march and get physically fit, not that he really needed the latter. On 17 November, Len was posted back to ACRC for a period of nearly seven weeks before being sent to RAF St Athan in preparation for embarkation to Canada on 4 January 1942.

Following a very rough sea crossing during which the engines broke down, leaving the ship drifting aimlessly at the mercy of huge waves, and many of the 500 RAF men on board frightened and very seasick, SS *Volundam* berthed at St John, New Brunswick on 19 January 1942.

Having disembarked, Len and his contingent were transported to No. 31 Personnel Depot, at Moncton, for processing, prior to being posted to No. 2 Manning Depot, at Brandon, Winnipeg, on 3 February. The contingent's next destination was No. 34 Elementary Flying Training School, located at Assiniboia, Saskatchewan.

> On arrival at Assiniboia, we immediately settled into our ground studies and flying training which was carried out on Tiger Moth aircraft. On completion of the EFTS course we moved further west to similarly named No. 34 Service Flying Training School at Medicine Hat, in Alberta, where we converted to twin-engined Oxford aircraft.

On 23 October 1942, LAC Len Miller qualified as a pilot, was presented with his flying brevet, and promoted to the rank of sergeant. The completion of the flying training in Canada saw the contingent return to 31 PDC at Moncton, prior to heading back to England, where their flying training would continue.

For the trip home, Len crossed into America and headed for New York, where he boarded RMS *Queen Mary,* accompanied not only by his own contingent but also 26,000 US troops. Compared to the outward journey, it took only about three-and-a-half days to complete the west–east crossing. Len had another reason to remember this voyage: 'The ship must have been sailing at about 38 knots; every time it zigzagged to avoid possible U-boats we were pinned against the walls by the *g*-force'.

When the ship docked at Southampton, on 23 November 1942, the officer of the RAF contingent, who was permanently based on the ship, called the men together and informed them that as they were the host country, the RAF would remain on board and clean up after the 'Yanks' had departed. When the officer started to issue out brooms and sacks, they were immediately tossed overboard and the officer very nearly went with them. Having finally got ashore, Len was posted to No. 7 Personnel Receiving Centre, at Harrogate, Yorkshire, where he spent the Christmas and New Year period awaiting a further posting.

Early 1943 saw Sergeant Miller moving around England to various RAF units in order to complete his training. Mid-April saw Len at No. 3 (Pilot) Advanced Flying Unit, South Cerney, Gloucestershire, prior to his being posted to No. 26 Operational Training Unit, at Wing, Buckinghamshire, in early July, where he converted to Vickers Wellington bombers. It was at the OTU that Len formed the nucleus of his crew, which consisted of himself as pilot, twenty-year-old Sergeant John Eastman, navigator; Sergeant Arthur Mathews, wireless operator; Sergeant George Mead, bomb aimer; and Sergeant Peter Slater, air gunner. The two remaining crew members required to make up a full crew complement, a second air gunner and the flight engineer, would join them later.

From RAF Wing, Len and his crew were posted to No. 1651 Conversion Unit at Waterbeach, Cambridgeshire, where Sergeant Alfred Pybus (from Newcastle) and twenty-two-year-old Sergeant Wilbert Cully joined the crew as flight engineer and rear gunner respectively. They became a close-knit team who lived, worked, and played together. Len related how, sometimes, on those late summer evenings, the seven of them would ride to the pub on two bicycles:

> This was achieved by tying the bikes together with rope. One bike carried four people and the other carried three. One person sat on the handle-bars, one stood and peddled the machine, one sat on the saddle, whilst the fourth person balanced on the rear wheel wing nuts. The second machine was ridden much the same way, but less one passenger. We used to hurtle around the countryside in this manner, much to the amusement of passers-by.

Apart from flying the mandatory training exercises, Len insisted the crew got to know the four-engined Stirling bomber intimately. When the aircraft was on the ground, he would have them practise ditching procedures and parachute dropping, by jumping from the escape hatches. In order that each man knew exactly how to open the hatches in the dark, Len had them do it with either their eyes closed or while wearing a blindfold. Finally, on 19 October 1943, Len and the crew were declared ready for operational flying duties and posted to 'A' Flight, XV Squadron, at RAF Mildenhall.

> Our first trip was a mining operation, or as they were more commonly known a 'Gardening sortie', to the Friesian Islands on the night of 24 October. We took off at 17.40 hours in Stirling BF533 LS-H, and headed for the 'planting' area. The weather deteriorated to such an extent that we could not carry out our mission, so I reluctantly turned the Stirling for home, with the mines still on board. Although I had followed orders, nobody was particularly pleased when it was discovered I had brought the mines back with me.

One month later, Len and the crew flew their second sortie, another mine-laying operation, this time to the Gironde estuary, in the Bay of Biscay. No. 3 Group Headquarters, RAF Bomb Command, had ordered the operation for which twelve aircraft were detailed, including two from XV Squadron.

As with the previous operation, the weather was bad, causing ice to build up on the wings. Len overcame the problem by reducing altitude and continued on to the 'planting' area. Their arrival over the Bay was greeted by bursts of flak, or strings of 'flaming onions' as the crews referred to them, which arced up into the night sky. Being a rookie pilot Sergeant Miller flew by the book, straight and level and at exactly the designated height. The 'onions' continued to arc up into the darkness and the crew commented on the poor sods who were being fired at.

Upon their arrival back at Mildenhall, Len was informed that a recall signal had been transmitted, but for some reason, Len's crew had not received it and they therefore were the poor sods being fired at. It would seem highly likely that Len's aircraft was the only one over the Bay of Biscay that night.

Apart from the various exercises that they undertook, as part of the on-the-job-training, Len and his crew only flew three operational sorties over enemy occupied territory before XV Squadron converted to Avro Lancaster bombers. During the first couple of weeks of December, the squadron's battle-weary Stirlings were flown to RAF Winthorpe, Nottinghamshire, where the aircraft were taken on charge, before the crews flew back to Mildenhall in an antiquated Handley Page Harrow aircraft, which had wicker passenger seats.

This period of time proved to be a busy one for both Len and the squadron. Not only was he granted a commission, which meant spending time purchasing new uniforms and associated items, but he also had to learn the protocol that went with the commission and all that entailed. The newly commissioned pilot officer also had to undertake conversion flying training, along with all the other members of aircrew, in order to fly the Avro Lancaster bombers with which XV Squadron were being re-equipped at that same time.

Although no entry has been recorded in the Operational Record Book indicating that XV Squadron participated in such an attack, on 1 January 1944 as part of the familiarisation training, Pilot Officer Miller flew as second pilot with Pilot Officer Greenwood on an attack against Berlin. The *Bomber Command War Diaries* confirm that a total of 421 Lancasters were detailed to attack the German capital on that date, and also record the fact that twenty-eight Lancasters failed to return from the operation.

Two weeks later, on the night of the 14th–15th, XV Squadron detailed twelve Lancasters for an attack against Brunswick. Flying Lancaster ED376, LS-F, Len took off at 4.55 p.m., bombed on the sky markers as instructed, and was back on Mildenhall's runway at 10.40 p.m. At the debriefing following the raid, Len and his crew reported the attack as a quiet trip with little flak and no fighters. This is in stark contrast to the official reports which indicate that German night fighters penetrated the bomber stream shortly after the latter had flown over the Dutch–German border and accounted for the loss of thirty-eight Lancasters.

During the early evening of 27 January, Len took off for an attack against Berlin but, due to the failure of the rear turret, he had to abandon the sortie and return to Mildenhall. The following day Len's crew was detailed for another attack against Berlin. During the day, he had been flight testing the aircraft to ensure all systems were working properly, which they were. However, when the aircraft was being prepared for the coming raid, for whatever reason the ground crew removed the armoured glazed screen which protected the flight engineer—an exercise that the pilot remembers was to have fatal consequences:

> I took off in R5904 at 00.20 hours and headed east. Shortly after crossing the coast over Cromer, the majority of the instruments failed, leaving me with the compass, altimeter and turn and bank indicator. A subsequent investigation revealed that when the temperature dropped at night, condensation froze in the tubes thus creating the problem. A quick deliberation and I decided to stay with the bomber stream and head for the 'Big City'. Berlin was obscured by very thin cloud, but we had no difficulty in seeing the target indicators, which appeared to be well concentrated. At 03.28 hours I was holding R5904 steady at 20,000 feet on the bombing run when I spotted a Ju 88 night fighter turning in to attack from low on the front port quarter, at a range of about 600 yards. As I warned the gunners, the enemy aircraft opened fire with cannon and machine guns. I swung the Lancaster into a side-slipping bank and the enemy's fire overshot. Aggressively, the Ju 88 broke away to starboard prior to commencing its second

> attack. Coming in from the starboard quarter it dived, and then climbed up towards us firing a long continuous burst.

Cannon fire struck the starboard mainplane and engines, but fortunately did not put the engines out of action. As the night fighter turned, it raked the length of the fuselage and starboard side of the tailplane. Len Miller lost a friend that night.

> Alf Pybus, my flight engineer, was struck in the head by a bullet and collapsed to the floor. The Ju 88 then came down and passed underneath us. As it emerged from under the tail, Peter Slater was waiting. He fired a long burst which appeared to go straight into the cockpit canopy and engines. The enemy aircraft reared up, turned onto its back and fell away, shedding fragments as we watched it silhouetted against the fires of the burning city below. Our troubles, however, were not yet over, for the mid-upper gunner reported another Junkers Ju 88 coming in for a head-on attack. The night fighter and the mid-upper gunner opened fire simultaneously; the enemy aircraft however did not press home the attack and was lost from view as it dived down on the port side. As I left the target area, and set course for Mildenhall, Peter Slater warned me he had spotted a single-engined fighter stealing up from below and dead astern. Having identified it as a Focke-Wulf Fw 190, Peter opened fire with several long bursts; the intruder turned and dived away without having fired a shot.

The gunners naturally remained at their stations and remained alert throughout the homeward journey, while the other crew members attended to Alf Pybus; yet Len had noticed that Alf had not moved since the initial attack.

> They put Alf on oxygen and wrapped him up to keep him warm; none of us could tell what his condition was. I was still at 20,000 feet and so decreased altitude in order to assist Alf's comfort. On the way down I tested the undercarriage and flaps; the former seemed to be alright but the latter did not work very well. As I reached base, the runway was ahead of me. I flew over the perimeter fence, crossed the threshold and lowered R5904 as gently as I could onto the runway. It was the smoothest landing I ever made, but sadly Alf was not to know; he was already dead.

Unfortunately, the aircraft was to spoil Pilot Officer Miller's efforts as, about 100 yards from the end of the runway, without warning, the port undercarriage collapsed, ripping the tyre to shreds. Sparks showered up into the air as the port propellers struck the concrete like giant grinding wheels, buckling the blades. Hinging on the semi-collapsed undercarriage, the aircraft pivoted off the runway, its port wingtip gouging a deep furrow in the grass.

Lancaster R5904 came to rest with the rear fuselage protruding across the runway, obstructing the path of the other aircraft behind it, a situation Len was aware of:

> I thought to myself, 'What the hell, she must be a write-off anyway' and pushed the throttles to maximum power. Slowly, the buckled machine edged forward, almost in a curving movement, still pivoting on the broken undercarriage leg. The airframe shuddered and vibrated from the strain as I kept the throttles open. Earth and debris was thrown everywhere as slowly and painfully R5904's tailplane cleared the runway. After the noise of the crash, the silence that descended over us was almost eerie. It seemed ages, but must have been only a few seconds, before the rescue crews were in action, their first duty being to place Alf Pybus on to a stretcher and get him into the waiting ambulance, albeit too late.

As a result of this action, although he was not aware of it at the time, Len was recommended for the award of a DFC.

The death of their flight engineer was a great loss. As a crew they were, by this time, a closely integrated team. They slept in the same billet and went everywhere together. When given short periods of leave, due to the fact distance precluded some of them from getting to their own respective homes and families, they went home with their pilot who lived in London. Following the tragic events over Berlin, they were given a period of leave, during which time they attended Alf Pybus' funeral, which took place at Newcastle-Upon-Tyne (All Saints) Cemetery.

On returning to RAF Mildenhall, they found a new aircraft awaiting them. Avro Lancaster serial LL801 was a Mk I model with Rolls-Royce Merlin 24 engines with paddle blade propellers, which meant the aircraft could carry about 1,000 lb more bombload than any other squadron aircraft and was certainly much faster.

Peter Slater had more than proved his worth as an air gunner and was a great asset to the crew. Apart from being a good friend to Len, with whom he shared a room, Peter was meticulous about the condition of the weapons he used. After every trip, be it an operation or exercise, Peter would remove the guns from the turret and clean them in their room. Len would often assist in this task, lest his friend sat up all night. When the cleaning task was completed, Peter would place the weapons in little canvas bags and store them under his bed; the following morning, he would check them again before replacing them in the turret.

Before the war, Peter (who was married with a young son) had been a policeman—a very short one as he was approximately 5 feet tall and quite thick-set. Due to a popular song of the day, he was affectionately known as

'Mr Five-by-Five'. Peter had a thin aquiline nose, piercing blue eyes which afforded him superb night vision, and very short hair. At the age of thirty-two, he was regarded as being quite old for aircrew and would have been the 'granddad' to younger members of the crew. When Peter wore his flying suit, he would literally waddle out to the aircraft which, due to his natural metabolism, would make him perspire a great deal. Len recalled how this could be much to Peter's discomfort:

> One night on a raid Peter had switched on his electrically heated flying suit. About half way out to the target, screams emanated from the rear turret. Peter had perspired so much he had short-circuited the suit and was giving himself electric shocks.

For some unrecorded reason, Peter Slater decided to transfer from the mid-upper turret down to the rear turret, a situation that Pilot Officer Miller was quite happy about. Len felt better knowing that his friend was guarding the rear of the aircraft and could almost sense when an enemy fighter was lurking in the darkness.

The crew returned to operations on 19 February, with their pilot wearing the ribbon of a Distinguished Flying Cross on his tunic. Although Len had been informed that the recommendation had been approved, it was not officially gazetted until the 22nd of the month. That night, the crew took LL801 to Leipzig but abandoned the sortie due to the failure of both the rear and mid-upper turrets. The bombload, a mixture of high-explosive and incendiaries, was jettisoned into the North Sea from an altitude of 21,000 feet. Apart from being the crew's first operation in LL801, and their first attack against Leipzig, it was also the first operational sortie they had flown with Sergeant Alf Beazley-Long, who, as a flight engineer, had joined the crew as Alf Pybus's replacement.

There were no mechanical problems a week later when they took Lancaster, LL801, to Augsburg, but there was a breakdown with the weather, which could have caused a catastrophe. Visibility over the target area was clear and the crews could see the red and green target indicators were well placed which, along with the lack of flak shells exploding around them, enabled the attacking force to deposit 2,000 tons of bombs accurately on the old city centre. Among those bombs was a 4,000-lb 'cookie' dropped by George Mead, the bomb aimer, who reported that it exploded on a railway junction, adding to the already burning fires and chaos. The job done, Len turned LL801 on a course for home, but as the aircraft flew west towards England, the weather began to deteriorate, with the cloud base getting lower and lower.

By the time they reached Mildenhall, the cloud base was down to about 300 feet and was accompanied by torrential rain. Len circled the airfield, flying on almost empty tanks. Although he knew other aircraft had been given priority landings, he called the tower asking for permission to land, sooner than later. The tower responded by telling Len to divert to Bourn airfield, some 8 miles away. Following the instruction, he reset the compass, pulled back on the control yoke and powered LL801 back up into the clouds, milling through the hoard of Lancasters from both XV and 622 Squadrons, all trying to land. Flying blind through the thick cloud and heavy rain, following the compass, Len waited until instinct told him to decrease height. He broke cloud dead in line with the end of Bourns' illuminated runway. Knowing the fuel had all but gone Len broke into a frenzy of activity, lowering the flaps, dropping the undercarriage and putting the props into fine pitch ready for an immediate landing. Simultaneously, he called the tower and flew over the threshold, putting LL801 on the rain-sodden runway. The tower was a bit late in responding and told him to turn right once he had landed, to which he instantly replied in exasperation, much to their surprise, 'I am now turning right'. As he made the manoeuvre all four engines died.

The first day of March began with Len being appointed to the rank of flight lieutenant. It ended with the newly promoted officer taking off with his crew at 11.40 p.m. for an attack against Stuttgart. The brilliant red glow of fires, started by the first bombers to arrive over the target, could be seen through the gaps in the clouds. Having commenced his bombing run, Len held LL801 steady in accordance with George Mead's instructions, until the latter called 'Bombs gone'.

As with all raids, George checked the bomb switch panel and, on this occasion, reported that two canisters of 4-lb incendiary devices had hung-up in the bomb bay. As George reported this fact to his pilot, Flight Sergeant Arthur Mathews, the wireless operator, on watch in the astrodome, yelled a warning of a Junkers Ju 88 night fighter approaching in a turn from astern at approximately 600 yards range. All thoughts of the two hang-ups in the bomb bay were forgotten as the pilot threw the Lancaster over in a corkscrew manoeuvre. Flight Sergeant Wilbert Cully and Sergeant Peter Slater (mid-upper and rear gunners respectively) traversed their turrets, sighted the enemy aircraft, and opened fire simultaneously. The night fighter returned fire which was seen to miss the Lancaster's mainplane as the bomber went into a dive and then banked to port. With the mid-upper and rear gunners maintaining their fire, the enemy aircraft was seen to peel over and dive away to the starboard quarter. The incident was recorded at the later debriefing, where the enemy aircraft was claimed as damaged. Having ascertained that neither aircraft nor crew had sustained any battle damage, Len turned for home. However, they still had to contend with landing at Mildenhall with two canisters of incendiary bombs on board, which they did safely at 7.45 a.m.

Although various training exercises and ferry trips were flown during the first two weeks of March, there were no operational sorties until the night of the 15th–16th, when LL801 and her crew were detailed for another attack against Stuttgart. Shortly after take-off, Peter Slater reported the rear turret had gone u/s, thus causing the sortie to be abandoned. Having jettisoned the bombload, Len turned the aircraft on to a reciprocal course and landed back at Mildenhall less than one hour after taking off.

The period between the end of March and the middle of April proved very quiet for Len and his crew. They flew a number of training exercises, but only four operational sorties, which warranted little or no comment; but that was about to change. On the night of 27–28 April, the crew were detailed for an attack on Friedrichshafen, as back-up to the Pathfinder Force.

When flying operational sorties, Len always wore engineers' overalls because they were made of Denim, with epaulettes and military style pockets. A number of small bar compasses had been sewn into the various seams, the theory being that if he were shot down, captured, and searched, if one of the compasses were found he would hopefully be able to retain one or two of the others. The rest of his survival kit included a hacksaw blade, concealed in one of his flying boots, a bag of pepper for use against dogs or anybody who sought to interfere with his freedom, chocolate bars, a small shaving kit, and a toothbrush. This was how Flight Lieutenant Miller was dressed that late April night.

Peter Slater's name was not on the crew battle order for the raid on Friedrichshafen. A few days earlier, he had jumped over a barbed wire fence, did not clear it, and almost left his testicles decorating the wire. Naturally, the medical officer had declared him unfit to fly and a young man by the name of Sergeant Robert Watson was drafted in to fly in Sergeant Slater's place.

While standing out at dispersal, prior to preparing for take-off, Len spoke with the newcomer and discovered it was the young air gunner's first operational flight. Len immediately decided to place Bert Cully back in the rear turret and have Watson fly in the mid-upper.

The squadron had detailed sixteen aircraft for the attack, all of which took off. Lancaster bomber LL801, LS-J, piloted by Len, was the second aircraft to leave Mildenhall, at 9.44 p.m. One by one, the aircraft took off, circled the airfield, formed-up in formation and climbed away. The route out that night took them over south coast at Shoreham, Sussex, across the English Channel and on a direct route across northern France to Friedrichshafen. Lancaster LL801 was approximately 80 miles from the target, near Strasbourg, when the crew first saw the flak arcing up into the sky, searching for the first wave of bombers.

Suddenly, and without warning, a Lancaster flying nearby exploded in a ball of flame, the light from which reflected off the metal surfaces of LL801. An eagle-eyed pilot of a marauding Luftwaffe night fighter saw the reflection and turned into an attacking position. The enemy pilot opened fire as Len

Right: Flight Lieutenant Len Miller, DFC, photographed in 1945. (*Author's collection*)

Below: Sergeant Len Miller, pilot, with his original crew. *Left to right back row*: Sgt Arthur Matthews, W/op; Sgt Wilbert Cully, A/G; Sgt Len Miller, pilot; and Sgt Alf Pybus, F/E. *Left to right front row*: Sgt George Mead, B/A; Sgt Johnson, Nav; and Sgt Peter Slater, R/G. (*Author's collection*)

Left: Pilot Officer Peter Slater, rear gunner on Len Miller's crew. The two men were the greatest of friends. (*Author's collection*)

Below: Avro Lancaster Mk I serial LL801 receives attention from the armourers at RAF Mildenhall. The aircraft was shot down by *Oberleutnant* Martin 'Tino' Becker, on the night of 27–28 April 1944. (*Author's collection*)

took evasive action, but the cannon fire raked the complete length of the Lancaster, striking the port outer engine and setting it ablaze. A fuel tank ruptured, causing flames to spread, which in turn left long tongues of flame streaming back from the trailing edge of the port wing. It was a night Len would never forget:

> Bert Cully in the rear turret was firing non-stop at the enemy aircraft. His guns were hammering away he must have fired 1,500 rounds in one burst. He was hurling obscenities and abuse with equal intensity, and then I heard him yell, 'I got the bastard'. Realising LL801 was doomed I ordered the crew to jump. George and Alf clipped on my parachute. While they went down to the forward escape hatch, I called the rest of the crew but there was no response. George yelled up to me that he could not open the hatch cover. In my frustration I kicked out with my legs and told him, through gritted teeth to get the bloody thing open. By this time the aircraft was going down in a dive, but as I kicked out, I must have pulled back on the control column, for the Lancaster started to level out. At the same instant the hatch gave way and George, who was leaning on it, went out with it.

In an effort to leave the stricken bomber, Len put the aircraft on auto-pilot, released his intercom cable and climbed out of his seat. It was then the pilot realised that Alf Beazley-Long was still sitting by the open hatch. Len gave Alf a shove and the flight engineer disappeared through the aperture into the night.

> I had a feeling that 'Mac' Mathews, the wireless operator, and John Eastman, the navigator, had not left the aircraft. I think they may have been killed in the first attack. I could also hear the gunners still firing and started to make my way down the aircraft when it suddenly lurched. I climbed back into my seat and tried to pull LL801 back on a more even keel. I re-connected my intercom and screamed a warning for them all to get out of the doomed aircraft, when the port wing folded and there was a hell of an explosion.

As Len regained his senses, he realised an eerie silence prevailed; he also realised that he was falling as one does in the darkness of a nightmare.

> I must have been catapulted out through the top of the aircraft, and rendered semi-conscious. I felt as though I was lying on a woolly cloud and, as my sight came back into focus, I could see the stars above me spinning round and round. I now began to tumble haphazardly and therefore reached for the parachute release handle to open my 'chute. Unbeknown to me, the shoulder harness straps had become unclipped and the parachute pack, still clipped to the harness straps,

> floated about two feet above my head. I managed to pull the pack down and yanked the canopy out manually. As I floated down I had time to take stock of the situation. Looking up into the bright moonlit sky I could see George and Alf above me. Returning my gaze earthwards I could see the fiercely burning wreckage of LL801 which, with the bombload still on board, had exploded on hitting the ground.

Len landed in the forest at Rheinwald, south of Strasbourg. The parachute canopy caught in the top of a spruce tree and he swung down into total darkness, hanging like a limp doll.

Recovering quickly from the shock of the incident, the downed pilot took a few moments to gather his thoughts and think about his predicament. He adopted a bear hug posture around the tree and gingerly pressed the harness release with the intention of edging his way down. Unfortunately, Len's lower leg got entangled in one of the parachute shrouds as he began his descent and he toppled backwards. After a short struggle with weight versus gravity, Len achieved his aim of freeing his leg and promptly fell headfirst to the ground—some 2 feet below: 'I remember I sat there thinking "Jesus Christ" and then, even in the seriousness of the situation, I saw the funny side of falling from the tree and began to laugh'.

The chiming of a clock, somewhere in the distance, caused Len to look at his watch. He could see it was broken and had stopped at ten-minutes-past-two. Interestingly, when *Oberleutnant* Martin 'Tino' Becker, the Luftwaffe night fighter pilot who shot down LL801, filed his combat report, he recorded the time of the attack as commencing at 1.35 a.m.; he also, although mistakenly, claimed the aircraft as a Halifax. *Oberleutnant* Becker went on to claim two more Lancasters shot down that night, again, claiming one of them as a Halifax. Flight Sergeant Wilbert Cully was also mistaken in claiming he had shot down the attacker; unfortunately, Cully did not survive the ordeal to learn of his mistake.

With his parachute firmly caught in the trees, Len cut away the parts he could reach and buried them, along with the harness, before edging away from his immediate landing area. Feeling fatigued and wanting to rest, he settled down in a holly bush, hoping it would afford him some protection. He was awoken at dawn by the chiming of the clock he had heard earlier and decided it was time to move on.

With his natural survival instincts taking over, Len waded slowly along a small stream until he thought it safe to climb back on to the bank, but the sound of people thrashing about in nearby undergrowth, obviously searching for him, made him change plans and course. It was then he decided to only move at dusk, which would enable him to disappear more quickly if the need arose.

It was only when Len looked at his silk scarf escape map that he realised he had landed near Schönau, a village close to the town of Marckolsheim, on the French side of the River Rhine. Utilising the map together with one of the bar compasses, and using minor roads and avoiding open fields, Len set off in a southerly direction, his aim being to try and reach Switzerland. On locating another stream and having ascertained all was safe, he took the opportunity to have a wash and shave, and a meal consisting of two squares of chocolate and a Horlicks tablet.

Resuming his journey, Len arrived at Neuf-Brisach, a town approximately 17 km south of Marckolsheim, during the evening of 29 April. Walking cautiously along the road, Len came up behind a German soldier who, apparently lost in his own thoughts, was slowly cycling along the road. Adjusting his pace, Len was able to keep the soldier in view until the latter dismounted, lent the bike against a wall and disappeared into a café. With a feeling of trepidation, Len made his move:

> As there was nobody about, I continued walking towards the bike. As I drew level with it, I placed my hands on the handle bars and kept going, pushing the bike along by the side of me. After about fifteen yards I leapt onto the saddle and peddled like bloody hell.

It was only when he tried freewheeling down a slope that Len realised the bike had a fixed-wheel and a back-peddle brake. However, he soon mastered the controls and continued on his way. Staying on the back roads Len continued south, heading for Mulhouse, where he arrived in the middle of the night. With no one around, and giving way to his self-confidence, Len happily cycled through the deserted streets until he came to an intersection with many roads radiating off it. In the middle of the intersection was a lamp post with various names inscribed on arms pointing in all directions. Unsure which way to go, the evader stood looking up these names to see if there were any he recognised. As he stood there, Len became aware of the sound of uneven footsteps approaching him, he knew it was too late to run and suddenly remembered the curfew; the airman froze as a German officer stepped out of the shadows and stood in front of him. The officer said something, obviously asking a question, the smell of Schnapps filling the air space between them as he stood in front of Len. Len understood one word the officer muttered: it happened to be one of the names Len saw on the signs above his head. The English officer quickly pointed in the right direction, and to Len's surprise, the German snapped, '*Danke*' and staggered off into the darkness. Len wasted no time in making his escape; he jumped on the bike and peddled away as fast as he could.

Having spent a restful night in some foliage and recovered from the shock of coming face to face with a German officer, Len resumed his journey. Little did he know that later that same day he was to encounter some more Germans—lots of them.

Len reached Altkirch that afternoon and confidently cycled straight through an archway, which he thought led to the town, but unfortunately it led into the courtyard of a local barracks. There before him lined up in ranks, for inspection, were the local German divisions. Taking advantage of the fact a small number of civilians were standing around watching the parade, Len dismounted and lent the cycle against the wall. Hoping his shaking legs were not too obvious, Len also lent against the wall while he regained his composure. He nonchalantly looked up at the German posters and notices on the wall, the only words of which he could read were '*Achtung*' and '*Verboten*'.

His confidence restored, Len wheeled the bicycle back through the archway, remounted and cycled on. Leaving Altkirch, he passed a number of German officers, some walking with young ladies and some strolling with comrades, but none of them took any notice of him.

Having ridden for some distance without a break, the downed airman decided to sit and rest a while.

> Against my better judgement, I pondered on my good fortune at not having been captured. My musing was interrupted by the distant sound of barking dogs. Shielding myself with undergrowth I spotted three Dobermans with their handlers, whom I took to be forestry guards. I liberally sprinkled pepper around then quickly jumped onto the bike and cycled away from the area.

Still heading in a southerly direction and getting closer to the Swiss border each day, Len was holed up in Wittersdorf when he began to give some thought as to how he should approach the frontier, which was only 10 miles away; his first decision was to ditch the bike and continue on foot.

Walking that last 10 miles took the evader through the villages of Feldbach, Bendorf, Winkle, and finally Lucelle on the French–Swiss border, arriving at the latter on 1 May. It was both dark and deserted when he reached Lucelle and his footsteps seemed to echo around him as he walked down the main cobbled street. Suddenly, he saw the frontier crossing point complete with sentry box and guard, directly ahead of him; he paused and then did an about turn.

The barrier Len had to cross consisted of two parallel wire fences approximately 10 feet apart and 8 feet high. Along the top of each were three rows of 'flying' barbed-wire, angled inwards. Between each fence, at regular intervals of some 2 feet, were posts the same height as the fence; except for the area of no man's land, this was the obstacle that stood between Len and Switzerland.

Len thought about the sentry who had ignored him when he did an about-turn but reasoned there must be other guards in the vicinity. Being cautious the born survivor hid himself in the undergrowth, only seconds before another sentry appeared. The latter about-turned and marched off back in the direction from which he had appeared. Len sat concealed in the undergrowth and waited patiently and, according to Len's calculations, approximately twenty minutes later, the sentry reappeared. When the sentry had marched off yet again, Len knew it was time to act.

> I decided to move further along, looking at the fence and surrounding area to find a suitable place to get across. Having got this far, I had no intention of getting caught now. At one point I found the wire of the fence nailed to a young tree. Using the wire as footrests and holding onto the tree, I gingerly climbed up and over the fence. My heart was thumping against my chest, and I felt sure the guard would hear it if he came near. I managed, by supporting myself on the tree, to reach and stand on the top of the first of the posts spanning between the fences. Using the tops of the other posts as stepping stones, with a fair amount of balance and a silent prayer I jumped from post to post and dived over the wire on the far side, hitting the ground in a forward roll. I lay exactly where I dropped, hardly daring to breathe the only noise still being the thumping of my heart. After a short while, I got up in a crouching position, ran forward a few yards, and dropped back to earth. I repeated this action two or three times until I was well clear of the wire. I rested a while in the foliage to regain my breath and take stock of the situation. I had become disorientated and to some degree was unsure of my location.

Taking stock of his situation, Len emerged from his hiding place and pursued a course down into a valley with a road just below him and a river beyond. As he climbed down to the road, Len became concerned about a building he spotted which looked very much like a blacked-out power station.

Having reached the road, he cautiously walked along it until he came to a large house, but it was not until he drew level with the building that he realised there was a sentry box outside it. In the same instant, a guard with a rifle stepped forward and challenged Len. Without hesitation, and with Len's survival instincts coming to the fore, he grabbed the guard by the throat.

> The sentry was somewhat shorter than I and as I slid my arm round his neck, I stretched him up onto his toes, the rifle falling from his grasp. As I closed my arm around his windpipe, applying more pressure, he slowly began to sink to the ground. To my horror I suddenly noticed emblazoned on the side of his steel helmet the white cross of Switzerland. I immediately released my grip and gently lowered the guard to the ground where, after a few minutes, he revived.

To Len's relief, there were no recriminations from either the guard or his colleagues who fed and entertained Len in the guard-house for the rest of the night, but only after he had given his name, rank and number. It was during the course of the evening that his instincts about the power station were proved correct and that he had done the right thing in avoiding it; it was occupied by German forces.

The following morning, normality returned when Flight Lieutenant Miller was escorted to Porrentruy, where he was interrogated by the Swiss Military Authorities, but the only information the officer volunteered was his name, rank, and number.

Len spent that night in a hotel, where he met several other servicemen who had crossed the border in much the same area as he had. A fellow flier Len met that night was Flight Sergeant Colin Campbell, an Australian air gunner who had been shot down on 30 March, flying with No. 467 (RAAF) Squadron, which flew Lancaster bombers out of RAF Waddington. Colin Campbell's aircraft, Lancaster M376, PO-O, had fallen to the guns of a Messerschmitt Bf 110, piloted by Major Martin Drewes. Helped by the French Resistance, Colin had made his way down from Belgium and crossed the border the night before Len. Four other members of Flight Sergeant Campbell's crew also managed to evade capture, while the remaining two were taken prisoners of war.

On 3 May, the 'captives' were taken to Olten, where they were placed in quarantine for six days, before being transferred to Bad Lostorf, where they were placed in quarantine for a further fourteen days. At the latter, their accommodation was in a medieval castle, or *Schloss*, complete with drawbridge and vast dining hall. The *Schloss* housed prisoners from all the fighting nations, including Germans; Len remembered one of them in particular:

> There was one particular German whom we called Adolph. Adolph was a weedy little character, who wore thick horn-rimmed glasses; he had decided Germany was finished and had therefore decided to make his escape to Switzerland. Adolph was by nature a scrounger and came in useful to the group to whom he attached himself.

Three weeks after arriving at the *Schloss* on 23 May, Len and Colin received a visit from the air *attaché* to the British Embassy in Bern. The latter took both the airman back to the Embassy with him, where they were introduced to the British Consul, before being given some money and taken out to buy some new clothes—a welcome respite as Len had previously discarded his overalls in favour of his RAF battledress.

A further two days later, the pair was moved again, this time to Montreux, where they were interned in an expensive hotel situated on the shore of Lake Geneva. Being active types, neither Len nor Colin liked being cooped up:

> Compared to some, we lived a life of luxury and yet it became very boring. I used to get up in the morning, look across the lake and say, 'What shall we do today?' I'd see the same bloody lump of rock and the same stretch of water that people now pay a fortune for, and I was bored to tears. Colin and I decided we were not going to have too much of this situation. We did not like or get on with 'Clots', our name for the Senior British Officer in charge of us, so we devised a plan to get away, but first we needed money. We were given a small allowance but not enough to save. We had been told we could take up any pastime we wished and the authorities would pay the expenses incurred. I decided to learn to play the piano, for which I was allowed out after hours three times a week, to visit an ageing Polish woman who taught me. Each time I had a lesson she would give me a bill which I would take back to the authorities, who then issued the money which I would hand over to the teacher at the next lesson. In the interim period, I used to add a figure to the total. This of course was deducted, by me, when the money was handed over to settle the account for the lesson. In this manner I quickly accumulated a fair sum of money, certainly enough to purchase maps, boots, a small rucksack and two rail tickets for Saint Croix, near the border on the north-west side of Switzerland.

On 12 August, Len Miller and Colin set out on the first leg of their homeward journey. They first took a train to Yverdon-les-Bains, where they changed for a connection to Saint Croix. On arrival at the latter, they walked down into the town, treated themselves to a good meal and then stocked up with necessary provisions. When the money ran out, Len and Colin set off, on foot, up the mountainside. Somewhere over the top, on the other side lay the French border. The climb presented no difficulties, but as they neared the frontier, Len thought he heard a dog barking:

> I heard barking and thought 'Bloody hell, they've got dogs out' and told Colin to run. We ran and ran but the barking stayed close to us. Out of breath, we had no choice but to stop and rest and in doing so saw that it was not a dog but a fox that was barking. We had obviously frightened each other and in our panic all taken off in the same direction.

Ignoring barking foxes, the pair managed to cross into France without hindrance, away from prying eyes and trigger-happy fingers.

Continuing in a westerly direction, Len and Colin arrived at Oye-et-Pallet, on the northern tip of Lac de Saint-Point. Skirting the town, they made their way down the west bank of the lake and headed for Vaux-et-Chantegrue, where they sat down under a tree; somewhat astounded, they awoke shivering in the cold light of dawn the next morning.

Their journey continued to take them on a westerly course, through Bonnevaux to Censeau. By the time they reached the latter, Colin was experiencing trouble with his feet and Len had to carry his friend piggy-back fashion. Although Len was a fit man, there was a limit to his endurance and, by the time they reached Andelot-en-Montagne, he felt he could not carry Colin any further.

As the two men sat discussing their situation, including the possibility of enlisting the help of local people, a small boy aged about seven came along. The lad stopped and looked quizzically at the two scruffy individuals, with his head on one side. Len tried asking, in his schoolboy French, for food and help but without saying a word, the boy ran off.

Fearing he and Colin could be in trouble if the lad spoke to the wrong people, Len looked for a solution and spotted a tree about 200 yards away, which looked like a suitable hiding place. Carrying Colin on his back, Len made his way to the tree where Colin reached up and pulled himself on to the lower branches. Len then hauled himself up and together they climbed up into the higher branches where the foliage was thicker, but still offered a good view down the road in the direction of which the boy had run. Sitting there, Len pondered on the thought that he had started his escape in a tree; he hoped it was not going to end in one.

Eventually, having ignored cramp-induced pain from squatting in the branches, Len saw two men ambling down the road towards them. They appeared to be engaged in casual conversation, but they kept glancing towards the hedgerows as they walked. As they got near the tree, they stopped, but casually kept on talking. Knowing they could not sit among the foliage forever, Len motioned to Colin to stay where he was and slowly climbed down. With hands stretched out from his sides, Len turned to face the men and informed them that he was an RAF officer seeking help. The Frenchmen agreed to help Len but then asked where his companion was. On Len's signal, Colin clambered down and painfully made his way towards them.

The two evaders were escorted to the house of a forestry worker near the village of Supt, east of Andelot-en-Montagne, where they were locked in a room and guarded by two men armed with machine guns. Knowing the Frenchmen would check their identities, both Len and Colin freely gave their names, ranks, and service numbers.

> The men were obviously part of the French resistance and were playing the situation very carefully. They must have sent a radio message to London, for some twenty-four hours later they returned to inform us that our identities had been confirmed.

The leader of the resistance group was identified as Captain Paul, a Frenchman by birth who spoke excellent English. He asked Len and Colin to join the group in an attack in Dijon, but both declined, stating it was important for them to return to their respective squadrons as soon as possible.

To help the Englishmen on their way, they were provided with a bicycle each and issued with false identity cards. Len's bore the name Louis Dupont, as a result of which he decided to adopt the character of a Frenchman with a terrible stutter and a bad limp, the latter being achieved by putting a small stone in one of his shoes. The ruse was put to the test when the pair was stopped by two German soldiers. Len quickly realised that Germans did not like people who stuttered and spat over them as they talked, so he ensured he did plenty of both.

Refusing to join a Communist Group the evaders had encountered, giving the same reason as they gave Captain Paul, the Englishmen were quickly passed on to a Free French Group, who were a much tougher and more active unit. This latter group was headed by an individual who used the codename 'Zabia'.

Len and Colin were to spend some time with the group, even becoming involved in their activities, a fact of which the authorities in London were aware, having received regular radio transmissions from Zabia. Both London and Len were also aware that as the Allies were advancing through France, some Germans unit were attempting to get back to the Fatherland by whichever route they could find open.

> One day, Zabia informed me that London had transmitted a message saying that two RAF Dakota aircraft were flying in loaded with men and equipment from a special unit to assist in cutting off the retreating German forces in our area; Zabia, Colin and I were then to return to England in one of the aircraft. At the appointed time, the two aircraft landed on the designated landing strip and disembarked soldiers and equipment. Speed being of the utmost importance we all lent a hand, and the first Dakota duly took off into the night. We assisted the soldiers with their equipment and then hurriedly clambered aboard the second aircraft. Just prior to take-off one of the engines coughed, spluttered and died. No amount of persuasion would coax it back to life. Fortunately, the aircraft was close to the airfield boundary, around which there was plenty of bushes and shrubbery. Whilst a signal was sent to London, informing them of the situation, the rest of the group frantically cut some branches from the trees and bushes in an effort to camouflage the aircraft as much as possible.

Amazingly, the aircraft remained undetected all the following day. That night, under cover of darkness, and an exchange of signals, another aircraft flew over and parachuted in the men from the RAF Commando Servicing Unit, whose job it was to repair the engine and return to England on board the aircraft. Len was feeling very apprehensive at this stage:

> Anxious about being discovered and impatient to get away, as the shadowy figures approached I blurted out, 'Where the hell have you been?' A somewhat

> puzzled voice asked, 'Is that you Len?' Equally puzzled I responded that it was, just as the leader of the team stepped forward. I was amazed to see it was my cousin. It transpired that my cousin was a sergeant mechanic and had been parachuting into trouble areas doing precisely the type of work he had now come to do.

Len's cousin and his team worked hard and fast and the aircraft was made ready for flight. As the foliage was removed from the aircraft, the area around the field was checked by Zabia's group. When given the signal, the pilot pushed forward the throttles, released the brakes, and lifted the aircraft into the air. Flight Lieutenant Len Miller DFC and Flight Sergeant Colin Campbell were going home.

12

No Illusions of Grandeur: Warrant Officer Bernard Dye

Bernard Dye was full of admiration for young RAF pilots, not least of all the young man, not much older than himself, who also sat on the top deck of the bus each morning. Resplendent in his RAF uniform, complete with pilots' wings above his left breast pocket, the young man sat regaling his friends with stories of his adventures in the 'wide blue yonder'. Bernard would eavesdrop as the bus meandered through the streets of Ipswich, taking him to his place of employment.

Although he wanted to be a pilot, Bernard was fully aware he would not make the grade. He had therefore decided that when his turn to join up came he would volunteer for aircrew training as an air gunner. Bernard had no illusions of grandeur—he read the newspapers and saw the stories of local lads who would never come home; he was aware of what the possible outcome might be.

When the young man in the uniform ceased catching the bus, Bernard thought the worst, but his esteem for the 'pilot hero' was shattered when he read in the local newspaper that the young man had actually been arrested for impersonating an RAF officer.

Bernard's wish came true when he qualified as an air gunner at No. 9 (Observer) Advanced Flying Unit, at Penrhos, North Wales. His final report, signed by Flight Lieutenant E. Johnison on behalf of the chief instructor and dated 31 July, read, 'Has worked hard, but still requires a lot of experience. Should improve and become a good gunner'.

Having qualified and been promoted to the rank of sergeant, Bernard was posted to No. 82 Operational Training Unit at Ossington, near Newark. The ten-week course comprised two weeks of ground studies and eight weeks of air training, but Bernard's career as an air gunner nearly came to an end before it had started due to an incident on his first flight out of Ossington. On the night of 21 August 1943, Bernard was occupying the turret of Wellington bomber HE332, coded 'J', which was being piloted by Flight Sergeant Shaw, a Royal

Australian Air Force pilot. The aircraft, which had taken off at 9.32 p.m. on a night-flying exercise, had been airborne for just over two hours and was making a low approach to Ossington's runway in preparation for landing, when the aircraft hit an obstruction. The Wellington bomber crashed at 11.37 p.m., killing two of the crew and injuring two others, while the remaining two men on board suffered severe shock. Bernard remembered the crash and the cause:

> The pilot had received a wrong QFE (air pressure at ground level reading) from the ground controller and had therefore set the barometer incorrectly. As the Wellington descended even lower it flew into the tops of some trees a short distance from the runway threshold. The aircraft was flung to the ground killing the navigator and the bomb aimer. The other four crew members, including me, were taken to the station sick quarters.

The two members of aircrew who were killed were Flying Officer Frederick G. Ingram, who was buried in Brighouse Cemetery, Yorkshire, and Sergeant Ronald W. Hughes, who was buried in Portsmouth (Milton) Cemetery; both were listed (at the time) as bomb aimers. The two injured aviators were the pilot and Flight Sergeant E. A. McCasker, RCAF. Sergeant Jennings and Sergeant Bernard Dye were recorded as the survivors who suffered severe shock. It was the diagnosis of severe shock that was enough to confine Bernard to bed for a few days.

Sitting up in bed on the third day, Bernard was wondering how things were in the outside world when suddenly, a commotion erupted out on the airfield. The noise of fire and ambulance vehicles racing past the station sick quarters, with bells ringing loudly, accompanied by the excited babble of voices, made Bernard curious as to what was going on. It was a male nurse who gave him the story.

> It transpired that Wellington, BK399, was sitting at its dispersal with the engines running, in preparation for a routine training flight. Flying Officer MacFarlane, the New Zealand instructor, and Sergeant Leslie Wheeler, the trainee pilot, were running through the final cockpit checks prior to taxiing out for take-off, when there was a sharp bang from within the fuselage. It became apparent that one of the crew had picked up the Very pistol and squeezed the trigger not knowing, in the best traditions of crime fiction, that the gun was loaded. Within minutes, the dope fabric-covered geodetic fuselage was ablaze, and ammunition was exploding all over the place. Two crash tenders and a domestic fire appliance were at the scene in minutes, but the fire had too great a hold. Fortunately, the whole crew escaped without injury, except to [their] pride. When I heard the story I said to the nurse, 'Good grief, I don't think I would want to fly with a crew like that'.

On being declared fit for duty, Bernard was instructed to report to the chief ground instructor. Standing in front of the CGI, a squadron leader, Bernard was informed that a number of crews required air gunners, particularly mid-upper gunners. The CGI had a board displaying photographs of all the crews requiring a gunner and actually invited Bernard to choose the crew he thought he would like to fly with. Bernard perused the images in front of him and then selected a crew. The CGI asked Bernard why he had chosen that particular crew, to which Bernard replied that he had trained with Sergeant Joe Hayes, the rear gunner, and would like to fly with him and his crew. The CGI responded by informing Bernard that that was the crew, headed by Sergeant Leslie Wheeler, who had set their aircraft alight. Bernard's heart sank, but he had made his choice.

Sergeant Wheeler and his crew, including Bernard, were posted to No. 1651 Conversion Unit, at Waterbeach, on 13 November 1943. It was at the CU that the crew converted to four-engined Stirling bombers, flying first with Pilot Officer Kinsella and then Sergeant Wheeler. The course consisted of flying 'circuits and bumps' and night cross-country exercises. It was while undertaking one of the latter exercises that the port inner engine cut and Sergeant Wheeler had his first real experience of landing the huge aeroplane on three engines.

During December, the crew were posted to XV Squadron, but due to the fact the squadron was in the process of re-equipping with Avro Lancaster bombers, the crew was directed to No. 3 Lancaster Finishing School at RAF Feltwell where the squadron's crews were undergoing conversion courses on the new aircraft.

On completion of the course at LFS, the crew reported back to Mildenhall. They spent their first week with XV settling in to the new accommodation and finding their way around the base. Further training both on the ground and in the air commenced on 8 January 1944. The ground exercises were of various content including escape and evasion exercises, which for Bernard came during the last week of the month:

> We aircrew members were driven out of the base in the back of a lorry, from which we could not see out off, and dumped some ten miles from the camp. The intention was for us to get back to Mildenhall without being caught by the police who were actively looking for us. I teamed up with Joe Hayes and together we set off. As we were walking down a narrow country road, we saw in the distance, a man in uniform riding a bike. We departed in opposite directions into the hedgerows either side of the road. The cyclist turned out to be a postman, who stopped his bike almost between the two of us, to relieve himself. Joe and I were both carrying 'thunder flashes' in our pockets, and I signalled to Joe I was going to light one. As the flare went off the postman, who had not finished his business, grabbed his mailbag, picked up his bike and made off down the road as fast as he could peddle.

Another exercise Bernard was engaged in was one of a flying nature, the outcome of which was not at all humorous, but very tragic and disturbing. During the day, on Thursday, 13 January 1944, a number of XV Squadron aircrews were getting

Left: Sergeant Bernard Dye, air gunner, was posted to XV Squadron but eventually completed his operational tour with No. 622 Squadron, also based at RAF Mildenhall. (*Author's collection*)

Below: Three members of Flight Sergeant Leslie Wheeler's crew are (*left to right*) Sgt Bernard Dye, A/G; Sgt Keith Hollingrake, F/E; and Sgt Joe Hayes, A/G. Sergeant Hollingrake completed a total of nineteen operational sorties before being killed in a flying accident on 21 June 1944. (*Author's collection*)

Bernard Dye (extreme right) was posted to No. 622 Squadron and completed a tour of 'ops' with Flying Officer Arthur Horton (third from left) and his crew. (*Author's collection*)

to know their new aircraft better and were undertaking various flying training exercises. Among those airborne were Bernard and his crew, and Flight Sergeant Houston, RCAF, and his crew. As they flew over the Wash, on the east coast of England, undertaking a loaded climb exercise, Bernard was horrified to see one of the engines on Lancaster ED826, LS-W, catch fire. Within seconds, from an altitude of 1,500 feet, the aircraft peeled over into a steep dive and plunged, in flames, into the sea. Although he witnessed the scene, Bernard found it hard to believe that the lives of six friends had been extinguished in such a short space of time; in making mention of them, Bernard named the six crew members.

> The pilot was Flight Sergeant Walter 'Wally' Houston, the navigator was Warrant Officer William 'Pappy' Hynes, the bomber aimer was Flight Sergeant Charles 'Christie' Christie, the flight engineer was Sergeant John 'Jock' Johnston, the wireless operator was Sergeant Kenneth 'Ken' Talbot and the air gunner was Sergeant Ronald 'Andy' Andrews.

Three of the crew (the pilot, the navigator, and the bomb aimer) were Canadians: from British Columbia, New Brunswick, and Ontario respectively.

The flight engineer was from Edinburgh, while the wireless operator and air gunner were English. The average age of these six men was just twenty-two years old. Having no known graves, they are remembered on the RAF Memorial located at Runnymede, near Egham, Surrey. They are also remembered as the first Lancaster crew lost by XV Squadron.

On the night of 20 February, the name of Sergeant Wheeler and his crew was recorded on the battle order for an attack on Stuttgart. Apart from butterflies in the tummy, everything seemed to be in order. The crew followed the usual routine of the pre-operation egg and bacon meal, attending the briefing, taking notes and recording specific and important details, and checking with the ground crew all was well with the aircraft.

One hour before take-off, Sergeant Wheeler and his crew were on board the aircraft, each man alone with his thoughts as he carried out the respective checks appertaining to his particular station. Happy all was well on board, the crew assembled outside the aircraft for a pre-op chat, joke, and smoke with the ground crew before take-off.

Having been given the signal they were going, the crews climbed back into their aircraft, started up the engines and taxied out. Sitting high on the back of the Lancaster, in the mid-upper turret, Bernard could see Lancasters in front and behind him, all snaking round the taxi track to the take-off point. Unfortunately, all did not go well and Bernard was to face another setback to the start of his operational career. Two of Bernard's fellow crew members called the pilot on the intercom and announced that they were not going on this operation. Sergeant Wheeler notified flying control and was immediately instructed to abort his take-off; he was also instructed to taxi back to the dispersal area, where the crew were met by the RAF police. Under guard, the whole crew were escorted to the Station Headquarters and paraded before Wing Commander Elliott, the Officer Commanding XV Squadron. Although the two crew members were arrested and subsequently court-martialled, an unassuming entry recorded in the XV Squadron Operational Record Book, possibly relating to the incident, simply read, 'Ten aircraft were detailed for operations, but one was later cancelled'.

No blame was attributed to Leslie Wheeler regarding the situation that occurred that night; in fact, shortly after he was promoted to the rank of flight sergeant, given a new crew and undertook two operational sorties before being killed in action during an attack against Berlin, on the night of 24–25 March.

Although it is not known what happened to the rest of Leslie Wheeler's original crew, in the interim period, Bernard Dye was posted to 622 Squadron; the latter having been formed from 'C' Flight, XV Squadron, back in August 1943. Bernard joined a crew headed by Flying Officer Arthur Horton, with whom he went on to complete a full tour of operational duty, logging up a respectable total of 305.55 hours flying time.

13

The First Hurdle: Flight Sergeant Harry Bysouth, DFM

Harry Bysouth was sitting in the mid-upper turret of Lancaster bomber ED383. The pilot had already made one attempt to land but decided to overshoot and go around again. As the aircraft emerged out of the gloom for a second attempt, Harry made a decision which probably saved his life. He opted to vacate the turret:

> At that moment, I decided to leave my turret. I climbed down and as my feet touched the fuselage floor the aircraft ran off the runway, the carriage sunk into the soft ground and the aircraft cart-wheeled over onto its back.

The last thing Harry remembered was being tossed about like a pea on a drum, to the accompaniment of splintering Perspex and wrenching metal. Slowly, he realised that the figure bending over him was that of Warrant Officer George Franklin, the navigator who, although slightly injured, was attempting to extricate Harry from the wreckage. At that moment, the crash crews arrived and cut away the debris around Harry before lifting him carefully on to a stretcher and placing him in an ambulance. Looking back out through the ambulance doors, Harry could see flames flickering over the mangled remains of ED383. As Harry watched, the image gradually disappeared as he receded into a state of unconsciousness. Sometime after the crash, he wrote in his logbook, against the entry for that particular flight, 'I will press on!' and that is exactly what he did.

Harry Bysouth was born in Tottenham, north London, on 2 December 1919. He attended All Hallows Boys School but was not a natural scholar. He enjoyed some lessons but struggled with others. He persevered with school until he reached the age of fourteen and then ventured out in the adult world.

On reaching his eighteenth birthday, he enlisted for service with a searchlight unit of the Territorial Army, based near his home. He remained part of this unit until July 1938, when he volunteered for service with the Royal Air Force. He was posted to Grantham for basic training before being posted to North Weald, Essex, as 615782 Aircraftman H. T. Bysouth, assigned to general duties.

Just prior to the outbreak of war, Harry was posted to a balloon squadron based at Dulwich, South London where he met a very attractive young lady named Renee Clark. Renee made quite an impact on Harry and they became very close friends; that is until the air force transferred Harry to a balloon squadron in Manchester.

Thinking about his future and his part in the war, Harry felt he could serve his King and Country in a far better capacity and, to that end, volunteered for aircrew training. It took about a year before he was called for interview, which took place in Manchester. Having been told he would be notified in due course, Harry was posted to another balloon site near the Barrett sweet factory at Wood Green. It was while he was in Manchester that Harry decided to make his relationship with Renee a permanent one; they married in November 1941.

Eventually, Harry received notification that his application for aircrew had been approved and was instructed to report to the Aircrew Receiving Centre at Viceroy Court, St John's Wood. His lack of academic qualifications, which he needed for pilot training, caught up with him at this point and he was sent to St John's College, Cambridge, for intensive tuition. Understandably, he found the going hard and could not keep up with the studies, so decided to remuster as an air gunner. He was initially sent to Brighton, but then went to Bridlington before finally being posted to No. 1 Air Gunnery School at Pembrey, where he arrived on 18 July 1943.

Harry's first experience of flight occurred eleven days after his arrival, when he flew on a Bristol Blenheim aircraft. He was to make a further sixteen flights with No. 1 AGS before converting to Wellington bombers with No. 1483 (Bomber) Flight at Newmarket. The transition to four-engined Stirling bombers was made at No. 1657 Conversion Unit at Stradishall. It was at Stradishall that Harry accepted the offer of joining Flight Sergeant Harold Richards' crew as mid-upper gunner. Their training complete, Richards and his crew were posted to No. 622 Squadron at RAF Mildenhall where, five days later, Flight Sergeant Richards, RNZAF, failed to return from an operation while flying his first sortie as a second pilot. Being without a captain to lead them, the crew were posted back to conversion unit, which for Harry meant being sent to No. 1651 CU at Wratting Common.

Harry undertook two training flights on 1 December, the pilot of the second flight being Sergeant Joseph 'Tony' Davis, from Shrewsbury. Harry began to fly regularly with Tony and got to like him very much. When Davis was posted to RAF Feltwell, for conversion to Lancasters, Harry had no hesitation in accepting the former's invitation to join the crew as mid-upper gunner. The rest of the crew consisted of Sergeant James 'Geordie' Carrott, navigator; Sergeant William 'Bill' Geraghty, bomb aimer; Warrant Officer George Franklin, wireless operator; Sergeant Ernest 'Mick' Harbidge, rear gunner; and Sergeant Doug Haydock, flight engineer.

Having successfully completed the conversion course, the crew were posted to XV Squadron at Mildenhall. For Harry, it was a case of *déjà vu* and he felt uneasy about it, but he got on with the job in hand.

The crew trained hard, completing numerous training exercises during their first month with the squadron. Tony Davis flew his first second pilot trip with an experienced crew and, much to Harry's relief, returned safely. Then, on the night of 20 February, the crew flew their first operational sortie: a trip to Stuttgart. Harry's feelings of uneasiness returned:

> I sat alone in the mid-upper turret high on the back of the Lancaster, my stomach churning, the back of my throat dry and various thoughts racing through my mind. 'You're on your own now, mate', a voice in my head told me. I endeavoured to remain calm as I thought, 'This is what I've trained for and now I'm here'.

As Tony Davis pushed the throttles forward and released the brakes, the Merlin engines roared, gathering power to lift the fuel and bomb-laden Lancaster off the ground. Once airborne, Harry rotated the turret back and forth, his keen but inexperienced eyes searching the darkness. A voice in his headphones broke Harry's concentration; somebody was stating he could smell petrol. The pilot first asked the flight engineer for his opinion, the latter confirmed the statement. Unsure how to handle the situation, the pilot then asked each individual crew member for their respective comments. By this time, Lancaster LL871 was out over the sea, and Tony Davis elected to return to base. It was a return that was not welcomed at Mildenhall:

> The whole crew was paraded before the officer commanding who gave us a good 'rollicking' for our actions. The smell of petrol was normal, due to the full fuel tanks and would have dissipated in due time. Because of our inexperience, however, no further action was taken, the lesson having been learned.

This was, for Harry at least, an inauspicious start to his tour of operations, bearing in mind the false start due to the loss of Flight Sergeant Richards, but unbeknown to Harry and the rest of the crew there was worse to come.

Bomber Command planned an attack against Augsburg for the night of 25 February, four nights after the crew's early return; the names of Sergeant

Davis and his crew were on the battle order. At 9.30 p.m. that night, Lancaster ED383 lifted off Mildenhall's runway with Tony Davis at the controls. Eleven aircraft had been detailed for the attack by XV Squadron, but one was cancelled prior to take-off and three abandoned their sorties *en route*, due to either aircraft or crew member malfunction.

The crew of ED383 carried out the respective duties as they headed for Germany, each man ignoring the strong smell of petrol and mindful of the previous raid. The city was a sea of flame, which could be seen from many miles away. For the 593 participating crews, including Harry's crew, who bombed without mishap, the attack went well.

Although the weather over the target had been clear with good visibility, the conditions over England began to deteriorate, with some crews being diverted to other airfields. As Sergeant Davis was preparing for a landing at Mildenhall, he received a signal diverting his aircraft to Lakenheath, where the weather was not much better and visibility was still poor. Sergeant Davis concentrated hard as he fought to keep the aircraft straight and level during approach to the runway. Suddenly, the excited voice of the flight engineer broke that concentration as he yelled a warning that the flaps would not fully extend. The pilot powered up the engines, aborted, and went around again, but the problem was still there. Doug Haycock warned Davis that they did not have enough fuel for another circuit and would have to land. It was at that moment that Harry made that life-saving decision; he climbed down from the mid-upper turret to take up his crash position.

The Lancaster hit the runway hard and fast, ran on to the soft ground of the overshoot and cartwheeled into a tangled mess of twisted metal. Sergeants Davis, Carrott, Geraghty, and Haydock were all killed instantly, while Mick Harbidge, who was trapped in the rear turret, died the next day. Harry was trapped in the wreckage and rescued by Warrant Officer Franklin, who had been thrown clear.

While lying in the station sick bay, in pain and in fear of what injuries he may have sustained, Harry asked for a drink, working on the principle that if it was refused he possibly had a stomach injury. He was, however, given a hot, sweet cup of tea, which allayed all his fears. He had sustained little more than facial cuts, bruising, and concussion. On being declared fit to travel, Harry was transferred to Littleport Hospital via Ely Hospital.

Having overcome the shock of the crash, James Franklin was making preparations to return to operational duties. Prior to flying on an air test, which all crews did on a regular, almost daily basis, he visited Harry in hospital:

> Franklin told me he was going up with Flight Lieutenant Jarvis, on an air test, as the usual wireless operator of that crew was sick. As Franklin left the

room he raised his hand in salutation and said, 'Don't worry, I'll be all right. See you later'.

Harry, who had still not overcome his own fears, experienced a deep feeling of apprehension, as he watched his friend saunter off swinging his flying helmet in a carefree way as he went. Harry wondered, with envy, how his friend could take this flight in such a light-hearted manner. Within sixty minutes of Franklin leaving, a loud explosion shook the airfield and a great pall of black smoke rose into the air. Flight Lieutenant Jarvis's aircraft had crashed; there were no survivors. Harry was devastated when he received the news. First Flight Sergeant Richards, then Davis and the crew, now Franklin; Harry felt lost and alone, his only comfort came from his young wife, Renee.

Following his discharge from hospital, Harry was given a period of leave, during which he carefully considered his future and decided to stay on operations, but he was not totally sure if he was ready to return just yet.

On his return to Mildenhall during mid-April, he experienced a chain of events that left him wondering if he had made the right decision. His first flight since the crash was as a passenger on a cross-country exercise with Pilot Officer Carl Thompson, on Lancaster LM465, the aircraft in which Thompson was to be shot down two months later. At the end of April, Harry flew a fighter affiliation exercise with Pilot Officer Thomas Jones; a week later Jones and his crew were dead. On the morning of 10 May, Flight Lieutenant Alan Amies, who required a gunner for his next operation that night, approached Harry and asked him if he would occupy the rear turret. Harry was unsure of his feelings; he even went to the MO's office with Amies but declined to see the doctor and declined the request to fly. Alan Amies feeling disgruntled walked off, never to be seen again; he failed to return from the raid. Cold shivers ran down his spine when Harry heard the news, He wondered if he were a jinx to other members of aircrew.

In his own mind, Harry had still not cleared that first hurdle of becoming operational. He was sent on leave, but informed that when he returned, he would be crewed-up. A tragic accident took Harry to his next crew.

During the early evening of Friday, 30 June 1944, seventeen Lancaster bombers from XV Squadron were flying in three vee formations over Ford, Sussex, when the last aircraft in the formation, Lancaster ME695, LS-Z, piloted by Flight Sergeant John French, was struck from below at 7.25 p.m. by Lancaster PB178, piloted by P/O Jack Hannesson, RCAF, from 514 Squadron, as the latter was trying to join the formation.

Although Flight Sergeant Andrew Pawlyk, Johnny French's rear gunner, was killed in the initial collision, miraculously, French managed to regain control of his shattered aircraft and execute a difficult but safe landing at RAF Ford, 2.25 miles north-west of Littlehampton, Sussex, without further

Above left: Sergeant Harry Bysouth's operational tour of duty got off to a shaky start, but he went on to be awarded a Distinguished Flying Medal. (*Author's collection*)

Above right: Sergeant Joseph 'Tony' Davis, pilot, was killed in a landing accident at RAF Lakenheath on 21 February 1944. (*Author's collection*)

Below: Front starboard view of the wreckage of Avro Lancaster ME695, LS-Z, following a mid-air collision with another aircraft. Note the Spitfire in the background. (*Author's collection via Adrian van Zantvoort, the Netherlands*)

Above: View of Avro Lancaster, ME695, LS-Z, from the rear port side, which crash-landed on the Fighter Command airfield at RAF Ford, Sussex, on 30 June 1944. (*Author's collection via Adrian van Zantvoort, the Netherlands*)

Below: The crew with whom Harry Bysouth (standing in doorway) completed a tour of operations. Flt Sgt J. Hope (sitting in doorway), Flt Lt John French (standing second from left), WO J. Raine (standing third from left), and WO Geoff Stubbings (sitting front centre). The two other crew members are known to be Plt Off. F. Smith and Plt Off. Harold Slingsby. (*Author's collection*)

death or injury to his crew. John French was an inexperienced pilot who was undertaking his second operational sortie, having been posted to XV Squadron only seventeen days earlier, on the 13th. Unfortunately, all but two members of the crew of Lancaster PB178, JI-P, were killed in the accident, the remaining two sustaining injuries.

On his return from leave, as he had previously been informed would happen, Harry was crewed-up in preparation for a return to operational flying. Apart from John French, the pilot, Harry's new crew consisted of Flight Sergeant Geoff Stubbings (navigator), Sergeant J. Hope (wireless operator), Flight Sergeant F. Smith (bomb aimer), Flight Sergeant Ron Wilson (mid-upper gunner), and Flight Sergeant Ted Pavey (flight engineer). As he read the battle order for the night of 28 July, Harry went cold; he had seen the target was recorded as Stuttgart. His first operation, the night they had returned early due to the smell of petrol, had been Stuttgart: 'I sat in the turret, my stomach churning, and the back of my throat dry, I said to myself, "I have been here before"'.

Perspiring slightly, Harry was breathing deeply, but evenly, trying to keep his mind on the job in hand. At 9.30 p.m., Lancaster LL923 lifted off the runway at Mildenhall, with John French at the controls. The aircraft had only been airborne for thirty-five minutes when the pilot announced there was a leak in the starboard petrol tank and they were returning to base. The bomb aimer jettisoned four 1,000-lb bombs over the Wash, from a height of 5,000 feet. Although Harry considered John French a confident man, his anxieties began again, and Harry offered up a silent prayer of 'Please, not again': 'I need not have worried, for even with two 1,000-lb and four 500-lb bombs still on board, John French made a smooth landing at Mildenhall'.

On 3 August, Harry participated in an attack on a flying bomb storage site at Bois De Cassen, north of Paris, France. The sortie was carried out in daylight, and both aircraft and crew returned to base safely. It was the first time Sergeant Bysouth had completed an operational sortie without incident; the air gunner felt he had finally cleared that first hurdle. Having cleared that hurdle, Harry went on to attack many targets in France and Belgium, the latter including a raid against the Luftwaffe night fighter airfield at St Trond, in support of Operation Anvil, the invasion of southern France by US and French forces.

Harry eventually completed a total of twenty-nine operations over France, Belgium, Holland, and Germany, and accumulated a total of 320.30 flying hours. In early September 1944, he was promoted to the rank of flight sergeant, and was recommended for the award of a Distinguished Flying Medal on 24 January 1945. The citation for Harry's DFM stated that Flight Sergeant Bysouth's operational career had been characterised by exceptional keenness and determination in the face of setbacks. It told how on the night of 25

January 1944, Harry had flown as mid-upper gunner on a sortie to Augsburg and how, on return, the aircraft had crashed and caught fire, leaving Flight Sergeant Bysouth and the wireless operator as sole survivors of the crew. The recommendation made mention of how, after two months in hospital, Harry had returned to the squadron and, by steady persistence in non-operational flying, had gradually regained his confidence. It told of another setback in June 1944, when the wireless operator who had escaped with Harry in January was killed in a local flying accident and that still refusing to give in, Flight Sergeant Bysouth persevered and in July 1944 was crewed up with Flight Lieutenant French with whom he completed his tour of twenty-nine operational sorties. It also mentioned how Harry had always shown himself to be an exceptionally enthusiastic and reliable air gunner who had won the complete confidence of his captain and gunnery leader. The citation concluded with a strong recommendation for the award of the Distinguished Flying Medal. The RAF Mildenhall Station Commander reiterated the comment that the award was strongly recommended and came with the final comment that Flight Sergeant Harry Bysouth had always shown that he possessed the utmost fortitude and devotion to duty.

14

Operations Manna and Exodus: Flight Sergeant D. A. 'Pat' Russell

Although he was only seventeen years old and still attending Hitchin Grammar School, on 29 November 1941, D. A. Pat Russell travelled to London to volunteer for pilot training with the RAF, at Adastral House, in the Aldwych area of London. Pat's application being accepted, he underwent medical examinations, sat various exams and appeared before a selection board. On being passed fit for flying training, he was attested and sent home, as an aircrew cadet on deferred service, until being called for training. The call came seven months later, on 29 June 1942, when Pat was instructed to report to Lord's Cricket Ground where he was 'one among thousands'.

Pat was billeted at No. 6 Hall Road, St John's Wood, just north-west of the cricket ground, where he shared a room with another cadet named Kenneth Griffiths. Unfortunately, having been posted to Canada for aircrew training, Kenneth Griffiths caught scarlet fever and, as a result, was invalided out of the Royal Air Force. Not being able to serve his country, the Welshman turned to acting and became a well-known character actor in many British post-war films; he also appeared in numerous television productions.

Having spent three weeks at St John's Wood, Pat made the first of a number of moves in quick succession; the first being to No. 26 Elementary Flying Training Wing at Theale in Berkshire. The airfield, situated 5 miles west of Reading, boasted four grass runways but no accommodation for cadets, necessitating Pat and his fellow students to live under canvas for a month. The next move was to No. 17 Initial Training Wing at Scarborough where he spent six weeks before moving to No. 9 Elementary Flying Training School at Ansty, 5 miles west of Coventry, Warwickshire. The latter was a grading school where cadets spent up to twelve hours flying Tiger Moth aircraft, to assess their potential, and to decide if it was worth sending them to Canada or Rhodesia for further flying training. The cadets then spent a month at the

Aircrew Despatch Centre, Manchester, before being moved to No. 1 RAF Regiment School. A further month later, the cadets returned to Manchester prior to boarding the *Empress of Scotland* for the journey to Canada.

On arrival on the North American Continent, Pat was posted to No. 3 Personnel Depot, Moncton, for two weeks before moving to No. 31 EFTS at De Winton near Calgary. Here, Pat and his fellow cadets put the Tiger Moth aircraft through its paces, before graduating to twin-engined Airspeed Oxford, at No. 36 Service Flying Training School at Penhold, located between Calgary and Edmonton.

Take-offs and general piloting of the Oxford presented no problem for Pat, his troubles started when he tried to land the aircraft. He persevered for six weeks, trying to master the problem but eventually, his instructors removed him from the course and sent him to No. 3 Manning Depot.

Pat remustered as a bomb aimer and started re-training at No. 8 Bombing and Gunnery School, Lethbridge, Alberta; his course included learning navigation, which Pat undertook at No. 2 Air Observer School, Edmonton. On graduating from both sections of the course, bombing and gunnery and navigation, Pat received his flying brevet and was promoted to the rank of sergeant; he was then sent back to No. 31 PD at Moncton to await a space on a troopship to the United Kingdom.

Back in the UK, Sergeant Russell continued to be moved around until he finally arrived at No. 14 Operational Training Unit at Market Harborough, where he became bomb aimer to a crew being formed by Sergeant Norman Waller; the rest of the all sergeant crew consisted of John Sheppard, navigator; Phil Smeeton, RAAF, wireless operator; Jack Turner, mid-upper gunner; and Paddy Kirrane, rear gunner. Unfortunately, as their training continued, for unrecorded reasons, Norman Waller was removed from the course, his place as captain of the crew being taken by Sergeant Doug Hunt, an Australian pilot from Mount Barber, South Australia.

From 14 OTU, the crew were posted (according to Pat) to ACCS at Balderton, 2 miles south of Newark-on-Trent, Nottinghamshire, but it is not recorded for what purpose or for how long.

The penultimate part of Pat Russell's training came at No. 1654 Heavy Conversion Unit at Wigsley, Nottinghamshire, where Pat and the rest of the crew were to be converted to four-engined Stirling bombers. However, the day the crew reported to Wigsley, the wireless operator went absent without leave, an action which resulted in the whole crew being sent back to Balderton. The errant crew member having satisfied his senior officers as to his reasons for going 'AWOL', Phil Smeeton was reinstated as wireless operator and instructed to report to No. 1668 Conversion Unit at Bottesford, Leicestershire, for conversion to Lancasters, along with the rest of the crew. It was at this time that Sergeant George Pitkin joined the crew as flight engineer.

Being declared ready for operational flying duties, Doug Hunt and his crew were posted to XV Squadron at Mildenhall, where they arrived on the penultimate day of 1944; the pilot wore the rank of flying officer, having recently been commissioned.

The air war Pat was to enter into was completely different to the one his predecessors had endured. The nightly bombing campaigns, with the fear of not knowing what lay in wait for them in the darkened skies over enemy-occupied Europe, had given way to daylight attacks. Both the Royal Air Force and the United States Army Air Force were now flying daylight operations and, thanks to technological advances in aircraft design, the fighters were able to escort the bombers to and from the majority of targets. Another added bonus in the bomber crews' favour was the fact the Luftwaffe fighters were less evident.

Having settled into the new surroundings at RAF Mildenhall, Pat and his crew were hoping for a short daylight raid on their first operation, like something in support of the advancing ground forces. However, on hearing that their designated aircraft was being fuelled with a maximum load of 2,154 gallons, and that an 8,160-lb bombload was being winched into the bomb bay, they realised their hopes had been shattered. They had in fact been detailed for a night attack against Munich, a round trip which would last eight hours and thirty-four minutes.

The battle order for the attack, dated 7 January 1945, when posted that morning, showed that the officer commanding XV Squadron, Wing Commander Nigel Macfarlane, would captain the aircraft, Lancaster HK648, LS-F, with Doug Hunt flying as second pilot.

Nigel Graeme Macfarlane, a Rhodesian by birth, had served with No. 218 Squadron prior to taking command of XV Squadron on 17 November 1944. This highly respected officer, who made it his policy to fly with every new crew on their first operational sortie, retired from the Royal Air Force on 18 April 1958, having completed twenty years' service and been awarded a Distinguished Service Order and made a Chevalier de l'Ordre de Léopold (Belgium).

As though flying an eight-and-a-half-hour night bombing raid against Munich on a first operational sortie would not induce a high degree of nervous tension in its own right, Pat and his crew had their commanding officer in attendance throughout the whole ordeal. For the duration of the flight, each crew member ensured they, individually, did not give their OC any cause for complaint, this included Pat. However, while actually carrying out the attack Pat, who was naturally flying in the bomb aimer's compartment, made a decision which was to earn him the silent wrath and displeasure of his crew:

> I was playing it by the book and as I couldn't see the target indicators over which we were briefed to bomb, I called a dummy run and instructed the pilot to go

round again. As we then had to turn back against the stream of several hundred other Lancasters I got the distinct impression that this was not a popular move.

The crew's hope for a short, daylight trip was granted on their second sortie, on the 11th, when twelve aircraft were detailed for an attack against Krefeld. Bomber Command had ordered a total of 152 aircraft from 3 Group to undertake a G-H (pulse radio navigational aid) raid on the railway yards in the eastern suburb of Uerdingen.

Pat released the bombload, consisting of one 4,000-lb high capacity bomb, ten 500-lb bombs, and four 250-lb bombs, on the first run over the target, so did not incur the displeasure of his crew on this sortie. However, with the target being obscured by 10/10th cloud, the results of their effort could not be recorded.

Two days later, on the 13th, Pat and his crew were detailed to join 157 other crews, again all from 3 Group, for an attack against the marshalling yards at Saarbrücken, which at that time was only just inside German lines. Thirteen of the aircraft being dispatched, including Lancaster LL854, LS-S, piloted by Flying Officer Doug Hunt, were from XV Squadron. As LL854 taxied out in preparation for take-off, Pat was in awe of the sight that unfolded on the airfield:

RAF Mildenhall resembled a car park at the end of a race meeting. There were dozens of Lancasters from both XV and 622 Squadrons swarming around the peri-track lining up for take-off. Most of the ground staff, having finished their work, took time out to watch the Lancasters get airborne. A small group of people around the flying-control caravan waved them off as each aircraft sped down the runway past the line up of 'bloodwagons' and rescue vehicles in case a Lancaster incurred trouble during its heavily laden take-off.

Watching his instruments carefully, and with George Pitkin sitting beside him assisting with the throttles, Flying Officer Hunt pulled back on the control column and Lancaster LL854 lumbered off the runway at 12.05 p.m.; the last of the squadron's aircraft to get airborne. In the bomb bay were a 4,000-lb 'cookie' and twelve 500-lb bombs. With this weight, plus the weight of the fuel load, the Lancaster climbed slowly towards the clouds 1,000 feet above the airfield:

We climbed through the cloud and gradually the gloom on the ground, of that January morning, gave way to ever brighter conditions until we emerged at 3,000 feet on top of a perfect layer of cloud, with blue sky and sunshine above. Over the Channel the cloud dissipated and I was, once we cleared the enemy coast, able to map read right up to the target, where I experienced the satisfaction of seeing our 'cookie' explode right in the centre of the marshalling yards. Crossing over the lines near Luxembourg, we thought we were having an uneventful trip, so much so

> that the skipper put LL854 onto auto-pilot and came down into my compartment in the nose of the aircraft. George Pitkin, the flight engineer, was however keeping an eye on things on the flight deck, when all of a sudden I thought I heard an engine splutter and without warning the aircraft went into a dive. We had inadvertently flown over the area between Dunkirk and Calais, which were still in German hands. The spluttering was in fact the noise of exploding flak, which was so close we could hear it above the throbbing of the four Merlin engines.

As a result of the flak, the aircraft sustained some damage, but it was only superficial. It was then that Phil Smeeton announced that a signal had been received, directing all XV Squadron aircraft to land at Predannack in Cornwall, due to inclement weather in East Anglia. This was interesting news to Pat, as his sister Sybil was serving there in the WAAFs, and he was now looking forward to seeing her and her friends.

Unfortunately, John Sheppard could not share Pat's happiness on hearing this news, as he had not got the appropriate maps or charts for the Cornwall and Devon area on board, which would have meant he could use the 'GEE' navigational aid. Instead, he would have to resort to more conventional method of taking fixes along the route. It was by now late afternoon or early evening and seven pairs of 'Mk I eyeballs' were staring out into the gloom looking for landmarks, as well as watching a stream of Halifax bombers going in the opposite direction, on their way out for the 'night shift'.

> Once again, we were above cloud, but as darkness set in we descended through it and found we were flying over the sea. At one point, we saw rockets being fired up towards us but didn't get the message at the time; we just noted the position. By the time our ETA had expired, Doug Hunt was convinced we had overshot and therefore turned the aircraft on to 090 degrees, which should have got us back over the UK. We were now below the cloud layer, which was by this time less than 1,000 feet above ground level. Added to this was the fact we were rapidly running out of fuel. Thirty-five minutes later, with the fuel gauge needles almost reading zero, we saw some searchlights on top of the cliffs with an airfield amongst them. We did not know which airfield it was until we were in the circuit, when Phil Smeeton announced he had a fix and it was in fact Predannack. After we landed we were informed that the rockets we logged were in fact part of the 'Granite' emergency system. The rockets had been fired from the Scilly Isles, twenty-five miles past Land's End and were to warn us that we were heading for New York and a watery grave!

It took three days for repairs to the aircraft to be completed at Predannack. Unfortunately for Pat, his sister was on leave, but he and his crew did enjoy the company of her friends during their enforced stay.

Their return journey to Mildenhall turned out to be an exhilarating one, when Doug Hunt flew back at a low level. Pat lay in his bomb aimer's compartment watching as the countryside of at least half a dozen counties unrolled beneath him.

Five days after their enforced stay at Predannack, on the 22nd, Pat and his crew flew their last sortie for the month of January, when they flew Lancaster HK648, LS-F, on an attack against the coking plant at Sterkrade, near Duisburg. The squadron detailed twelve aircraft for the attack, with Flying Officer Hunt and his crew being recorded, again, as the last ones to take off from Mildenhall at 5.07 p.m. The target, which was clearly marked by the Pathfinder Force, was bombed by the attacking crews who dropped a mixture of high-explosive, medium-capacity, and general-purpose bombs. Pat and his crew, their task satisfactorily completed, turned for home and returned to Mildenhall where they landed at 9.58 p.m.

Following a possible period of leave, Pat returned, along with his crew, to operational duties on the night of 2 February, when XV Squadron detailed fourteen aircraft for an attack against the military barracks at Wiesbaden. It was to be a busy night for Bomber Command, with a total force of 507 aircraft attacking the town. A further 369 aircraft detailed were to attack oil refineries at Wanne-Eickel, while a third force comprising of 261 aircraft headed for Karlsruhe. Although Wiesbaden was blanketed by cloud, most of the bombloads were recorded as hitting the town. The Bomber Command Loss Cards record that a combined total, for all three raids, indicate that thirty-four aircraft failed to return to their respective bases, although at least two of the losses are known to have been as a result of a mid-air collision. There were no such problems for Pat and his crew, who landed back at RAF Mildenhall at 2.53 a.m. on the morning of 3 April.

Pat must have been doing something right as, during that first week of February he was promoted to the rank of flight sergeant, but he made no mention of having a celebratory beer or two with his crew.

Flight Sergeant Russell participated in a number of operational sorties during February 1945, including attacks against the Hansa Benzol plant at Dortmund, Wanne-Eickel, the Hohenbudberg railway yards at Krefeld, Dresden, and Wesel; some of these targets were attacked more than once.

Between 27 February and 16 March, neither Pat nor his crew are recorded as having undertaken any operational sorties. Yet when the crew were detailed for a daylight attack against Dortmund on the 17th, Pat's position as bomb aimer was occupied by Flight Sergeant E. Naldrett. Flight Sergeant Naldrett was an experienced bomb aimer with eight operational sorties to his credit; he was initially reported 'missing' in action on 4 December 1944, after his aircraft crash-landed behind Allied lines, while flying with Flying Officer Robert Ostler. The aircraft, PA170, LS-N, had sustained damage from debris as the result of

Above: A crew photograph taken at No. 14 Operational Training Unit, Market Harborough, during the summer of 1944, shows front row, *left to right*: Sgt Paddy Kirrane; Sgt Doug Hunt, RAAF; and Sgt John Sheppard; back row, *left to right*: Sgt Phil Smeeton, Sgt Jack Turner, and Sgt D. A. Pat Russell. (*Author's collection via the late Pat Russell Collection*)

Left: Sgt Pat Russell checking the bomb sight on Lancaster NF953. (*Author's collection via the late Pat Russell Collection*)

Above: Avro Lancaster NG358 displays a bomb tally of forty operational mission symbols under the front cockpit canopy. The horizontal stripes on the tail fins are yellow 'G-H' leader markings. (*Author's collection via the late Pat Russell Collection*)

Below: Members of XV Squadron take a break resting on the panniers containing food sacks, which are waiting to be loaded into the bomb bay of Lancaster NG444 in preparation for a 'Manna' operation. (*Author's collection*)

Former prisoners of war wait anxiously near the crew entry doorway, ready to board Lancaster ME455 for the journey back to England. (*Author's collection*)

ME455
LS

another Lancaster, HK626, LS-W, exploding in mid-air. Flight Sergeant Naldrett returned to the United Kingdom and rejoined XV Squadron in March 1945.

Whatever the reason for Pat's absence from flying, he was back with his crew for an attack against a Benzol oil plant, at Hattingen, south of Essen, on the 18th. The crew took off just before midday, dropped their bombs without incident and were home in time for tea.

The next attack, on the morning of 21 March, could have had a different ending when the crew went to Munster. Fourteen aircraft from XV Squadron joined a total force of 160 Lancaster bombers from 3 Group, for a raid against railway yards and a nearby railway viaduct. Although Pat had vivid memories of the incident, no comment was recorded in the operational record book:

> We were some miles from the target when we first saw the box barrage of ack-ack bursts. The sky was clear and the flak seemed intense. As I released the bombload there was a terrific bang and the Lancaster shuddered. I heard Phil Smeeton cry, 'The starboard outer is on fire'. George Pitkin hit the propeller feathering switch and pushed the Graviner fire extinguisher button, while I prepared to make a hasty exit.

Fortunately for Pat, the fire was doused and the aircraft flew home safely on three engines. The ORB did however mention, 'Two aircraft returned each with a feathered engine, and landed safely'. One of the aircraft was recorded as Lancaster NG358, LS-H, piloted by Flight Sergeant Noel McLennan, who lost power in the port inner engine on his way to the target. The other aircraft, which was not identified, could possibly have been HK772, LS-A, flown by Pat and his crew.

During the closing stages of the war, XV Squadron commenced a new type of operation one none of the crews had trained for, they were to fly to the target unarmed, at very low level, drop their loads and return to base. These operations were codenamed 'Manna'.

During September 1944, the Allies had been making such good progress with their advance into Holland, that the Dutch envisaged an early end to the occupation by the German forces. Unfortunately, this was not to be the case and it was to be another seven months before the deadlock was broken. Action taken by the 2nd Tactical Air Force and the Dutch Resistance had rendered the railway system unserviceable and food supplies could not be conveyed to the western areas such as Amsterdam, Rotterdam, or The Hague. In early April 1945, negotiations were convened between the Allies, the Dutch Resistance and the Germans as to how food could be supplied to the starving Dutch population. The outcome was Operation Manna, which allowed British bomber aircraft to fly at 500 feet and drop a total of approximately 6,500 tons of food on designated areas. The first four areas agreed were the Hague Racecourse and the airfields at Valkenburg, Waalhaven, and Ypenburg. While it was agreed that the German forces would not open fire at the British aircraft and that the latter would not be armed, some air gunners felt it prudent to arm the turrets. In the event, several cases of small arms fire were reported by returning British aircrew.

Consignments of flour, powdered egg, dried milk, biscuits, and chocolate were packed in sacking and placed in specially designed panniers, which were released by the bomb aimer utilising the bomb release mechanism. Pat undertook his first Manna operation at the end of April:

> On 29 April 1945, twelve crews from XV Squadron were detailed to fly individually to an airfield one mile south of Rotterdam. We were briefed to fly out of Mildenhall at 12.39 hours, in Lancaster, HK693, with five panniers of food supplies in our bomb bay. On this first trip we did not know what to expect in the form of a reception by the Germans. We flew across Holland at an altitude of about 200 feet and could see the crowds out in the streets waving anything they could lay their hands on. Here and there the green uniforms of the Wehrmacht stood out; needless to say they were not waving. In fact, several aircraft came back with bullet holes in them. A Lancaster from 622 Squadron lost an engine and two members of aircrew were injured by trigger-happy 'Prussians'. After our previous operations when we were dropping nasties on Germany, from 21,000 feet, the Manna flights were a joy for several reasons; firstly, we now had official instructions to fly low, which was not normally allowed, but was highly enjoyable, we no longer expected to be shot at by either fighters or flak, and finally, we were caught up in the obvious excitement of the crowds below.

On hearing the low distinct drone of approaching aircraft, which then appeared over the rooftops like a swarm of hornets, the people around Rotterdam rushed out of their houses to watch. When the Lancasters opened their bomb doors and the food sacks began tumbling out, those on the ground went wild—waving, cheering, laughing, and crying. To the Dutch recipients, these operations became known as 'the droppings', but other names and titles soon started to be heard, as Pat remembered:

> Although the operations were codenamed Manna, the British newspapers called us 'Flying Grocers', whilst we aircrew referred to them as 'Spam Trips'. The latter gave rise to us bomb aimers being known as 'Spamardiers'. Whilst we endeavoured to drop supplies in the designated areas, some food fell in other locations due to hang-ups in the bomb bay.

It was one of those stay packs that fell towards a young Dutch girl and her friends as they watched the unfolding event. Realising what was about to happen, a German soldier dived forward pushed the girl to the ground and protected her with his body. The soldier's action saved the girl's life, but he forfeited his own when he was struck on the head by a heavy food pack.

Fourteen aircraft were dispatched by XV Squadron for another Manna operation on 1 May, when Pat again marvelled at the obvious excitement he could see near the drop zone—on this occasion, a large sports field near The Hague. At the appropriate moment, Pat released the precious cargo of five panniers, all of which fell to earth without mishap.

Flight Sergeant Russell completed two more Manna operations, one on 2 May the other on the 7th. A few storm showers were encountered on the route out during the latter sortie, but on both occasions, the panniers were delivered safely to the accompaniment of the rousing cheers of a grateful population.

Tuesday, 8 May 1945, was declared Victory in Europe Day. German forces in north-west Germany, the Netherlands, and Denmark had signed an act of surrender, on Lüneburg Heath, a few days earlier on the 4th.

The war may have been declared won, but there were still tasks to be completed. On the 10th, Pat and his crew were detailed, along with fourteen other crews, to participate in yet another type of operation codenamed 'Exodus'. They were dispatched to Juvincourt-et-Damary, northern France, where they landed and embarked twenty-four passengers on each Lancaster. These passengers were all ex-prisoners of war who were to be flown back to reception centres in southern England, where they were processed, had medical health checks, given fresh clothing, and fed. The following day, XV Squadron detailed sixteen aircraft and crews for the same purpose; Pat and his crew among them. On this occasion, they delivered their charges into Tangmere, before returning to Mildenhall.

On 12 May, fifteen aircraft left Mildenhall at lunchtime and again flew to Juvincourt-et-Damary for another Exodus operation; Pat and his crew took off at 1.05 p.m. All the aircraft and crews stayed overnight, with the intention of flying back late morning on the 13th. The former prisoners of war eagerly formed themselves into groups of twenty-four men and boarded the aircraft as instructed. All XV Squadron's aircraft took off safely, except one, PP672, piloted by Flight Lieutenant Bagenal; the aircraft crashed on take-off and burst into flames. Although the aircraft was burnt out, both the crew and all passengers escaped without injury.

On landing back at Mildenhall, Flight Sergeant Pat Russell's tour of operations with XV Squadron came to an end, but not his tour of duty; Pat was posted to a further twelve RAF stations before being demobbed on 10 September 1946.

Having been trained as a bomb aimer, Pat's greatest memory of the war was that he had the opportunity to drop the gift of life, in the form of those food packs, from the bomb bay, to the starving Dutch people. He always felt a great sense of pride in this achievement and often returned to Holland, where he joined in the annual Manna reunions.

15

A Collection of Memories: They Also Flew

Most XV Squadron veterans, when asked about their specific tour of operational duty during the turbulent years of 1939–1945, will give a standard answer that their tour or time was no different to anybody else's; nothing out of the ordinary happened. Then, with a glint in the eye or a little chuckle, they will recall the odd incident, which at the time could have had serious consequences, but when brought to mind years later are told with an element of humour.

One such story was related by Flight Sergeant Frank Watson, a wireless operator who, at the time, flew with Pilot Officer Charles Woodley and his crew. The incident occurred on 2 October 1943:

> We took off from Mildenhall in Stirling BK818, LS-O, at 17.35 hours on that Saturday evening, for a 'Gardening' (mining-laying) operation in the Skagerrak, the strait between Norway and the Jutland peninsula of Denmark. During the flight, which was to last over seven hours, we were caught in an electrical storm. St Elmo's fire danced all over the aircraft, engulfing it in blue flames six feet high. Lighting struck the trailing aerial, ran up it, earthing on the winding out handle and causing it to burn through. On landing back at Mildenhall, I informed the ground crew chief that I had lost my aerial. The chief immediately produced his notebook and pencil and proceeded to fine me five shillings (equivalent to nearly £8.00 in 2017). As so many aerials were being lost in trees and church steeples due to W/Ops forgetting to wind them in before landing, it was the custom to fine the guilty party. I immediately put the chief in the picture and invited him to view the damage. A further note was made in his book and he mumbled in a disgruntled voice, 'I'll have to report it anyway', but I never heard anymore [*sic.*] about it.

A more serious incident had befallen Frank's crew five days earlier, on the evening of Monday 27 September, but Frank still made light of it.

Pilot Officer Woodley was at the controls of Stirling BK719, having taken off from Mildenhall at 7.50 p.m., for an attack against Hannover. Bomber Command had detailed a total force of 683 aircraft comprising 312 Lancasters, 231 Halifaxes, 111 Stirlings, twenty-four Wellingtons, and five Boeing B-17s, with BK719 being one of eleven Stirlings dispatched by XV Squadron.

The Stirling was renowned for its lack of ability to gain altitude, and as BK719 crossed the target area it was struck by a bomb from above—an experience Frank Watson was never to forget:

> On the Hannover raid we were in the third wave. As we crossed the target area a string of bombs fell from a Lancaster overflying us. One of the bombs went through the wing and main petrol tank.

The Stirling immediately heaved over and fell into a spin, out of control. The compass toppled and the altimeter spun crazily round unwinding the altitude reading, as the rest of the instrument panel needles flickered back and forth across the dials in rapid movement.

Pilot Officer Woodley finally managed to recover from the spin and regain control of the aircraft, with the burning city of Hannover now only 3,000 feet below him. Climbing steadily, the pilot managed to regain some of the lost height and set course for home, a journey which kept the flight engineer busy, again as Frank remembered: 'We nursed the aircraft back to Mildenhall by changing the petrol tanks and regulating the fuel supply all the way home'. Back at RAF Mildenhall, when filling in his logbook, Frank simply recorded, 'Hannover—Quiet Trip'.

Another XV Squadron veteran, Sergeant Frank Diamond, a navigator who flew with New Zealander Flight Lieutenant Hugh Wilkie, never forgot the night their aircraft lost a propeller: the night of 11–12 June 1943. Short Stirling BK470 was one of 783 aircraft detailed for an attack against Düsseldorf and had taken off from Mildenhall at 11.39 p.m. Hugh Wilkie headed towards the target with no indication about what the night might hold; in fact, all was going well until a Mosquito inadvertently unleashed a load of target markers approximately 14 miles to the north-east of the city. This action led to some of the main force bombers dropping their loads in open countryside.

Pilot Officer Wilkie flew in over the target at 12,000 feet and dropped his bombs on the correct markers, without hindrance from either flak or the prowling enemy night fighters which some of the crew had spotted during the bombing run.

Having turned on to a course for home, Hugh Wilkie was advised that there was another Stirling flying close to them, but neither he nor the gunners paid any attention to it until it opened fire at them. The port outer engine sustained damage, putting the constant speed unit out of action. Frank Diamond witnessed what happened next:

> Being ensconced inside the fuselage, I thought we'd been hit by flak. The port outer engine started to roar and scream. I looked out of the window on the port side, just as the aircraft went into a dive. The engine was going mad and started to vibrate. I remember John Ledgerwood, the mid-upper gunner, who had a perfect view of the port outer, saying, 'It looks as if it's about to come off', at which point the propeller, complete with boss, sheared off and cart-wheeled up and over the top of John's turret.

Pilot Officer Wilkie hauled the de-stabilised aircraft back on course and tried to gain some of the lost altitude, a difficult task with an aeroplane which had trouble climbing even with four engines. The gyro-compass had toppled and was swinging wildly, leaving Hugh Wilkie to urgently call for a course for home. Frank's navigational training was to prove invaluable on this occasion:

> The loss of the port outer meant no power to the GEE navigational aid, which in turn meant we would have to use Astro-navigation. Wilkie took the aircraft above cloud, whilst I climbed up into the astrodome. I told the pilot that if he kept Polaris on the starboard side we must be flying west. I took three fixes and plotted a course which, thanks to the excellent training I received in America, proved correct.

Noticing a gap in the clouds, Wilkie descended and dropped down through the aperture. Below and ahead of him, he saw Mildenhall's flashing identification beacon.

Ten days later, on the night of 21–22 June, fate smiled kindly again on Frank Diamond and his crew as they headed for an attack on Krefeld. Pilot Officer Wilkie was holding Stirling BF470 steady at 17,000 feet, over 10/10th cloud. Their position was approximately 15 miles from the target, which they were approaching from the south-west. The crew were expressing apprehension about the lack of both searchlights and flak activity, when suddenly 'Jock' Palmer, the rear gunner, yelled a warning of 'fighter'. Identified as a Junkers Ju 88, the enemy aircraft positioned itself on the Stirling's rear port quarter, where it lined-up for an attack. When the night fighter was at a range of about 800 yards, Sergeant Palmer instructed his pilot to take evasive action. As the Stirling lurched to port, Palmer opened fire with short bursts of machine gun fire, which it was later claimed hit the mainplane of the Ju 88. The twin-engined fighter followed the twisting, turning, bomber down in a dive, firing bursts of poorly aimed cannon fire as it did so. Hugh Wilkie dipped one wing and then the other in a series of steeply swinging banks to port and starboard, having been informed by the rear gunner that the German aircraft had passed somewhere underneath them. These manoeuvres enabled the gunners to see the fighter and fire at it when it appeared in their respective sights. After several minutes, which seemed like an eternity to the crew, the Ju 88 was seen to peel over and dive down into the cloud below. The only thing left to do now was for Frank Diamond to get BF470 back on course for Krefeld.

Sergeant John James Sparrow was a mid-upper gunner, who was posted to XV Squadron, along with his crew, in early July 1943. Their first two operational sorties, both mine-laying operations, passed without incident, but that was to change on the night of 10–11 August, when the crew participated in an attack against Nuremberg. The pilot, Flight Sergeant Lewis, pushed forward the throttles, released the brakes and Stirling BF460 rolled down the runway gathering speed and lifted into the night sky; take-off was logged as 10.26 p.m.

RAF Bomber Command dispatched a total of 653 aircraft, which included thirteen Stirling bombers from XV Squadron. Although 9/10th cloud was reported to a height of 12,000 feet, the flight out was uneventful. Crews reported dummy fires in the Mannheim area, but all crews reported bombing on the green target indicators. Their bombing run complete, aiming-point photo taken, and bomb doors closed, Flight Sergeant Lewis turned BF460 on to a heading for home. All was quiet and it seemed as though the homeward journey was going to be as uneventful as the outward leg; that is until they reached the French–Belgian border. It was a nightmare John Sparrow would never forget: 'Without warning, out of the darkness, a Messerschmitt Bf 110 night fighter opened fire. Its' first burst of cannon fire slammed into the nose and starboard wing of the Stirling, immediately setting the bomber afire'.

The enemy aircraft executed a tight turn in towards the now blazing bomber, to inflict the *coup de grâce*, but so fierce was the fire that the flames illuminated the incoming night fighter, giving both John Sparrow in the mid-upper turret and Sergeant Sheppard, the rear gunner, an opportunity to return fire. John Sparrow claimed hits on the night fighter, piloted by *Leutnant* Johannes Hager, of 6 *Gruppe*, *Nachtjagdgeschwader* 1, which the mid-upper gunner said peeled over and dived away.

Due to the raging fire, there was no time for rejoicing; Flight Sergeant Lewis had given the order to bail out and there was no time to lose. Clambering down from his turret, John Sparrow clipped on his parachute and fought his way to the rear escape hatch. As he got there he saw Sergeant Cave, the wireless operator, and Sergeant Bryne, the navigator, make good their escape, John quickly followed. Unfortunately, the rest of the crew were to perish, including Sergeant Poole, the bomb aimer, who is thought to have jumped, or fallen, from the aircraft without his parachute.

John Sparrow landed north of Givet, near the Meuse River on the French–Belgian border. He spent thirty-eight days at liberty, until a local person betrayed him to the Gestapo. Having been savagely treated by the latter, he spent the rest of the war as a prisoner of war but that, really, is another story.

Owen Sylvestre, who was born in Trinidad, is only one of two black men known to have served with XV Squadron during the Second World War. Flight Sergeant Sylvestre was an excellent pilot, with a love of low flying that resulted in him having to face the wrath of his commanding officer on more than one occasion. However, his low-flying skills could work to his advantage and get him out of trouble, as George Allom (Owen Sylvestre's bomb aimer) could testify:

> Returning from a daylight raid on the Ruhr towards the end of summer 1944, we began to trail behind the main [bomber] stream until eventually we were flying alone. Gradually we lost height and flew over Brussels at a fairly low altitude. We continued our journey home flying 'on the deck', heading towards Knokke on the Belgium coast. I warned the skipper that according to that morning's *Daily Express* newspaper, Knokke was still occupied by German forces.

The German anti-aircraft gunners were not slow in opening fire at the low-flying Lancaster but were not, seemingly, very good at aiming at the incoming aircraft. Tracer followed the bomber, trying to keep pace with it, as it flashed over their heads. Shrapnel rattled against the skin of the aircraft as shells burst near the aircraft's flight path. Sergeant George Allom remembers his pilot's next move:

> As we flashed over, we heard a few 'pings' on the fuselage, but the skipper knew how to deal with the situation and took the Lancaster right down to sea level once we had crossed the coast. The enemy guns were then unable to be trained on us due to elevation and depression restrictions. We flew home at sea level, but found it necessary to gain altitude to cross our coast.

On the night of 16–17 August 1944, 461 Bomber Command aircraft attacked the port and industrial areas of Stettin. Fourteen Lancasters were detailed by XV Squadron for the attack, including ME848, LS-N, piloted by Flight Sergeant Sylvestre. Approaching the target area, with his crew at their respective battle stations, Owen Sylvestre commenced his bombing run, being guided to the aiming point by George Allom.

With fires raging in and around the port area, looking out through the glazed nose blister of the Lancaster, George could see a kaleidoscope of changing colours of flame dancing on the ground beneath him. With the searchlights scanning back and forth, the battle was brought to the night sky with flak bursting in and around the bomber stream. As always, without warning, the blue ray of a master beam caught ME848 in its glare. George was very concerned:

> As we were running into the target, we got caught by a radar controlled beam. The skipper reacted immediately by pushing the 'kite' into a dive and escaped the tenacious beam before the other manually controlled beams could lock onto us.

The crew had had a lucky escape, but there was a further dice with death shortly after they had returned to their allotted task. Both Owen Sylvestre and Ernie Fitch, the mid-upper gunner, became aware there was another Lancaster flying fairly close to them to their port side. Keeping a wary eye on the situation, Ernie Fitch's night vision was suddenly destroyed when their flying companion erupted in a fireball of light and flame, as the bombload blew-up following a direct hit from flak. Fortunately, ME848 survived the incident and returned safely to Mildenhall.

One of those occasions that found Flight Sergeant Sylvestre standing to attention in front of the officer commanding was due to the pilot's decision to fly over Ernie Fitch's home:

> We had taken the Lancaster on an air test and flew down to Welwyn Garden City, where Ernie lived. Owen dropped the nose of the aircraft and made a low pass

Sergeant Frank Watson, wireless operator (extreme left) seen with his first crew headed by Sqn Ldr Charles Woodley, who is standing next to him. (*Author's collection*)

Above left: Sergeant John Sparrow, later warrant officer, was shot down, evaded capture, and was betrayed to the Gestapo after thirty-one days of freedom. (*Author's collection*)

Above right: Sergeant George Allom, bomb aimer, always got a thrill from the low-flying antics performed by his pilot. (*Author's collection*)

Below left: Flight Lieutenant William 'Bill' Prune, XV Squadron mascot. Bill Prune's obituary appeared in a local Suffolk newspaper, following an altercation with a lorry. (*Author's collection*)

Below right: Flying Officer Billy Goat, formerly owned by Flt Lt Len Miller, but later became the XV Squadron Mascot. (*Author's collection*)

Flight Sergeant Kay Godfrey, WRAF (second left), with Section Officer Grace Archer on her left, following their return from a Baedecker trip across Germany and the Low Countries, to see first-hand the destruction wrought by Bomber Command (*Author's collection*)

> over the latter's house. Unfortunately, the aircraft's serial number was recorded and obviously reported, for the minute we got back to the station the skipper was ordered to report to the OC's office.

During his tour of duty with XV Squadron, George Allom, like most of his aviator colleagues, collected many memories, but there were two sorties that he particularly remembered. The first was a daylight operation against oil storage depot at Bordeaux, on 5 August, when the participating crews were ordered to fly at low level. Owen Sylvestre loved it and George Allom remembered it with youthful exuberance:

> We flew at low level to Land's End, on the deck all the way, including flying down the runway of an airfield in the area and out over the cliffs. Dropping down to wave top height, we flew south until we were west of Bordeaux, with sea water splashing up onto my nose blister. Smashing! We climbed to 3,000 feet to bomb the target and then flew north, overland, to home.

The second operation that left a lasting impression on George's mind again included the sea. It occurred on 3 October 1944, when a total of 259 Bomber Command aircraft attacked the sea wall defences on the island of Walcheren, Holland. The squadron detailed eleven Lancasters for the operation.

The aiming point was the wall around the Westkapelle area, which was heavily defended by German coastal batteries guarding the entrance to the River Scheldt. The plan was to flood the area and thus submerge and render non-effective some of the German gun emplacements. The attack was successful and a wide breach was made in the wall. George Allom was, as expected, in the bomb aimer's compartment of ME848 and had an excellent view of the attack:

> We were on a daylight raid bombing the dykes to flood Walcheren Island. It was spectacular watching the water pour through the breaches in the dykes. At Middleburg, some of the houses were standing out above the level of water, as were some of the gun emplacements. Although they were surrounded by water they were still firing like hell.

Those emplacements that had not been deluged with water endeavoured to repel the attack, but it was all in vain. All participating aircraft returned safely to their respective bases.

When reminiscing about their time on an operational squadron during the Second World War, both pilots and members of aircrew will, at some stage, undoubtedly make mention of that gallant and dedicated group who toiled to keep their aircraft fully functioning and in the air: the ground crews. Close bonds were often formed between the aircrew and ground crew of a particular aircraft, but behind the scenes was a vast number of both men and women who were involved in repairing, servicing and preparing the aircraft for their operational sorties, whether it was night or day. Some served away from the aircraft in administrative positions and manual tasks, such as intelligence, administration, motor transport section, the photographic section, maps and charts section, and parachute training and packing sections; the list goes on.

As far as members of the ground crews were concerned, they 'owned' the aircraft, the aircrews only borrowed them to undertake their nightly forages across enemy territory. Having completed all pre-flight inspections, the pilot was required to sign Form 700, as it was known, before the crew chief would release the aircraft into the pilot's custody.

When an aircraft returned from an operational sortie with battle or flak damage, or defective instruments, it was the airframe fitters, instrument fitters, and armourers who all carried out their respective duties in an efficient manner that earned them the respect of everyone, from the station commander down. These men, especially those below the rank of corporal, were affectionately known to many as 'erks'.

Air tests were an everyday occurrence on front line airfields and, in the case of bomber aircraft, often gave the ground crews the opportunity to fly. As with the aircrews, the ground crews also have their memories of flying; Tony Godfrey of Gil Marsh's ground crew was one of them:

> I remember one occasion flying with Gil Marsh on an air test, when two single-engined fighters approached us. They positioned themselves on either side of the Stirling and we identified them as American P-47 Thunderbolts. For a few minutes we flew in formation with them, but it soon became evident they wanted to play games. One of the Thunderbolt pilots waggled his wings at us and Gil Marsh responded by doing the same with the Stirling. The fighter boys obviously opened their throttles, because their aircraft began to pull slightly ahead of us. Not to be outdone Gil applied full throttle to all four Bristol Hercules engines which powered the Stirling. The engines responded and the bomber accelerated away, leaving the American fighter pilots to find somebody else to play with.

On another occasion, when Tony Godfrey was flying with Gil Marsh, their youthful exuberance very nearly got them into trouble, as again, Tony remembered:

> We were flying along reasonably low when somebody on board spotted a hay rick with a number of figures on it, which we took to be Land Army Girls. Gil was urged to give them a bit of a show, and standing the Stirling almost vertically on its wingtip turned the huge bomber back towards them. Gil levelled out and was so low that he was almost cutting the stubble with the propeller blades. As the aircraft approached the hay rick we realised the figures were men, possibly Italian prisoners of war, who either flung themselves to the ground or took to their heels. At the last moment, Gil Marsh pulled back on the control column and lifted the aircraft up and over the great mound of hay. To his horror, and mine, there in front of the aircraft was a row of trees, the tops of which were lined up with the cockpit. Much to our relief the trees disappeared just under the nose of the Stirling.

A less glamorous side of Tony Godfrey's work and certainly in no sense humorous, was the night Gil Marsh's aircraft returned from an attack against Berlin, during which the pilot was severely wounded, and Tony had the unenviable task of hosing out the cockpit floor in order to wash away Gil Marsh's blood.

The majority of Leading Aircraftman Percy Pluck's RAF service was undertaken with XV Squadron, having joined them at RAF Wyton; he remained with the squadron when it relocated to RAF Bourn and then to RAF Mildenhall. Percy, or 'Duke' as he was known to some of his friends, was an aircraft electrician with a wealth of knowledge, having worked on a number of different types of aircraft, including Bristol Blenheims, Vickers Wellingtons, Stirling bombers, and Avro Lancaster bombers. Percy was gifted with a jovial personality and a great sense of fun, which sometimes helped when the realities of war were brought on to the airfield:

> I remember one night the bombers were returning from a raid. As one of the Lancasters was making its final approach an enemy 'intruder' aircraft came in from

> behind him and opened fire with his cannons. The shells slammed into and around the rear turret in which the rear gunner was still sitting. What a mess it made of him.

Death was never far away and could come without any assistance from the enemy, neither was it choosy about rank or status as was witnessed by Percy Pluck, on Monday, 30 August 1943:

> Wing Commander J. D. Stevens, together with a corporal airframe fitter, took off from Mildenhall in a Boulton Paul Defiant aircraft for a local flight. The aircraft stalled, crashed and caught fire. Both men were killed. The fitter was found hanging upside down in the turret.

The aircraft, Defiant N1643, developed engine failure almost immediately after take-off due to a coolant leak, which apparently seeped into the cockpit and affected the pilot.

Flight Lieutenant William Prune and Flying Officer William Goat were two other characters on XV Squadron who, rumour has it, got their fair share of flights. William Prune, a Bulldog, was the much-loved squadron mascot. Although it is recorded he had his own logbook and undertook at least fourteen flights, no one would ever lay claim to have taken him aloft as part of their crew.

Apart from being included in the squadron's group photographs or crews' end of tour photographs, Bill Prune's favourite pastime was to chase motorcycles and endeavour to bite the front tyre, a ritual that was only concluded when the rider was dislodged from his machine. Unfortunately, Bill tried this trick on a lorry, which duly ended his career when he ran in front of it.

William Goat ('Billy' as he was familiarly known) was, as his name implies, a goat, or rather a kid. His guardian was Flight Lieutenant Len Miller, DFC, who acquired him after an alcohol-fuelled party. The young goat rarely left Len's side, especially if the latter was wandering around the airfield. Sometimes, on air tests, Len would take Billy along for the ride, much to the annoyance of the ground crews, one of whom expressed his displeasure:

> The goat developed a liking for Empire Tape, which was used for binding or repairing cables. He went on a few flights but was grounded after eating the tape during one of the flights, which of course we then had to replace all over again.

Len also remembered his friend with affection: 'We, as a crew, enjoyed Billy's company and would all "act the goat" when we were with him. We would get down on all fours and headbutt him, a game which Billy thought great fun'. Following the loss of Bill Prune, and after Flight Lieutenant Miller had been shot down, the squadron adopted Billy as its mascot, although some crews tried to claim him as their own.

The Women's Auxiliary Air Force (WAAF) made an enormous contribution towards the war effort in general and the Royal Air Force in particular. They carried out their work with dexterity and enthusiasm, in the knowledge that they were helping the cause towards victory, freedom, and peace. Although some WAAFs managed to get airborne in the bombers, such flights were against regulations and unofficial. However, at the end of the war, all members of Bomber Command ground crew got the opportunity to fly on the bombers over France, Belgium, Holland, and Germany. These flights were known as 'Baedeker' flights and gave members of ground crew, in all the various sections and departments, the opportunity to see the damage inflicted in occupied Europe and Germany by Bomber Command. One lady who took advantage of this opening was Flight Sergeant Kay Godfrey, a senior NCO in the Intelligence Section:

> I was lucky to go on one of these flights with Section Officer Grace Archer and one or two others. It was wonderful; I lay on my stomach in the nose of the aircraft for most of the trip. The heart-rending sight was over Holland, where in some places all one could see were church steeples and tree tops, following the flood to keep the Germans out. On our return, we had our photograph taken with the crew.

Hostilities in Europe officially ceased on 8 May 1945. The whole country celebrated and RAF Mildenhall was no different. Kay Godfrey was at Mildenhall and always remembered the celebrations:

> I was at Mildenhall on VE night. Everything was quiet on the WRAF site so thought I would take a walk across to the main camp. What pandemonium! The boys were going wild and had started a large bonfire outside the barrack block. I also saw some of our girls there, but decided to ignore the fact. Group Captain Ken Batchelor, the Station Commander, was trying to restore order and was brandishing a pistol to no avail. He then shouted at me to get my girls to bed. I told him that was impossible on my own, and suggested we got them singing to calm them down. When I returned to the WRAF site, I found somebody had started a fire there. I put it out with an extinguisher and gave them a stern telling-off, reminding them that it was still work as usual in the morning.

The war in Europe was over but for those who participated in the long fight the memories would remain. It is thanks to the many veterans who have shared their experiences of the Second World War that their stories can be passed on to future generations.

APPENDIX I

XV Squadron List of Awards 1939–1945

(I) denotes granting of an immediate award
(NYHL) denotes New Year's Honours List
(BHL) denotes Birthday Honours List

Name	Rank	Award	Gazetted Date
Alderson, Peter	Sgt	DFM	22 November 1940
Aleandri, Anthony A.	Fg Off.	DFC	13 April 1945
Allen, George	WO	DFC	17 October 1944
Anderson, Sidney A.	WO	DFC	25 May 1945
Angus, RCAF, John	FS	DFM	18 February 1944
Armstrong, RCAF, Arley W.	FS	DFM	14 November 1944
Bagan, Michael J.	WO	DFC	17 April 1945
Baigent, RNZAF, Cyril H.	AFL	DFC	2 November 1942
(Later Acting Wing Commander C. H. Baigent, DSO, DFC and Bar, RNZAF)			
Baker, Kenneth J.	Sgt	DFM	15 October 1943 (I)
Baker, RCAF, Richard P.	AFL	DFC	13 October 1943
Baker, William C.	Sgt	DFM	22 November 1940
Ball, RAAF, Clive W.	Plt Off.	DFC	27 March 1945
Banks, RAAF, Ronald R.	WO	DFC	17 April 1945
Barford, Alfred E.	FS	DFM	16 February 1945
Barr, Leslie R.	AFL	DFC	26 May 1942
Barr, Leslie R.	Flt Lt	Bar to DFC	7 August 1942
Barrass, John	Plt Off.	DFC	13 August 1943
Barrett, Arty. E.	FS	DFM	23 March 1945
Barron, RNZAF, James F.	FS	DFM	26 May 1942
Bell, RAAF, Ronald J.	Plt Off.	DFC	12 December 1944
Bell, Walter J.	AFL	DFC	14 July 1944

Bennitt, Neville A.	AFO	DFC	7 August 1942
Bentley, Leslie	Sgt	DFM	16 November 1943 (I)
Bicknell, Stanley	FS	DFM	13 October 1944
Bishop, Douglas R.	Sgt	DFM	8 December 1944
Boards, Douglas	Sgt	DFM	20 August 1943 (I)
Boggis, Peter J.	Fg Off.	DFC	9 January 1942
Bolduc, RCAF, Williard J.	Plt Off.	DFC	30 June 1944
Bone, DFM, David	AFL	DFC	17 July 1945
Box, Alfred J.	Sgt	DFM	13 September 1940
Briggs, Edward W.	Sgt	DFM	10 February 1941 (I)
Brooks, Oliver V.	Plt Off.	DFC	19 May 1944
Brown, John H.	WO	DFC	17 April 1945
Brown, Victor W.	FS	DFM	17 July 1945
Buchanan, RAAF, Ivor S.	AFL	DFC	13 April 1945
Bull, DFM, Bernard C.	Plt Off.	DFC	25 May 1945
Burns, Norman W.	AFO	DFC	25 September 1945
Burrett, John R.	Plt Off.	DFC	20 February 1945
Bushell, Jack R.	Sgt	DFM	6 June 1941 (I)
Bysouth, Henry T.	FS	DFM	22 May 1945
Cage, RAAF, Vernon	AFL	DFC	22 May 1945
Cameron, RNZAF, Robert W.	ASL	DFC	13 April 1945
Camp, Philip	Sgt	DFM	22 October 1940
Cantrell, RCAF, George. A.	Fg Off.	DFC	13 October 1944
Capel, RAAF, Daniel L.	Plt Off.	DFC	20 February 1945
Carden, Patrick D.	ASL	DFC	8 December 1944
Child, Percy R.	FS	DFM	13 October 1044
Clark, Denis E.	Flt Lt	DFC	12 January 1943
Clark, Frank	Sgt	DFM	20 April 1943
Claydon, Geoffrey M.	AFL	DFC	14 July 1944
Cochrane, Archibald G.	AFO	DFC	22 August 1941
Cook, Reginald J.	Sgt	DFM	13 February 1942
Cope, DFM, John	AFL	DFC	20 April 1943
Cope, Philip H.	Plt Off.	DFC	18 February 1944
Cowell, RAAF, John	AFO	DFC	13 October 1944
Cox, Joseph	Wg Cdr	DFC	24 December 1940
Cox, Douglas R.	AFL	DFC	16 January 1945
Craddock, Arthur R.	AFL	DFC	14 June 1943
Craven, David	Sgt	DFM	15 June 1943
Crowe, RNZAF, Leonard W.	Fg Off.	DFC	20 July 1945
Cunningham, John R.	Sgt	DFM	27 October 1942
Curtis, Paul	Sgt	DFM	29 December 1942
Davis, Ronald F.	Sgt	DFM	19 July 1940 (I)

Dengate, RAAF, Frank H.	AFL	DFC	13 October 1944
Denton, DFM, F.	WO	DFC	20 February 1945
Devine, Peter	Sgt	DFM	18 May 1943
de Willimoff, RNZAF, Jesse J.	AFL	DFC	11 April 1944
Diggins, William W.	Sgt	DFM	2 October 1942 (I)
Dollisson, RAAF, John T.	AFL	DFC	22 May 1945
Dorie, RCAF, John E.	FS	DFM	13 August 1943
Dorsett, Kenneth T.	Sgt	DFM	17 April 1945
Doyle, Denis P.	Sgt	BEM	17 March 1941
Dunlop, Kenneth	Fg Off.	DFC	25 May 1945
Du Preez, Cornelius J.	Sgt	DFM	15 May 1942 (I)
Egri, RCAF, William E.	FS	DFM	15 December 1942(I)
Elias, Lancelot B.	Fg Off.	DFC	13 October 1944
Ell, RCAF, Joseph	Fg Off.	DFC	14 November 1944
England, Anthony W.	Fg Off.	DFC	17 July 1945
Escreet, Raymond F.	Sgt	DFM	15 June 1943
Fabian, DFC, RNZAF, John C.	AFL	Bar to DFC	19 May 1944
Ferguson, William. M.	AFO	DFC	19 January 1945
Fisher, Stanley	Fg Off.	DFC	13 October 1944
French, John W.	AFL	DFC	22 May 1945
Gabel, RCAF, Goldwin W.	Plt Off.	DFC	15 October 1943
Galley, John G.	Sgt	DFM	22 August 1941
Gallop, George	Flt Lt	DFC	8 December 1944
Gaylor, Joseph W.	Sgt	DFM	5 May 1943 (I)
George, Lionel H.	Fg Off.	DFC	19 May 1944
George, William H.	AFL	DFC	22 October 1940
Gericke, RAAF, Philip K.	FS	DFM	15 February 1944 (I)
Gibson, DFC, John A.	ASL	DSO	16 March 1944
Gilmour, Robert S.	Plt Off.	DFC	22 November 1940
Goodall, RCAF, Gordon L.	FS	DFM	12 January 1943
Grimshaw, Edwin	Plt Off.	DFC	17 October 1944
Grover, Edmund F.	Plt Off.	DFC	17 October 1944
Halkett, RCAF, Alexander	FS	DFM	6 November 1942 (I)
Hall, (RCAF), William	AFL	DFC	23 March 1945
Hamilton, RCAF, Frank	FS	DFM	15 December 1942 (I)
Hardy, Richard H.	FS	DFM	9 January 1942 (I)
Haycock, Dennis H.	AFL	DFC	1 June 1945
Hayden, RNZAF, Andrew A.	Flt Lt	DFC	17 July 1945
Hayles, Raymond P.	FS	DFM	15 February 1944 (I)
Hearne, Richard A.	FS	DFM	14 November 1944
Henzel, RNZAF, Edward S.	Fg Off.	DFC	17 October 1944
Hislop, John	Fg Off.	DFC	16 February 1945

Houlgrave, Clifford	FS	DFM	17 July 1945
Hunter, Robert E.	LAC	DFM	9 July 1940
Hurt, RNZAF, Homer C.	Fg Off.	DFC	20 February 1945
Irwin, RNZAF, William A.	Plt Off.	DFC	20 April 1943
Jackson, Francis C.	Sgt	DFM	20 April 1943
Jennings, RAAF, Roy D.	AFO	DFC	25 May 1945
Jessop, William	Sgt	DFM	22 October 1940
Johnston, RNZAF, Maurice	AFL	DFC	17 October 1944
Jones, Evan T.	Fg Off.	DFC	8 December 1944
Jones, Harold A.	Fg Off.	DFC	20 July 1945
Jones, Henry R. (BEF)	Cpl	DFM	23 July 1940
Jones, Robert J.	FS	BEM	24 September 1941
Kendall, William H.	Plt Off.	DFC	27 March 1945
Klufas, RCAF, William J.	AFL	DFC	15 October 1943
Lamason, DFC, RNZAF, Philip J.	ASL	Bar to DFC	27 May 1944
Lambert, Ronald	WO	DFC	26 May 1942
Lawrence, Kenneth A.	Flt Lt	DFC	18 January 1944
Lay, DFC and Bar Douglas J.	AWC	DSO	3 December 1942
Lithgow, SAAF, James A.	Fg Off.	DFC	16 February 1943
Lowe, Desmond	WO	DFC	17 April 1945
Lown, Reginald F	AFL	DFC	16 November 1943
MacDonald, John C.	AWC	DFC	9 July 1940
MacDonald, DFC	WC	AFC	11 June 1942 (BHL)
MacDonald, DFC, AFC, John C.	AGC	Bar to DFC	16 March 1943
Macfarlane, Nigel	AWC	DSO	17 July 1945
Macmonagle, RCAF, William D.	FS	DFM	12 January 1943 (I)
Mahler, John N.	ASL	DFC	22 November 1940
Mansel-Pleydell, David	Fg Off.	DFC	19 May 1944
Marpole, John	Flt Lt	DFC	22 May 1945
Marriott, RAAF, Louis H.	AFL	DFC	22 May 1945
Marshall, RAAF, Laurence W.	Fg Off.	DFC	13 April 1945
McAlpine, William E.	Plt Off.	DFC	29 December 1942
McCaffery, RCAF, Elmore H.	AFL	DFC	6 November 1942
McFadden, RAAF, Desmond R.	Fg Off.	DFC	27 March 1945
McLachlan, RAAF, Edward W.	Plt Off.	DFC	20 February 1945
Meades, Harry	Sgt	DFM	2 October 1942 (I)
Megginson, Robert R.	Sgt	DFM	22 October 1940
Megginson, DFM, Robert	ASL	DFC	15 October 1943
Menaul, Stewart, W.	ASL	DFC	22 August 1941
Menaul, DFC, Stewart W.	AWC	AFC	1 January 1943 (NYHL)
(Later Air Vice-Marshal Stewart Menaul, CB, CBE, DFC, AFC, MiDx5)			
Mephan, Douglas W.	Sgt	DFM	13 July 1943

Midgley, RCAF, Durward	AFL	DFC	31 December 1943
Miles, RCAF, Harold T.	Fg Off	DFC	6 November 1942
Miller, Leonard A.	Plt Off.	DFC	22 February
Mitchell, RCAF, Francis E.	Sgt	DFM	12 January 1943
Moore, RAAF, Edward J.	AFL	DFC	14 July 1944
Morris, William M.	ASL	DFC	18 July 1941
Muirhead, Albert W.	Fg Off.	DFC	12 October 1944
Munns, Robert	Fg Off.	DFC	10 February 1943
Musgrove, RCAF, Gerald	Fg Off.	DFC	12 December 1944
Nettleton, Peter A.	AFL	DFC	16 January 1945
Noonan, RNZAF, Russell T.	FS	DFM	11 June 1943
Oakeshott, Alan R.	AFL	DFC	30 July 1940
O'Conner RCAF, Howard J.	FS	DFM	7 May 1943 (I)
O'Donnell, Charles A.	Sgt	DFM	22 October 1940
Ogilvie Bruce B.	Wg Cdr	DSO	9 January 1942
Orchard, RAAF, Edgar	WO	DFC	17 November 1944
Ordish, C. Brian	AFL	DFC	9 February 1943
Ostler, Robert	AFL	DFC	20 April 1945
Palmer, RNZAF, Thomas R.	Fg Off.	DFC	17 April 1945
Parke, William C.	AFL	DFC	8 December 1944
Parkins, Dennis A.	AFL	DFC	23 June 1942
Pavely, Robert	ASGT	DFM	22 November 1940
Pawley, Norman J.	Sgt	DFM	20 July 1943 (I)
Payne, Barry G.	ASL	DFC	13 April 1945
Pearce, Stanley	Sgt	DFM	20 April 1943
Pepper, Maurice S.	Sgt	DFM	10 February 1942 (I)
Perry, RAAF, Wesble K.	AFL	DFC	12 February 1945
Peters, RAAF, Kenneth W.	Sgt	DFM	14 May 1943
Phillips, Eric J.	Fg Off.	DFC	15 October 1943
Phillips, Robert H.	Fg Off.	DFC	29 December 1942
Pidsley, SAAF, Douglas W.	Maj.	DFC	10 November 1942
Pierce, RCAF, Thomas W.	Fg Off.	DFC	12 January 1943
Pincott, Kenneth M.	FS	DFM	19 May 1944
Poole, William T.	Plt Off.	DFC	19 January 1945
Potter, George A.	Sgt	DFM	13 July 1943
Powell, Ernest G.	Sgt	DFM	12 January 1943
Prewer, Walter F.	WO	DFC	25 May 1945
Putt, Albert J.	AFL	DFC	23 September 1941
Rainton, Dennis	FS	DFM	14 November 1944
Raymond, Cuthbert	AFL	DFC	6 June 1941
Redhead, Sidney C.	Sgt	DFM	13 September 1940
Reid, RAAF, Victor C.	WO	DFC	17 November 1944

Renner, RNZAF Irvine W.	Plt Off.	DFC	14 May 1943
Roach, RCAF, Wilfred	Sgt	DFM	18 August 1943
Rudall, H. T.	F/O	CDG	1945
Russell, J. V.	FS	CGM	25 October 1943
Sargent, Roderick A.	Plt Off.	DFC	17 October 1944
Schofield, Arthur	Plt Off.	DFC	20 July 1945
Scott, David R.	AFL	DFC	31 December 1943
Sellick, DFC, Boyd D.	Wg Cdr	Bar to DFC	26 May 1942
Sellwood, RAAF, Alan C.	AFO	DFC	25 May 1945
Shiells, James R.	FS	DFM	1 June 1945
Shoemaker, RCAF, Wilbert A.	Plt Off.	DFC	7 August 1942
Sim, RAAF, Gordon L.	Plt Off.	DFC	17 April 1945
Sleeman, RAAF, John. W.	AFL	DFC	13 April 1945
Smale, RCAF, John L.	Sgt	DFM	17 August 1943
Sneddon, Walter	FS	DFM	17 October 1944
Soderquist, RCAF, Delbert	FS	DFM	15 December 1942 (I)
Spannier, RCAF, Edward	WOII	DFC	17 October 1944
Sparks, RNZAF, Mervyn	AFL	DFC	13 October 1944
Stephens, William J.	Sgt	DFM	30 July 1940
Stewart, RAAF, Sidney W.	AFL	DFC	16 February 1945
Stokes, Geoffrey W.	AFL	DFC	24 October 1944
Stone, Raymond A.	Sgt	DFM	9 July 1940
Stubbins, Geoffrey A.	Plt Off.	DFC	25 May 1945
Sutcliffe, John	Sgt	DFM	30 July 1940
Swales, DFM, Ian	Fg Off.	DFC	13 March 1942
Swent, RCAF, William H.	Plt Off.	DFC	19 January 1944
Sykes, Arthur K.	AFL	DFC	13 August 1943
Sylvestre, Owen O.	FS	DFM	20 February 1945
Tait, RCAF, George B.	Plt Off.	DFC	15 June 1943
Tanton, Peter A.	Sgt	DFM	19 August 1941(I)
Taylor, Albert E.	Sgt	DFM	30 July 1940
Thomas, Glyn	FS	DFM	27 March 1945
Thomas, RAAF, Norman L.	FS	DFM	16 November 1943 (I)
Thompson, Charles E.	Plt Off.	DFC	19 July 1940
Tilson, RCAF, Henry 'Hank'	Fg Off.	DFC	1 January 1943
Towse, Wilfred	Sgt	DFM	10 July 1943 (I)
Trehearne, Vernon	Sgt	DFM	30 July 1940
Trent, RNZAF, Leonard H.	AFL	DFC	9 July 1940
Turner, RAAF, William D.	Fg Off.	DFC	27 March 1945
Vernieux, RAFO, Cyril A.	Fg Off.	DFC	9 January 1942
Ware, Geoffrey	Plt Off.	DFC	14 June 1943
Warren, RCAF, Earle F.	FS	DFM	12 January 1943 (I)

Watkins, DFC, DFM, William	AWC	DSO	7 November 1944
Watson, Frederick J.	Sgt	DFM	20 August 1943 (I)
Watson, Francis J.	Plt Off.	DFC	25 May 1945
Waugh, Robert	Fg Off.	DFC	20 August 1943
Webster, Peter F.	ASL	DFC	9 July 1940
Wellings, John	FS	DFM	17 November 1944
Whiskie, Leslie	FS	DFM	25 September 1945
Wilkie, RNZAF, Hugh C.	AFL	DFC	27 July 1943
Williams, John	Fg Off.	DFC	24 April 1945
Woodhouse, William J.	Plt Off.	DFC	17 October 1944
Woodruff, Dennis C.	AFL	DFC	15 February 1944
Wright, DFC, Frederick	Flt Lt.	Bar to DFC	13 April 1945
Wright, Herbert H.	Sgt	DFM	29 December 1942
York, John R.	Fg Off.	DFC	13 October 1944

APPENDIX II

XV Squadron Second World War Roll of Honour

All dates of death are those recorded by the Commonwealth War Graves Commission.

Adams, Ernest	Sgt	F/E	RAFVR	08.05.44	19
(The above-named casualty was born Ernest Richards.)					
Adkins, Henry	Sgt	B/A	RAFVR	08.12.42	31
Aiken, Ronald	Sgt	A/G	RAFVR	21.10.41	24
Aitken, Robertson	W/O	A/G	RAFVR	08.06.44	22
Allen, Reginald	P/O	Pilot	RAFVR	12.06.43	Unk.
Amies, Alan	F/L	Pilot	RAFVR	12.05.44	21
Amos, Orison	F/S	Nav	RNZAF	03.03.43	30
Anderton, James	Sgt	Pilot	RAFVR	23.09.43	28
Andrews, Ronald	Sgt	Unk.	RAFVR	13.01.44	21
Appleby, Eric	Sgt	F/E	RAFVR	29.01.44	20
Apps, Percy	F/S	W/AG	RAF	19.09.42	21
Archibald, William	P/O	Nav	RAFVR	14.02.43	Unk.
Armer, George	Sgt	Nav	RAFVR	02.03.43	30
Armstrong, James	F/S	W/Op	RAAF	08.06.44	22
Arnott, Kenneth	P/O	Obs	RAFVR	16.07.42	22
Arnott, Patrick	Sgt	B/A	RAFVR	26.05.43	19
Ashcroft, Francis	F/S	Nav	RAFVR	16.07.44	Unk.
Ashdown, Richard	F/S	Pilot	RAF	26.02.43	21
Ashill, Rev. Denis	S/L	Chap.	RAFVR	29.12.42	30
Atkinson, Sam	Sgt	F/E	RAFVR	16.09.42	19
Attenborrow, Eric	Sgt	W/Op	RAFVR	16.07.43	22
Austin, Ronald	LAC	A/G	RAF	25.05.40	21
Avent, Douglas	Sgt	Obs	RAF	12.05.40	22

Bagg, Arthur	F/S	Obs	RCAF	09.03.43	22
Baillie, John	Sgt	F/E	RAF	09.05.42	26
Baker, Herbert	Sgt	Nav	RAFVR	12.05.44	Unk.
Ball, John	F/L	Pilot	RAF	08.08.44	24
Bamber, Hugh	P/O	Pilot	RAF	07.07.40	19
Bance, Eric	Sgt	F/E	RAFVR	08.12.42	30
Bannister, Harry	F/S	Pilot	RAFVR	11.09.42	31
Banyer, James	F/S	B/A	RAFVR	05.05.43	33
Barber, George	Sgt	Pilot	RAFVR	04.07.43	21
Barkshire, Albert	Sgt	A/G	RAFVR	08.08.44	37
Barnes, Robert	F/S	W/AG	RAFVR	23.04.44	22
Barrett, Denis	Sgt	Pilot	RAFVR	16.07.42	21
Barrett, William	F/S	W/AG	RAF	13.08.41	26
Barrie, Charles	Sgt	A/G	RAFVR	29.10.42	22
Barton-Smith, BSc, Hugh	F/S	Pilot	RAFVR	28.08.42	26
Bassett, Thomas	F/O	Pilot	RAF	12.05.40	22
Batchellor, Cecil	Sgt	Obs	RAFVR	29.06.41	23
Bate, Howard	Sgt	F/E	RAFVR	16.11.44	25
Batham, Raymond	Sgt	A/G	RAFVR	29.01.44	19
Baxter, William	Sgt	A/G	RAF	18.05.40	22
Beard, Harold	Sgt	Obs	RAF	04.08.40	24
Beare, Royston	Sgt	Pilot	RAFVR	15.06.45	22
Beazley, Harry	P/O	B/A	RCAF	08.06.44	26
Bebbington, Richard	Sgt	Pilot	RAFVR	03.09.42	24
Beck, George	Sgt	B/A	RAFVR	31.07.43	20
Bee, Charles	F/S	A/G	RCAF	19.09.42	22
Bell, John	Sgt	A/G	RAFVR	11.06.44	20
Bell, DFC. Walter	F/L	Pilot	RAFVR	21.07.44	25
Belton, Robert	Sgt	A/G	RAFVR	04.09.43	24
Benjamin, Thomas	Sgt	A/G	RAFVR	08.05.44	21
Benny, John	Sgt	Pilot	RAFVR	27.09.43	Unk.
Benson, Charles	P/O	Pilot	RNZAF	20.02.44	29
Bente, John	Sgt	F/E	RAF	18.12.41	27
Bentley, Sidney	Sgt	F/E	RAF	13.10.41	Unk.
Bergin, Joseph	F/S	Nav	RNZAF	21.01.44	33
Bessette, Bertie	F/S	A/G	RCAF	16.04.43	21
Beswick, Arthur	Sgt	A/G	RAF	29.10.42	21
Beverton, Harry	F/S	A/G	RAFVR	12.09.44	Unk.
Bidgood, Harry	Sgt	W/AG	RAFVR	09.03.42	19
Billington, Edward	F/O	B/A	RAFVR	22.03.43	21
Birchall, Albert	P/O	A/G	RCAF	19.09.42	Unk.
Bird, Peter	P/O	Pilot	RAFVR	11.05.41	20

Blackburn, John	Sgt	Nav	RAFVR	17.04.43	Unk.
Blackhall, William	LAC	Gdcw	RAF	13.06.43	34

(Died of malaria in Solomon Islands while on attachment to No. 1 Fighter Maintenance Unit, RNZAF.)

Blackmore, Lester	Sgt	W/AG	RAFVR	13.08.42	23

(A probable error in the XV Squadron ORB records that Sgt L Blackmore and Sgt D Jeans, who flew with the same crew, have the same service number: 798522.)

Blanchard, Rex	Sgt	A/G	RAFVR	03.10.43	19
Bland, Ernest	Sgt	A/G	RAFVR	26.03.44	20
Blignaut, Jochemus	Sgt	Pilot	RAFVR	08.12.42	Unk.
Bliss, John	Sgt	W/Op	RAFVR	18.11.43	20
Bloomer, Peter	Sgt	Obs	RAF	25.05.40	22
Bond, William	Sgt	Pilot	RAFVR	30.05.42	26
Booth, Alfred	F/S	B/A	RAFVR	16.11.44	22
Booth, Neville	F/L	Pilot	RAFVR	18.05.42	25
Booth, Reginald	Sgt	W/AG	RAFVR	01.10.42	Unk.
Borrett, Arnold	Sgt	A/G	RAAF	19.02.43	25
Bottomley, Handley	Sgt	A/G	RAFVR	24.08.43	Unk.
Bovett, George	F/O	W/Op	RAFVR	08.08.44	Unk.
Bowden, Peter	F/O	B/A	RAF	18.11.43	20
Bowen, David	Sgt	F/E	RAFVR	27.09.43	21
Bowen, John	Sgt	F/E	RAFVR	21.04.44	20
Bowen, William	Sgt	F/E	RAFVR	02.03.43	27
Bowers, Henry	Sgt	W/Op	RAFVR	15.08.40	23
Bowers, Robert	Sgt	A/G	RAFVR	18.11.43	19
Bowyer, Clifford	S/L	Pilot	RAFVR	14.05.43	21
Bradford, Jack	P/O	Pilot	RAFVR	31.08.43	23
Bragg, Wilfred	Sgt	F/E	RAF	08.04.43	23
Brandt, Augustus	Sgt	Obs	RAAF	07.04.42	30
Brennan, James	Sgt	A/G	RAFVR	21.07.44	23
Brennan, Patrick	F/L	A/G	RAFVR	19.02.43	Unk.
Briggs, James	Sgt	A/G	RAFVR	24.03.44	21
Brock, Derek	Sgt	F/E	RAFVR	31.08.43	20
Brockett, William	Sgt	F/E	RAFVR	27.08.44	30
Brodie, William	Sgt	Pilot	RAF	09.05.42	22
Bromley, Thomas	Sgt	A/G	RAF	17.04.43	22
Brook, Philip	F/S	A/G	RAAF	01.09.43	20
Brookes, BA. Joseph	Sgt	Obs	RAFVR	06.11.42	27
Brookfield, Thomas	Sgt	A/G	RAFVR	21.07.44	21
Brophey, Burton	Sgt	A/G	RCAF	26.03.44	19
Brown, Dennis	Sgt	Nav	RAFVR	31.07.43	21
Brown, Douglas	Sgt	F/E	RAFVR	29.06.41	21

Brown, Herbert	Sgt	F/E	RAF	04.05.43	Unk.
Brown, James	P/O	Pilot	RAFVR	16.09.42	22
Brown, Maurice	F/S	A/G	RAFVR	21.04.44	20
Brown, Roy	W/O	Pilot	RAFVR	16.01.45	25
(Died in the Far East and buried in Taukkyan War Cemetery, Rangoon, Burma.)					
Brown, Thomas	Sgt	F/E	RAF	19.09.42	24
Broyd, Stanley	Sgt	F/E	RAF	08.08.41	33
Bryne, Philip	Sgt	F/E	RAF	26.07.42	28
Buchanan, James	Sgt	F/E	RAF	01.10.42	21
Bunce, Gordon	F/O	Pilot	RAF	18.12.41	Unk.
Burcham, Alfred	P/O	Nav	RAFVR	29.01.44	26
Burgess, James	Sgt	A/G	RNZAF	06.11.42	31
Burke, Wilfred	S/L	Pilot	RAF	08.06.40	31
Burkill, Clifford	F/S	W/Op	RAFVR	09.03.443	34
Burrell, George	Sgt	W/AG	RAFVR	20.06.44	Unk.
Burton, Frederick	Sgt	A/G	RAFVR	11.04.43	20
Burtt, Marcus Heppell	Sgt	W/AG	RAFVR	27.08.42	Unk.
Busby, Peter	Sgt	F/E	RAFVR	12.08.42	18
Bushell, DFM. Jack	P/O	A/G	RAFVR	19.07.41	33
Butcher, Sidney	Sgt	A/G	RAFVR	06.11.42	20
Butler, Robert	P/O	Pilot	RAFVR	21.01.44	23
Butterworth, John	Sgt	W/AG	RAFVR	18.05.42	22
Cairns, John	Sgt	A/G	RAFVR	12.05.44	20
Calder, James	P/O	Pilot	RNZAF	18.11.43	25
Campbell, Daniel	P/O	Obs	RNZAF	11.04.41	25
Campbell, Donald	F/S	A/G	RCAF	26.06.43	20
Campbell, DFC. James	F/O	Nav	RAFVR	01.11.44	23
Campbell, Robert	F/O	Pilot	RAAF	23.07.41	27
Canday, Charles	Sgt	A/G	RAFVR	06.07.44	37
Cantwell, Christopher	Sgt	A/G	RAFVR	15.06.44	24
Care, Donald	Sgt	B/A	RAFVR	02.03.43	21
Carlyle, William	Sgt	Unk	RAF	10.03.45	24
(Possibly on attachment—name and squadron recorded on the Malta Memorial)					
Carmichael, Ernest	Sgt	A/G	RAFVR	16.07.44	19
Carrott, James	F/S	Nav	RAFVR	26.02.44	21
Carruthers, Carl	F/S	W/AG	RCAF	09.03.42	21
Carson, Lawrence	F/O	B/A	RCAF	19.02.43	29
Carter, John	W/OII	A/G	RCAF	07.10.43	20
Caselton, Victor	Sgt	F/E	RAFVR	04.09.43	20
Cash, Noel	Sgt	A/G	RAFVR	19.05.42	Unk.
Cato, Hugh	Sgt	Pilot	RAAF	05.11.44	21
Cavanagh, William	LAC	W/Op	RAF	12.05.40	22

Caveney, Thomas	Sgt	A/G	RAFVR	03.03.43	20
Chalker, Charles	Sgt	F/E	RAF	04.07.43	20
Chalmers, Frederick	F/O	B/A	RCAF	20.02.44	21
Chambers, William	Sgt	A/G	RAFVR	30.05.42	21
Champ, Wilfred	Sgt	W/Op	RAFVR	12.06.43	21
Chancellor, BA Roland	P/O	Unk.	RAFVR	18.12.41	24
Chandler, William	F/S	B/A	RAAF	25.05.44	20
Channer, Richard	Sgt	B/A	RAFVR	27.04.41	24
Chapman, Kenneth	F/S	Pilot	RNZAF	06.11.42	24
Chapman, MiDx2, Maurice	F/O	Pilot	RAFVR	26.06.43	24
Chapman, Paul	F/L	Pilot	RAF	18.05.40	23
Charbonneau, Ivan	F/S	Pilot	RCAF	09.05.42	20
Chatteris, William	F/O	Nav	RAFVR	10.03.45	25
Chave, Owen	F/L	Pilot	RAFVR	14.02.43	30
Childs, Jack	F/S	Nav	RAFVR	18.11.43	33
Childs, John	F/L	Pilot	RAFVR	28.07.43	21
Christie, Charles	F/S	B/A	RCAF	13.01.44	24
Church, Cecil	Sgt	Nav	RAFVR	22.03.45	23
Clarke, Ronald	F/O	Pilot	RAF	11.06.40	20
Clarke, George	P/O	Pilot	RAFVR	27.01.44	Unk.
Clayton. Henry	Sgt	A/G	RAFVR	16.11.44	24
Cleaver, Donald	Cpl	Gdcw	RAFVR	29.10.42	36
Clegg, Herbert	Sgt	Obs	RAFVR	27.08.42	28
Close, James	Sgt	Nav	RAFVR	04.07.43	21
Cobby, Arthur	Sgt	F/E	RAF	31.07.43	21
Cobell, Walter	Sgt	A/G	RAF	13.04.42	Unk.
Cockburn, William	F/S	W/AG	RAF	23.07.41	Unk.
Colbourn, Cecil	Sgt	Obs	RAF	18.05.40	26
Colbourne, Victor	P/O	Pilot	RAF	13.10.41	Unk.
Cole, Edward	F/O	B/A	RCAF	23.09.43	20
Cole, James	LAC	Gdcw	RAFVR	30.08.43	28
Cole, Raymond	Sgt	W/AG	RAFVR	27.09.43	21
Collins, Norman	Sgt	Nav	RAFVR	24.08.43	Unk.
Condron, John	Sgt	W/Op	RAFVR	26.06.43	23
Conn, William	Sgt	W/AG	RAFVR	14.08.41	27
Cook, James	Sgt	F/E	RAF	14.02.43	34
Cooley, Peter	Sgt	A/G	RAFVR	22.03.45	20
Coop, Samuel	Sgt	Obs	RAFVR	03.09.42	Unk.
Cooper, Ernest	LAC	W/AG	RAF	12.05.40	20
Cooper, Francis	F/S	Pilot	RAFVR	07.04.42	Unk.
Cope. George	Sgt	W/Op	RAFVR	22.03.45	21
Corbett, John	Sgt	W/AG	RAFVR	08.08.41	24

Cordell, Ronald	Sgt	Nav	RAFVR	27.09.43	20
Cornell, Eric	P/O	Pilot	RAFVR	24.08.43	21
Cowen, Leon	Sgt	F/E	RAF	16.09.42	Unk.
Cowie, James	F/L	Pilot	RCAF	09.02.45	22
Cowlrick, Andrew	W/O	Pilot	RNZAF	03.06.42	26
Crapp, Francis	Sgt	Nav	RAFVR	08.12.42	20
Crawford, Bernard	F/O	Pilot	RNZAF	19.02.43	26
Creed, William	Sgt	A/G	RAFVR	03.09.42	25
Crighton, Frederick	Sgt	W/AG	RAFVR	03.06.42	21
Criswick, Maurice	Sgt	A/G	RAFVR	04.07.43	31
Crone, John	F/O	Pilot	RAAF	17.01.45	21
Cronk, Gavin	W/OII	B/A	RCAF	12.05.44	29
Cross, William	F/S	Pilot	RCAF	09.03.42	20
Crowe, Robert	Sgt	A/G	RAFVR	25.07.44	20
Crozier, Alexander	F/S	W/AG	RNZAF	23.06.43	25
Cully, Wilbert	F/S	A/G	RAFVR	28.04.44	22
Curry, David	Sgt	F/E	RAFVR	18.11.43	25
Curtis, Eric	P/O	Pilot	RAFVR	22.07.43	Unk.
Dale, Herbert	W/C	Pilot	RAF	11.05.41	33
Dalton. Frank	Sgt	W/Op	RAFVR	04.07.43	21
Davidson, Frank	F/S	W/AG	RCAF	19.09.42	21
Davie, James	F/S	A/G	RCAF	04.07.43	28
Davies, Kenneth	Sgt	F/E	RAF	18.07.41	22
Davis, Frederick	Sgt	A/G	RAFVR	29.06.43	22
Davis, Joseph	F/S	Pilot	RAFVR	26.02.44	23
Davis, Norman	Sgt	W/Op	RAFVR	11.06.44	23
Davis, Roy	Sgt	F/E	RAF	22.06.43	20
Davis, Vincent	F/O	Pilot	RAAF	04.12.44	22
Dawson, Leon	Sgt	A/G	RCAF	12.06.43	20
Dawson, Thomas	Sgt	A/G	RAFVR	28.07.43	27
Dawson-Jones, Francis	F/O	Pilot	RAF	18.05.40	23
Day, Peter	F/O	Nav	RAFVR	09.02.45	21
Dean, William	Sgt	F/E	RAFVR	26.03.44	20
Dee, William	Sgt	F/E	RAFVR	22.03.45	20
Dench, Francis	P/O	Pilot	RAF	13.08.40	22
Devereux, Sidney	Sgt	W/AG	RAFVR	29.06.43	22
Devitt, Robert	Sgt	W/AG	RAFVR	23.09.43	20
Devlin, Richard	Sgt	F/E	RAFVR	17.01.45	31
Dickinson, George	F/S	B/A	RAFVR	09.02.45	21
Dickinson, William	Sgt	A/G	RAFVR	04.07.43	33
Dickson, Harry	Sgt	W/AG	RCAF	13.08.41	20
Dillicar, John	F/L	Pilot	RNZAF	31.07.43	26

Dillingham, Horace	P/O	Nav	RAF	04.07.43	22
Disley, Ronald	P/O	Pilot	RAFVR	09.03.42	37
Dobson, Alan	Sgt	W/Op	RAFVR	09.02.45	23
Dobson, Herbert	Sgt	A/G	RAFVR	07.10.43	21
Dobson, William	F/L	Pilot	RAAF	11.06.44	30
Dolan, Stephen	Sgt	F/E	RAFVR	05.01.45	Unk.
Dolby, Harold	F/S	W/AG	RAFVR	21.04.44	22
Dombrain, Peter	P/O	Pilot	RAAF	01.06.44	21
Donaldson, George	Sgt	A/G	RAFVR	27.08.44	22
Doughty, Harry	Sgt	A/G	RAFVR	30.05.42	28
Douglas, Stanley	Sgt	Nav	RAuxAF	28.07.43	29
Douglass, Albert	Sgt	Pilot	RAFVR	19.05.42	31
Douglass, Peter	F/O	Pilot	RAF	12.05.40	Unk.
Dove, Cyril	P/O	Pilot	RAFVR	15.02.41	20
Doyle, Francis	F/O	Pilot	RAFVR	30.05.42	Unk.
Drew, BA (Hons), Robert	F/S	B/A	RAFVR	06.11.42	31
Duncanson, Williamson	Sgt	A/G	RAFVR	28.08.43	35
Dunk, Thomas	F/O	A/G	RAFVR	08.06.44	32
Dyer, Bruce	F/S	W/Op	RAAF	27.08.44	20
Dyer, DFM, MiD. Headley	P/O	Pilot	RAF	16.09.41	26
Earley, Bernard (BSc(London), DFM, MiD.)	F/L	Pilot	RAFVR	02.11.44	24
East, David	Sgt	A/G	RAFVR	25.04.42	25
Easthorpe, Frederick	W/O	Nav	RAFVR	08.06.44	22
Eastman, John	Sgt	Nav	RAFVR	28.04.44	20
Eccles, Joseph	Sgt	Nav	RAFVR	04.07.43	36
Edmonds, Harold	Sgt	W/AG	RAF	19.05.42	28
Edwards, Thomas	AM.II	Gdcw	RAF	19.05.42	Unk.
Edwards, William	P/O	Obs	RAF	23.05.40	Unk.
Eldridge, Gordon	Sgt	A/G	RAFVR	19.09.42	21
Ellis, Alfred	Sgt	A/G	RAFVR	19.02.43	Unk.
Elton, Percy	Sgt	F/E	RAFVR	03.03.43	21
Emberson, Thomas	P/O	Pilot	RAFVR	04.05.43	Unk.
Entwisle, Herbert	W/O	W/Op	RAFVR	15.02.44	24
Ethelston, John	P/O	B/A	RAFVR	19.02.43	Unk.
Evans, David	F/L	F/E	RAFVR	21.07.44	Unk.
Evans, Ivor	Sgt	W/AG	RAFVR	13.10.41	Unk.
Evans, Kenneth	Sgt	Obs	RAFVR	09.05.42	Unk.
Evans, Robert	Sgt	W/AG	RAFVR	16.09.42	22
Evans, Sidney	Sgt	F/E	RAFVR	11.08.43	33
Eve, Percy	Sgt	W/AG	RAFVR	19.07.41	21
Ewen, Thomas	F/S	Pilot	RAFVR	07.10.43	29

Exelby, MiD. Raymond	F/S	W/AG	RAF	18.12.41	21
Fagg, Ernest	LAC	W/Op	RAF	18.05.40	23
Fagg, John	Sgt	F/E	RAFVR	08.06.44	23
Faint, Reginald	Sgt	A/G	RAFVR	27.08.44	27
Farrelly, James	Sgt	F/E	RAF	08.03.43	20
Fenley, John	F/O	Nav	RAFVR	20.02.44	22
Ferguson, David	Sgt	F/E	RAF	18.12.41	22
Ferguson, Isaiah	P/O	Pilot	RAFVR	16.06.42	Unk.
Fiddes, Henry	P/O	B/A	RAFVR	17.04.43	30
Fisher, Charles	S/L	Pilot	RAF	29.10.42	30
Fitzgerald, John	F/S	A/G	RCAF	26.07.42	19
Flaherty, Michael	Sgt	B/A	RAFVR	24.05.43	30
Forrest, William	P/O	A/G	RCAF	21.02.44	29
Forster, Kenneth	Sgt	A/G	RAFVR	16.09.42	24
Fortune, Herbert	Sgt	W/AG	RAFVR	17.04.43	25
Fothergill, Wilfred	Sgt	Pilot	RAF	21.04.44	23
Fowler, Ronald	Sgt	W/AG	RAFVR	19.02.43	30
Fowler, Thomas	Sgt	A/G	RAFVR	12.06.43	21
Frame, William	Sgt	B/A	RAFVR	24.08.43	29
France, Ralph	P/O	Nav	RNZAF	31.08.43	20
Francis, Edward	Sgt	Nav	RAFVR	07.10.43	27
Frankish, Claude	P/O	Pilot	RAFVR	12.05.40	25
Franklin, George	W/O	W/Op	RNZAF	21.09.44	24
Franklin, James	Sgt	A/G	RAFVR	16.11.44	Unk.
Frazer, John	P/O	Obs	RAFVR	27.08.42	22
Frearson, Frederic	F/O	W/A	RAFVR	02.11.44	22
Freedman, Harry	F/O	A/G	RAFVR	17.01.45	20
Friend, George	Sgt	F/E	RAF	23.07.41	20
Frost, Arthur	Sgt	A/G	RAFVR	18.07.41	28
Fuller, William	F/O	A/G	RAFVR	17.01.45	19
Funnell, John	F/L	Pilot	RNZAF	21.04.44	33
Furness, BA. John	P/O	Nav	RAAF	04.12.43	22
Gard, Gilbert	Sgt	A/G	RAFVR	18.11.43	29
Garfit, Joseph	Sgt	F/E	RAFVR	29.06.43	32
Garrett, Leslie	Sgt	A/G	RAFVR	12.12.44	39
Garvey, Peter	Sgt	Pilot	RAF	15.08.40	22
Gearing, Leonard	Sgt	F/E	RAFVR	01.06.44	19
Geraghty, William	Sgt	B/A	RAFVR	26.02.44	22
Gericke, DFM. Philip	F/S	A/G	RAAF	29.01.44	20
Gerrard, Robert	P/O	B/A	RCAF	23.04.44	23
Gibbons, Anthony	F/S	A/G	RCAF	31.07.43	22
Gibbs, Sidney	Sgt	A/G	RAFVR	27.09.43	Unk.

Gibson, Raymond	F/O	Nav	RAFVR	28.04.44	Unk.
Gilchrist, Campbell	F/S	A/G	RCAF	06.07.44	22
Gill, Albert	Sgt	W/AG	RAFVR	08.06.44	22
Gilson, Edmond	W/OII	Obs	RCAF	28.08.42	20
Gladwell, Willis	F/O	Nav	RCAF	06.07.44	22
Gladwin, Lewis	F/S	Pilot	RCAF	14.02.43	21
Glanfield, John	F/S	A/G	RAAF	13.06.44	30
Glenday, Lindsay	F/O	Nav	RNZAF	16.09.43	33
Goddard, Kenneth	F/O	W/AG	RAFVR	25.04.44	24
Gold, Edmund	F/S	W/AG	RAFVR	07.10.43	22
Golder, Reginald	F/S	A/G	RAAF	07.04.42	24
Golding, James	Sgt	A/G	RAFVR	27.04.41	24
Golub, Michael	F/L	Pilot	RCAF	06.07.44	22
Gomersal, Ernest	Sgt	A/G	RAFVR	28.07.43	19
Goodchild, Cyril	Sgt	Nav	RAFVR	19.02.43	19
Goodridge, Noel	P/O	W/Op	RAAF	15.06.44	20
Goodwin, George	Sgt	A/G	RCAF	13.10.41	24
Gorbett, Edward	F/S	W/Op	RAFVR	24.08.43	21
Gordon, James	P/O	A/G	RAF	25.05.40	30
Gough, Sydney	F/O	A/G	RAAF	13.06.44	32
Gould, Edgar	Sgt	W/AG	RAFVR	11.04.42	Unk.
Gould, John	Sgt	W/AG	RAFVR	16.04.43	21
Goulding, Clarence	F/S	A/G	RNZAF	18.12.41	29
Graham, Leslie	Sgt	F/E	RAFVR	03.10.43	22
Grant, Robert	Sgt	A/G	RAFVR	21.06.44	Unk.
Grant, William	Sgt	A/G	RCAF	29.06.41	29
Gray, Angus	Sgt	Obs	RAF	13.08.40	20
Gray, Roderick	F/S	Pilot	RNZAF	31.08.43	22
Green, William	Sgt	A/G	RAFVR	16.09.43	Unk.
Greenbeck, Stanley	Sgt	W/AG	RAFVR	19.09.42	25
Greenwood, John	Sgt	A/G	RAFVR	17.04.43	28
Gregory, John	Sgt	A/G	RAFVR	09.02.45	22
Grove, William	F/L	Pilot	RAFVR	24.03.44	24
Grundy, Robert	F/S	Pilot	RAFVR	18.08.43	21
Guild, Edward	P/O	Pilot	RAFVR	16.09.41	Unk.
Gunn, Kelsall	Sgt	F/E	RAF	28.08.43	Unk.
Gunning, Frank	Sgt	Obs	RAF	12.06.40	19
Gurr, Anthony	P/O	Pilot	RAFVR	08.04.43	20
Gustafson, Roy	F/S	B/A	RCAF	07.10.43	21
Guy, John	Sgt	F/E	RAFVR	25.04.44	21
Gwynne, Lloyd	F/O	B/A	RNZAF	23.06.43	30
Habgood, George	P/O	Pilot	RAF	30.09.39	20

Haigh, Ronald	Sgt	F/E	RAFVR	01.09.43	28
Hains, Gordon	P/O	Pilot	RAFVR	20.06.42	25
Hales, Ronald	Sgt	A/G	RAFVR	08.06.44	20
Hall, Hubert	Sgt	Pilot	RAF	12.05.40	27
Hall, James	Sgt	A/G	RAFVR	08.04.43	Unk.
Hall, John	Sgt	Pilot	RAFVR	04.07,43	21
Hall, DFC, MiD. John	S/L	Pilot	RAF	18.05.42	24
Hall, Joseph	Sgt	A/G	RAFVR	09.02.45	32
Hammond, John	Sgt	Obs	RAF	12.08.42	Unk.
Hanberger, Peter	Sgt	A/G	RAFVR	04.05.43	20
Hance, John	F/S	W/Op	RAAF	05.11.44	23
Hannah, Wilfred	F/S	Pilot	RNZAF	06.11.42	24
Hansford, Albert	F/S	A/G	RCAF	02.10.42	34
Harbridge, William	Sgt	A/G	RAFVR	26.02.44	19
Hare, Thomas	W/OII	Pilot	RCAF	07.04.42	22
Harriman, Douglas	P/O	Pilot	RAF	25.05.40	20
Harris, Victory	F/L	Pilot	RCAF	26.02.43	24
Harris, Willis	F/L	Pilot	RNZAF	15.02.44	23
Harrison, Ernest	F/O	B/A	RAFVR	25.07.44	31
Harrison, Jack	Sgt	W/Op	RAFVR	11.04.43	21
Haswell, George	Sgt	F/E	RAF	08.06.44	21
Hathaway, Maurice	F/S	A/G	RAFVR	09.02.45	22
Hawkins, John	F/O	Pilot	RNZAF	23.06.43	28
Hawthorn, Kenneth	Sgt	F/E	RAF	28.08.42	22
Haycock, DFC. Dennis	F/L	Pilot	RAFVR	17.04.43	22
Haydock, Douglas	Sgt	F/E	RAFVR	26.02.44	24
Hayes, Eric	Sgt	W/AG	RAFVR	03.06.42	24
Hayes, George	Sgt	Obs	RAFVR	19.09.42	32
Hayles, DFM. Raymond	F/S	W/Op	RAFVR	21.02.44	21
Haywards, Frederick	F/S	W/Op	RAFVR	08.06.44	28
Head, Peter	Sgt	W/AG	RAFVR	29.10.42	21
Hearn, Douglas	F/S	W/Op	RAFVR	16.11.44	22
Heathcote, George	P/O	Nav	RNZAF	21.04.44	35
Heathcote, MiD. Gilbert	F/L	Pilot	RAF	18.12.41	30
Heathcote, Roy	Sgt	W/AG	RAFVR	19.09.42	21
Helyar, Roy	Sgt	A/G	RAFVR	13.08.42	22
Henderson, Ian	F/S	W/AG	RAF	19.09.42	Unk.
Henderson, Duncan	F/O	Pilot	RAF	25.05.40	23
Henderson, William	Sgt	A/G	RAFVR	05.11.44	20
Hendry, Dennis	Sgt	A/G	RAFVR	27.09.43	Unk.
Henson, George	Sgt	Obs	RCAF	13.08.41	22
Heurtley, John	F/S	W/AG	RNZAF	20.06.42	23

Heward, William	Sgt	W/AG	RAFVR	28.04.44	Unk.
Higgins, Clarence	P/O	Obs	RAF	11.09.42	28
Higgins, Robert	Sgt	Pilot	RNZAF	13.04.42	31
Higginson, Alfred	Sgt	Pilot	RNZAF	18.07.41	24
Highland. William	F/S	A/G	RAAF	03.10.43	21
Hill, Eric	F/S	Pilot	RAAF	04.09.43	25
Hill, Hugh	P/O	A/G	RCAF	16.12.42	Unk.
Hills, Michael	F/O	Nav	RAFVR	11.06.44	Unk.
Hipps, Arnold	P/O	Obs	RAFVR	19.07.41	25
Hoggard, Robert	F/O	Pilot	RAAF	02.11.44	21
Hohnen, Michael	P/O	Pilot	RAF	04.08.40	19
Holborrow, Richard	F/S	W/Op	RAFVR	21.01.44	20
Holden, Alfred	Sgt	Pilot	RAFVR	28.07.43	19
Holdsworth, John	Sgt	Obs	RAFVR	07.07.40	Unk.
Holland, Frank	F/S	B/A	RAFVR	24.03.44	29
Hollingshead, Ronald	Sgt	Obs	RAFVR	14.09.40	20
Hollinrake, Keith	Sgt	F/E	RAFVR	21.09.44	20
Holmes, Arthur	Sgt	Obs	RAF	24.05.40	20
Holmes, Russell	P/O	W/AG	RCAF	16.12.42	Unk.
Holt, Blake	Sgt	B/A	RAFVR	31.10.44	31
Honeybill, Ernest	Sgt	F/E	RAFVR	18.08.43	28
Hood, Louis	F/S	A/G	RAFVR	08.06.44	27
Hood, Walter	Sgt	Pilot	RNZAF	29.10.42	23
Hooker, Allan	F/S	A/G	RAAF	01.09.43	20
Hopkins, Reginald	Sgt	Obs	RAF	18.05.40	29
Hopkins, William	Sgt	F/E	RAF	27.08.42	Unk.
Hopson, David	F/O	Pilot	RAFVR	19.02.43	20
Horton, George	F/O	Nav	RAFVR	08.05.44	29
Horton, Leslie	Sgt	A/G	RAF	26.07.40	21
Houghton, Eric	F/S	Pilot	RNZAF	25.07.44	22
Hounsome, Harry	W/O	F/E	RAFVR	05.11.44	25
Houston, Walter	F/S	Pilot	RCAF	13.01.44	24
Howitt, Ian	Sgt	B/A	RAFVR	13.09.44	22
Howland, Harold	F/S	Pilot	RAFVR	02.03.43	26
Howson, Paul	F/O	B/A	RAFVR	19.02.43	Unk.
Hudson, Colin	Sgt	Nav	RAFVR	18.08.43	Unk.
Hughes, Philip	P/O	A/G	RAFVR	14.09.40	22
Hughes, Robert	Sgt	A/G	RAFVR	25.05.44	19
Humm, Harry	Sgt	W/AG	RAFVR	13.04.42	22
Humphries, Douglas	Sgt	B/A	RAFVR	04.07.43	22
Hunt, James	LAC	Gdcw	RAFVR	29.12.42	31
Hunt, Leslie	F/L	Pilot	RCAF	04.07.43	22

Hunter, Russell	F/O	W/Op	RCAF	22.06.43	21
Hunter, Thomas	Sgt	A/G	RAFVR	13.09.44	19
Hunter, William	Sgt	F/E	RAFVR	02.11.44	21
Hurley, Max	P/O	Pilot	RAAF	20.02.44	20
Hurworth, George	Sgt	A/G	RAFVR	15.02.41	22
Hussey, John	F/O	B/A	RAFVR	29.01.44	23
Hutton, George	Sgt	A/G	RAFVR	23.06.43	Unk.
Hutton, Grantley	Sgt	F/E	RAFVR	16.12.42	Unk.
Hyde, Donald	Sgt	A/G	RAFVR	16.04.43	22
Hynes, William	W/OII	Nav	RCAF	13.01.44	23
Hyrons, Albert	Sgt	F/E	RAFVR	02.03.43	Unk.
Ingle, DFC. Ray	Lt	Air Obs	SAAF	31.07.43	25
(Lt Ingle was attached to XV Squadron, RAF, from South Africa House)					
Jackson, Arthur	Sgt	Nav	RAFVR	24.03.44	22
Jackson, Bernard	F/O	Nav	RNZAF	31.07.43	23
Jackson, DFM. Francis	Sgt	F/E	RAF	29.12.42	22
Jager, William	F/S	B/A	RAAF	21.01.44	25
James, Clifford	Sgt	F/E	RAF	19.02.43	Unk.
James, Leslie	Sgt	B/A	RAFVR	16.04.43	22
Jamieson, Gerald	F/O	B/A	RCAF	06.07.44	34
Jamieson, Lawrence	F/S	B/A	RNZAF	01.06.44	26
Jarvis, Alfred	Sgt	W/AG	RNZAF	06.11.42	22
Jarvis, Arthur	F/L	Pilot	RAFVR	21.06.44	29
Jeans, Donald	Sgt	W/AG	RAFVR	13.08.42	25
(A probable error in the XV Squadron ORB records that Sgt D Jeans and Sgt L Blackmore, who flew with the same crew, have the same service number: 798522.)					
Jeeves, Dennis	Sgt	Pilot	RAFVR	19.07.41	Unk.
Jeffrey, George	Sgt	Obs	RCAF	08.08.41	24
Jeffreys, Kenneth	Sgt	W/Op	RAF	18.12.41	31
Jenkins, Thomas	Sgt	A/G	RAFVR	22.03.45	36
Jennings, William	Sgt	A/G	RAFVR	05.05.43	Unk.
Johnson, John	Sgt	F/E	RAF	24.03.44	28
Johnson, William	F/S	A/G	RCAF	16.09.42	29
Johnson, William	Sgt	A/G	RAFVR	29.06.43	20
Johnson, William	P/O	Pilot	RCAF	24.05.43	21
Johnston, John	Sgt	Unk.	RAFVR	13.01.44	19
Jones, Ernest	F/S	Pilot	RAF	12.05.44	24
Jones, Frank	P/O	Obs	RAF	30.07.40	32
Jones, Howell	Sgt	B/A	RAFVR	26.02.43	20
Jones, John	Sgt	A/G	RAFVR	02.03.43	21
Jones, Martin	Sgt	W/Op	RAFVR	06.07.44	27
Jones, Maurice	Sgt	Obs	RAF	11.06.40	23

Jones, Philip	F/O	B/A	RAFVR	08.05.44	23
Jones, Thomas	P/O	Pilot	RAFVR	08.05.44	21
Jones, Trevor	Sgt	F/E	RAFVR	16.09.41	22
Jordan, Albert	F/S	A/G	RAFVR	21.04.44	Unk.
Jordon, Sidney	Sgt	B/A	RAFVR	27.09.43	Unk.
Judd, George	F/O	Pilot	RAFVR	31.07.43	Unk.
Keeble, Kenneth	Sgt	W/AG	RAFVR	19.02.43	20
Keen, Jack	P/O	Pilot	RAFVR	29.06.43	27
Keen, Richard	F/S	Nav	RAFVR	13.09.44	29
Kelley, Alfred	F/S	A/G	RCAF	08.12.42	22
Kendall, Alfred	Sgt	A/G	RAFVR	16.09.42	32
Kennedy, Frederick	F/O	Obs	RCAF	30.05.42	29
Kennedy, Frederick	Sgt	A/G	RAFVR	29.06.43	23
Kent, James	Sgt	A/G	RAFVR	16.09.42	20
Kieswetter, Emerson	P/O	Obs	RCAF	16.12.42	24
Kimber, John	Sgt	W/AG	RAFVR	08.04.43	Unk.
King, Desmond	Sgt	A/G	RAFVR	28.04.44	20
King, Edward	Sgt	A/G	RAFVR	19.09.42	19
Kingston, Harry	Sgt	A/G	RAFVR	13.04.42	24
Kirk, Charles	Sgt	Nav	RAFVR	08.06.44	21
Kite, Cuthbert	LAC	Gdcw	RAFVR	01.07.41	25
Knipe, Humphrey	Sgt	W/AG	RAFVR	09.05.42	20
Knox, Kenneth	Sgt	A/G	RAFVR	05.11.44	20
Lacy, John	Sgt	F/E	RAF	16.04.43	22
Lake, Aston	P/O	Nav	RAFVR	12.06.43	20
Lake, George	Sgt	Nav	RAFVR	17.01.45	31
Lamb, Frederick	Sgt	A/G	RAFVR	13.10.41	Unk.
Lamb, James	Sgt	B/A	RAF	02.03.43	21
Lambert, Frederick	Sgt	B/A	RAFVR	08.04.43	20
Lambie, William	F/O	Nav	RAFVR	05.05.43	28
Land, James	P/O	Pilot	RCAF	19.09.42	22
Lander, Robert	Sgt	Nav	RAFVR	04.09.43	22
Law, Ian	F/O	Nav	RCAF	02.11.44	21
Lawrence, Hector	S/L	Pilot	RAF	18.05.40	26
Lawrence, Victor	F/S	W/AG	RAF	28.08.42	20
Lawson, Ralph	Sgt	W/Op	RAFVR	04.09.43	20
Lax, Frederick	Sgt	F/E	RAF	03.02.43	21
Leadley, Thomas	P/O	B/A	RAFVR	31.08.43	21
Leah, Edmund	F/O	Nav	RAFVR	08.08.44	21
Lee, David	P/O	Nav	RAAF	05.11.44	25
Lee, Samuel	F/O	B/A	RAFVR	12.12.44	32
Lee, Stanley	Sgt	B/A	RAFVR	28.04.44	27

Lemky, Ronald	W/OII	B/A	RCAF	13.06.44	23
Letbe, Thomas	Sgt	Nav	RAFVR	11.04.43	Unk.
Levesque, Fernand	F/S	A/G	RCAF	22.08.42	Unk.
Lewis, Aubrey	F/S	Pilot	RNZAF	11.08.43	30
Lewis, David	Sgt	F/E	RAF	19.05.42	Unk.
Lewis, Donald	P/O	Obs	RNZAF	23.07.41	23
Lewis, Victor	F/S	B/A	RAAF	27.03.44	28
Lilley, Alfred	Sgt	A/G	RAFVR	08.06.44	19
Lilley, Geoffrey	P/O	B/A	RAFVR	02.11.44	23
Ling, John	Sgt	Obs	RAFVR	29.10.42	22
Lockhart, Henry	Sgt	W/AG	RAFVR	16.07.42	23
Logan, Kenneth	Sgt	B/A	RAFVR	27.08.44	28
Long, Arthur	F/S	Nav	RAAF	01.06.44	21
Long, Clarence	F/O	Nav	RCAF	19.02.43	Unk.
Long, Joseph	Sgt	F/E	RAFVR	07.10.43	27
Long, Sydney	Sgt	B/A	RAFVR	31.07.43	26
Longworth, Herbert	Sgt	F/E	RAFVR	24.03.44	27
Loudon, Arthur	Sgt	F/E	RAFVR	11.04.43	22
Lovell, Robert	Sgt	A/G	RAFVR	17.10.42	23
Lowe, James	P/O	B/A	RAAF	04.12.44	22
Lowrie, Robert	Sgt	F/E	RAF	19.09.42	19
Lucas, Eric	Sgt	A/G	RNZAF	11.05.41	26
Ludgate, John	Sgt	A/G	RAFVR	28.08.42	21
Lutwyche, Percy	Sgt	Nav	RAFVR	08.04.43	20
Lyons, Henry	F/O	Nav	RCAF	24.05.43	32
MacAulay, Wilfred	Sgt	A/G	RAFVR	23.06.43	21
MacDougall, Allan	W/O	Pilot	RAAF	12.09.44	26
MacKenzie, Walter	F/S	Obs	RCAF	16.09.41	25
Macklin, William	Sgt	F/E	RAFVR	19.02.43	Unk.
MacLennan, John	W/O	B/A	RCAF	16.07.44	Unk.
Maddock, Frederick	F/S	A/G	RCAF	25.05.44	21
Maginn, Henry	Sgt	A/G	RAF	11.09.42	29
Malcolm, John	Sgt	F/E	RAFVR	09.02.45	19
Malley, Donald	Sgt	A/G	RAFVR	28.08.43	Unk.
Maloney, Terence	Sgt	W/AG	RAF	04.07.40	18
Mansfield, Sidney	Sgt	A/G	RAFVR	11.09.42	20
Margetts, Edward	Sgt	W/AG	RAFVR	27.08.42	20
Markovitch, Alfred	P/O	F/E	RAFVR	02.11.44	21
Marsh, Charles	Sgt	F/E	RAFVR	21.02.44	27
Marsh, Roy	F/L	Pilot	RAFVR	12.12.44	21
Marsh, Thomas	P/O	Pilot	RAFVR	26.03.44	20
Marshall, Sydney	F/O	Pilot	RAAF	18.07.41	24

Martin, James	Sgt	A/G	RAFVR	22.06.43	21
Martin, William	Sgt	A/G	RAFVR	02.03.43	Unk.
Masters, James	P/O	Pilot	RAF	23.05.40	19
Masur, Dennis	P/O	A/G	RCAF	27.08.42	21
Mathews, Arthur	F/S	W/Op	RAFVR	28.04.44	Unk.
Matlock, Elmer	F/S	W/AG	RCAF	08.03.43	21
Matthews, Glyndwr	Sgt	B/A	RAFVR	29.06.43	19
Matthews, Martyn	Sgt	B/A	RAFVR	22.03.45	22
Matthews, William	Sgt	A/G	RAAF	27.02.43	26
Matthews, William	Sgt	F/E	RAFVR	06.07.44	22
Maycock, Ronald	Sgt	Nav	RAFVR	18.05.42	21
Mayor, Gordon	Sgt	W/AG	RAFVR	18.07.41	22
McAusland, Kenneth	F/S	Pilot	RAFVR	13.08.42	27
McCallum, Donald	Sgt	A/G	RAFVR	09.03.42	29
McCallum, Eric	F/S	A/G	RNZAF	24.03.44	20
McCallum, John	P/O	Obs	RAFVR	18.07.41	Unk.
McCaughey, Peter	F/O	B/A	RAFVR	11.04.43	22
McCauseland, William	F/S	Pilot	RCAF	12.08.42	21
McCosh, Hargrave	P/O	Obs	RAFVR	06.04.41	Unk.
McDonnell, Patrick	LAC	W/AG	RAF	12.05.40	23
McGovern, John	Sgt	A/G	RAFVR	20.06.42	30
McGrane, James	Sgt	W/Op	RAFVR	03.03.43	22
McIntosh, Alexander	Sgt	F/E	RAFVR	29.10.42	Unk.
McIntosh, Robert	F/S	Nav	RAFVR	24.03.44	Unk.
McKay, Ronald	P/O	Pilot	RNZAF	13.04.42	22
McKay, William	F/O	Pilot	RAAF	25.05.44	21
McKie, Kenneth	Sgt	F/E	RAFVR	13.09.44	33
McKillop, Robert	Sgt	B/A	RNZAF	16.12.42	25
McLaggan, Alexander	P/O	Obs	RAFVR	27.06.40	20
McLaren, James	Sgt	Obs	RAFVR	20.06.42	22
McMaster, Gordon	F/S	A/G	RAAF	20.02.44	25
McMillan, Roderick	W/OII	Nav	RCAF	13.06.44	25
McNee, John	Sgt	A/G	RAFVR	13.09.44	Unk.
McNulty, Peter	Sgt	A/G	RAFVR	04.05.43	Unk.
McQueen, Alastair	F/L	Pilot	RAFVR	09.02.45	Unk.
McQuillan, Francis	F/S	Pilot	RAFVR	22.06.43	21
McRae, Donald	P/O	B/A	RCAF	21.06.44	21
McSparron, Ernest	Sgt	W/AG	RAFVR	30.05.42	Unk.
McWalter, Thomas	Sgt	A/G	RAFVR	31.03.41	22
Meijer, Adolph (Dutch Cross of Merit)	PO	W/AG	RAFVR	03.03.43	36
Mellor, Harry	F/O	Obs	RAFVR	02.03.43	31

Melville, Robert	P/O	Pilot	RAAF	16.07.42	25
Meredith, James	F/O	Pilot	RNZAF	02.10.42	24
Meredith, Owen	P/O	W/Op	RAAF	02.11.44	21
Merrie, John	Sgt	F/E	RAFVR	28.07.43	27
Metaxa, Anthony	Sgt	Pilot	RAFVR	30.06.41	Unk.
Middlemas, Neville	Sgt	Obs	RAF	12.05.40	26
Middleton, Kenneth	Sgt	A/G	RAFVR	31.07.43	19
Millar, John	Sgt	A/G	RAFVR	02.11.44	26
Millen, Frank	P/O	Pilot	RCAF	16.12.42	21
Mills, Terence	Sgt	A/G	RAFVR	12.08.42	Unk.
Milner, Joseph	W/OI	Pilot	RCAF	01.09.43	Unk.
Minns, Douglas	F/O	Pil/BA	RAFVR	21.08.44	22
Mitchell, Arthur	Sgt	Pilot	RAFVR	23.07.41	23
Mitchell, Desmond	P/O	A/G	RAFVR	24.08.43	20
Mobbs, Richard	Sgt	A/G	RAFVR	13.06.44	20
Moffat, Robert	P/O	Obs	RAFVR	08.06.40	20
Moffat, William	F/O	Pilot	RAFVR	03.03.43	21
Mohr-Bell, Harold	P/O	Pilot	RAFVR	13.10.41	Unk.
Monteith, John	P/O	Pilot	RCAF	19.02.43	20
Moorcroft, Albert	Sgt	A/G	RAFVR	03.06.42	22
Moore, Donald	W/O	W/Op	RAFVR	13.09.44	Unk.
Moran, William	F/L	Pilot	RAAF	27.08.44	20
Morelly, Max	W/OII	Obs	RCAF	16.09.42	21
Moroni, Hubert	Sgt	A/G	RAFVR	20.02.44	21
Morris, Frederick	Sgt	F/E	RAFVR	30.05.42	23
Morris, Frederick	Sgt	F/E	RAFVR	24.08.43	19
Morris, George	W/O	A/G	RAFVR	02.11.44	23
Morris, Hugh	Sgt	W/AG	RAFVR	26.05.43	20
Morrison, George	Sgt	A/G	RAFVR	08.08.44	19
Moss, George	Sgt	A/G	RAFVR	02.03.43	19
Moss, Leonard	Sgt	W/AG	RNZAF	28.08.42	28
Mounteney, Archibald	Sgt	W/AG	RAFVR	09.05.42	Unk.
Mugridge, Herbert	Sgt	A/G	RAFVR	04.05.43	20
Muir, John	F/O	W/AG	RAFVR	14.02.43	25
Mumford, Ronald	Sgt	Obs	RAF	16.09.42	Unk.
Munn, Stanley	Sgt	A/G	RAFVR	04.07.43	35
Munt, Victor	Sgt	W/AG	RAFVR	09.05.42	24
Murphy, Patrick	Sgt	A/G	RAF	30.07.40	22
Murray, Louis	2nd/Lt	Air/Obs	Army	26.02.42	23
(Attached from 120 Heavy Ack-Ack Regiment)					
Murray, Robert	P/O	W/Op	RAAF	12.12.44	33
Myland, DFC. Douglas	P/O	Pilot	RAFVR	04.09.40	24

Needham, Arthur	Sgt	W/AG	RAFVR	16.09.41	21
Needham, Frank	F/O	Pilot	RAFVR	08.08.41	29
Newell, Alfred	Sgt	W/Op	RAFVR	26.03.44	Unk.
Newlyn, Raymond	P/O	W/Op	RAFVR	29.01.44	21
Newman, Jack	P/O	Nav	RAFVR	19.09.42	Unk.
Newman, Raymond	P/O	B/A	RAFVR	26.05.43	25
Newport, Jack	F/S	Pilot	RAFVR	23.06.43	20
Newton, Frederick	P/O	Pilot	RAAF	22.03.45	24
Niall, Alexander	W/O	Pilot	RNZAF	16.09.43	30
Nicholls, James	Sgt	A/G	RAFVR	14.02.43	21
Nicholls, Robinson	Sgt	F/E	RAFVR	16.07.42	Unk.
Nicholson, George	F/L	Pilot	RAFVR	09.03.42	Unk.
Nicholson, Robert	Sgt	A/G	RAFVR	18.05.42	23
Nicklin, Arthur	F/S	B/A	RAFVR	05.01.45	22
Nixon, Frederick	F/S	B/A	RCAF	12.08.42	26
Nixon, George	Sgt	F/E	RAFVR	03.06.42	21
Nixon, Thomas	F/S	A/G	RAFVR	15.06.44	19
Noel, John	Capt	Air/Obs	Army	13.04.42	35
(Attached from the Royal Artillery)					
Norris, Raymond	Sgt	W/Op	RAFVR	01.06.44	21
Nuttall, Norman	Sgt	W/Op	RAFVR	11.05.41	20
Nystrom, Stanley	F/S	A/G	RAAF	01.06.44	21
Oakes, Fred	W/OII	B/A	RCAF	21.07.44	20
Oakley, Albert	F/O	Pilot	RAF	12.05.40	25
Oakley, Edward	Sgt	W/AG	RAFVR	07.04.42	27
O'Hara, Leonard	P/O	Pilot	RAFVR	16.09.42	24
Oliver, Richard	Sgt	A/G	RAFVR	08.12.42	29
O'Mara, Sidney	Sgt	A/G	RAFVR	29.06.41	21
O'Neill, William	F/S	Pilot	RCAF	18.12.41	34
Orchard, Leslie	Sgt	F/E	RAFVR	19.07.41	21
Orchard, Thomas	Sgt	A/G	RAFVR	26.05.43	18
Ordish, DFC. Charles	F/L	Pilot	RAFVR	31.12.42	23
O'Riordan, Dennis	Sgt	F/E	RAFVR	26.05.43	Unk.
Orr, Thomas	Sgt	Obs	RAFVR	16.09.42	28
Osman, Patrick	Sgt	A/G	RAFVR	18.12.41	Unk.
Oswin, Arthur	Sgt	A/G	RAFVR	28.08.42	Unk.
Overend, Norman	F/O	Pilot	RNZAF	12.09.44	21
Overend, William	Sgt	B/A	RAFVR	03.09.42	22
Oxenbridge, Edward	Sgt	Pilot	RAFVR	19.02.43	21
Palmer, Edward	P/O	A/G	RCAF	03.09.42	Unk.
Palmer, William	F/L	Pilot	RAFVR	08.06.44	Unk.
Parker, Geoffrey	F/S	A/G	RAFVR	21.06.44	20

Parkhouse, Evan	Sgt	A/G	RAFVR	05.01.45	Unk.
Paterson, John	Sgt	A/G	RAFVR	24.09.44	19
Patterson, Eric	P/O	Pilot	RCAF	28.08.42	20
Pattison, Leslie	P/O	W/AG	RAFVR	05.05.43	28
Paul, Frank	Sgt	A/G	RAFVR	08.06.44	23
Pavely, DFM, Robert	P/O	Nav	RAF	26.06.43	22
Pawlyk, Andrew	F/S	A/G	RCAF	30.06.44	22
Payne, Gerald	Sgt	A/G	RAFVR	28.08,42	19
Payne, Norman	F/S	A/G	RAFVR	20.05.42	26
Peach, Dermott	Sgt	F/E	RAFVR	25.05.44	20
Pearsall, P. F. G.	Sgt	F/E	RAFVR	13.06.44	Unk.
Pelham, Maurice	Sgt	F/E	RAFVR	13.06.44	20
Penmen, David	Sgt	W/AG	RAFVR	18.12.41	21
Perring, Clive	P/O	Nav	RAFVR	16.04.43	22
Perrin, Edward	Sgt	Obs	RAF	12.05.40	23
Perry, Harry	F/S	B/A	RCAF	04.09.43	24
Peters, Jack	F/S	A/G	RAF	18.12.41	21
Peters, Thomas	Sgt	W/AG	RAFVR	16.09.43	21
Petrie, Peter	Sgt	W/AG	RAF	04.09.40	30
Peuleve, David	Sgt	W/AG	RAF	12.06.40	21
Phillips, John	F/S	W/AG	RCAF	09.03.42	21
Phillips, Sidney	Sgt	A/G	RAFVR	26.02.43	21
Phillips, Simon	F/O	Pilot	RNZAF	13.07.44	22
Piche, Kenneth	P/O	Pilot	RCAF	16.04.43	21
Pittard, Ronald	Sgt	F/E	RAFVR	26.05.43	22
Pittendrigh, Wilfred	Sgt	W/AG	RAFVR	11.09.42	21
Plumb, Stanley	Sgt	F/E	RAFVR	11.05.41	23
Ponting, Roland	Sgt	Unk	RAF	29.10.42	Unk.
Poole,Frank	Sgt	B/A	RAFVR	11.08.43	Unk.
Porteous, Kenneth	F/S	A/G	RAFVR	21.01.44	28
Portsmouth, Robert	Sgt	A/G	RAFVR	11.08.43	19
Powys-Jones, Hugh	Sgt	Obs	RAF	04.09.40	22
Price, William	Sgt	A/G	RAFVR	04.09.43	19
Priddle, Terence	F/S	B/A	RAFVR	05.11.44	22
Prime, Norman	Sgt	F/E	RAFVR	11.09.42	Unk.
Prior, Albert	Sgt	Obs	RAF	13.04.40	28
Pritchard, William	Sgt	W/Op	RAFVR	02.03.45	26
Probert, William	F/S	W/AG	RCAF	19.09.42	24
Pryke, George	Sgt	F/E	RAFVR	29.06.43	21
Purry, Ronald	F/L	Pilot	RAAF	15.06.44	21
Pybus, Alfred	Sgt	F/E	RAFVR	29.01.44	27
Pye, James	Sgt	F/E	RAFVR	19.09.42	21

Quinn, George	P/O	Pilot	RAFVR	03.09.42	Unk.
Radcliffe, George	W/O	A/G	RAFVR	11.06.44	21
Ragless, John	F/O	B/A	RAFVR	15.02.44	27
Ralph, Basil	F/S	A/G	RAuxAF	15.02.44	33
Ralph, Joe	P/O	Pilot	RAF	30.09.39	19
Rampton, Albert	P/O	Obs	RAFVR	09.03.42	24
Ramsey, Ian	F/S	W/Op	RNZAF	31.07.43	31
Ratcliffe, Edward	F/O	Nav	RAFVR	19.02.43	30
Rate, Bernard	Sgt	B/A	RAFVR	28.07.43	Unk.
Raymond, Lloyd	F/S	A/G	RCAF	23.09.43	Unk.
Read, George	F/O	A/G	RAFVR	31.08.43	Unk.
Reardon, Glyndwr	Sgt	W/AG	RAFVR	11.02.41	Unk.
Recchia, Raymond	Sgt	W/AG	RCAF	29.10.42	20
Rees, Thomas	Sgt	F/E	RAFVR	11.06.44	21
Reid, Frank	F/S	A/G	RAAF	01.06.44	21
Reid, George	Sgt	A/G	RAFVR	07.07.40	28
Relph, Henry	Sgt	B/A	RAFVR	12.06.43	30
Rennie, Charles	F/S	Nav	RAFVR	27.08.44	22
Renshaw, Richard	P/O	Pilot	RAFVR	29.06.41	Unk.
Reynolds, Thomas	F/L	Pilot	RAFVR	25.07.44	21
Richards, John	Sgt	Obs	RAFVR	19.09.42	Unk.
Richardson, Jack	Sgt	W/Op	RAFVR	19.02.42	Unk.
Riordan, Lex	P/O	W/Op	RAAF	17.01.45	20
Ripley, Jack	P/O	Pilot	RCAF	08.03.43	21
Roberts, Edwin	Sgt	Obs	RAF	12.05.40	20
Robinson, Charles	P/O	Pilot	RAF	26.07.40	21
Robinson, John	Sgt	F/E	RAFVR	28.08.42	23
Robinson, John	F/S	B/A	RAFVR	11.06.44	29
Rodway, George	Sgt	W/Op	RAFVR	04.05.43	22
Rogers, Peter	Sgt	Nav	RAFVR	26.02.43	22
Rolfe, Ronald	Sgt	F/E	RAFVR	15.06.44	21
Rolls, Henry	Sgt	A/G	RAF	15.08.40	19
Rose, David	F/S	A/G	RAFVR	20.06.42	26
Ross, Robert	F/S	W/AG	RAFVR	08.08.41	25
Rowley, Kenneth	Sgt	W/AG	RAFVR	08.08.41	24
Rugless, George	F/S	W/Op	RAAF	05.01.45	22
Russell, CGM. Joseph	F/L	Pilot	RCAF	21.02.44	24
Russell-Collins, Charles	F/S	Pilot	RAFVR	19.09.42	Unk.
Rutherford, George	Sgt	B/A	RAFVR	04.05.43	28
Ruthven, James	F/S	Pilot	RCAF	18.12.41	24
Ryan, John	F/O	Obs	RCAF	18.05.42	30
Ryan, Thomas	F/S	B/A	RCAF	01.09.43	Unk.

Salter, Harry	F/L	Pilot	RAF	29.10.42	34
Sanders, Frederick	F/L	Pilot	RNZAF	16.11.44	22
Saunders, Arthur	P/O	Pilot	RAFVR	29.06.43	Unk.
Scarisbrick, Leonard	Sgt	W/Op	RAFVR	16.09.43	22
Scott, Horace	Sgt	W/Op	RAFVR	13.06.44	21
Scrase, Edgar	Sgt	A/G	RAF	13.08.40	19
Seeley, Duncan	W/OII	A/G	RCAF	19.02.43	21
Self, Alfred	Sgt	B/A	RAFVR	14.02.43	21
Sharman, Peter	Sgt	F/E	RAFVR	05.05.43	21
Sharman, Peter	Sgt	W/AG	RAFVR	28.08.42	20
Sharp, Frank	Sgt	W/AG	RAFVR	18.05.42	21
Sharp, Reginald	Sgt	Unk	RAFVR	19.05.42	22
Shaw, Wilfred	Sgt	W/AG	RAFVR	26.02.43	21
Shea, Victor	F/S	B/A	RCAF	04.07.43	20
Shearer, Robert	Sgt	A/G	RAF	18.12.41	Unk.
Shearer, William	Sgt	A/G	RAFVR	24.09.44	22
Sherratt, Harold	Sgt	A/G	RAFVR	03.03.43	19
Shewen, John	Sgt	F/E	RAFVR	04.12.44	19
Shiells, DFM. James	P/O	Pilot	RAFVR	16.04.43	31
Shoesmith, DFC, Wilbert	P/O	Pilot	RCAF	26.07.43	Unk.
Shoesmith, Terence	Sgt	A/G	RAFVR	13.08.42	Unk.
Shortland, Wilfred	Sgt	Obs	RAF	12.05.40	28
Sills, MiD, James	P/O	W/Op	RAF	24.03.44	24
Simcox, James	P/O	Nav	RAFVR	13.06.44	22
Simpson, Grenville	Sgt	W/AG	RAFVR	15.02.41	25
Sinclair, Anthony	Sgt	W/AG	RAFVR	01.03.43	20
Skelton, Robert	Sgt	W/Op	RAFVR	08.12.42	27
Skilbeck, Robert	P/O	W/Op	RAAF	04.12.44	20
Skillen, Robert	Sgt	F/E	RAFVR	16.09.43	20
Sleven, Arthur	Sgt	A/G	RAFVR	21.02.44	20
Slingsby, Harold	P/O	A/G	RAFVR	03.02.45	38
Smith, Allen	Sgt	A/G	RAFVR	26.06.43	Unk.
Smith, Augustus	Sgt	B/A	RAFVR	24.03.44	Unk.
Smith, DFM. Charles	P/O	Obs	RAF	18.12.41	23
Smith, Charles	W/OII	Obs	RCAF	26.05.43	22
Smith, Cyril	Sgt	F/E	RAFVR	21.01.44	33
Smith, Frank	Sgt	W/AG	RAFVR	11.05.41	21
Smith, Glen	F/S	A/G	RNZAF	28.08.42	22
Smith, Leonard	Sgt	A/G	RAFVR	26.05.43	Unk.
Smith, Paul	Sgt	Pilot	RAFVR	15.02.41	Unk.
Smith, Philip	F/L	Pilot	RAFVR	24.09.44	31
Smith, Ronald	Sgt	Pilot	RAFVR	30.06.41	27

Smith, Thomas	Sgt	W/AG	RAFVR	19.09.42	21
Snead, Frederick	Sgt	W/AG	RCAF	16.09.41	20
Soper, Sinclair	F/L	Pilot	RCAF	28.04.44	26
Soper, Thomas	Sgt	W/Op	RAFVR	30.05.42	19
Sparkes, Eric	Sgt	F/E	RAFVR	15.02.44	20
Spenceley, Frederick	Sgt	F/E	RAFVR	20.06.42	21
Spencer, Ronald	Sgt	W/Op	RAF	11.06.40	19
Spice, Maurice	F/S	Nav	RAFVR	26.03.44	Unk.
Spooner, Daniel	P/O	Nav	RAFVR	05.05.43	31
Spriggs, Anthony	Sgt	F/E	RAFVR	18.05.42	22
Spriggs, Eric	F/S	Nav	RAFVR	21.06.44	22
Stark, George	Sgt	A/G	RAFVR	02.10.42	27
Steer, Reginald	Sgt	W/AG	RAFVR	13.04.42	22
Stephen, Raymond	W/OII	F/E	RAFVR	29.07.44	24

W/OII Raymond Stephen was struck and killed by lightning, while in captivity as a POW

Stephens, Arthur	Sgt	Nav	RAFVR	22.06.43	25
Stephens, DFC. John	W/C	Pilot	RAFO	30.08.43	25
Stephenson, George	Sgt	A/G	RAFVR	07.04.42	27
Stevenson. Charles	F/O	Nav	RNZAF	16.11.44	23
Stevenson, Ian	F/O	B/A	RNZAF	16.09.43	27
Stocks, Thomas	Sgt	A/G	RAFVR	14.02.43	19
Stone, Noel	Sgt	B/A	RNZAF	17.10.42	32
Storie, Richard	F/S	A/G	RAFVR	30.06.41	19
Stowell, James	P/O	Pilot	RNZAF	05.05.43	25
Strachan, Robert	Sgt	F/E	RAAF	13.08.41	Unk.
Strickland, Algernon	Sgt	A/G	RAFVR	09.05.42	22
Stringer, George	F/S	A/G	RAFVR	23.09.43	20
Stringfellow, John	Sgt	Nav	RAFVR	01.09.43	19
Stubbs, Thomas	Sgt	A/G	RAFVR	13.06.44	20
Stuckey, Victor	P/O	Nav	RAAF	12.12.44	27
Sturgess, John	P/O	A/G	RCAF	13.08.42	21
Summers, Andrew	Sgt	A/G	RAFVR	21.01.44	24
Surridge, Gordon	Sgt	W/AG	RAFVR	28.04.42	25
Sutherland, Ian	F/O	Unk	RAF	04.08.40	21
Swainston, John	Sgt	F/E	RAFVR	12.12.44	23
Sweatman, Peter	F/L	W/Op	RAFVR	21.07.44	20
Sykes, Clifford	Sgt	A/G	RAFVR	16.07.44	20
Symondson, Sidney	Sgt	W/AG	RAFVR	19.07.41	Unk.
Takideli, Alexander	P/O	Pilot	RAF	12.06.40	20
Talbot, Edward	F/S	A/G	RAFVR	28.08.42	30
Talbot, Kenneth	Sgt	Unk.	RAFVR	13.01.44	21

Tanner, Arthur	Sgt	Pilot	RNZAF	17.10.42	22
Tarbin, Dennis	Sgt	F/E	RAFVR	16.07.44	19
Taylor, Guy	Sgt	Pilot	RAFVR	13.08.41	Unk.
Taylor, Kenneth	Sgt	W/AG	RAFVR	07.04.42	20
Taylor, Stanley	Sgt	A/G	RAFVR	04.12.44	20
Taylor, Thomas	F/S	W/AG	RCAF	17.10.42	Unk.
Temperton, Evan	P/O	A/G	RNZAF	03.02.45	22
Thomas, Douglas	Sgt	A/G	RAFVR	29.06.43	Unk.
Thomas, Hamilton	Sgt	F/E	RAFVR	23.09.43	31
Thompson, Allan	Sgt	A/G	RAFVR	24.03.44	24
Thompson, Carlton	P/O	Pilot	RCAF	13.06.44	22
Thompson, Clifford	Sgt	W/AG	RAF	23.05.40	19
Thompson, George	Sgt	W/AG	RAF	08.06.40	Unk.
Thompson-Horan, Robert	Sgt	F/E	RAFVR	07.04.42	Unk.
Thomson, Ivan	F/O	Pilot	RCAF	26.05.43	21
Thomson, John	Sgt	A/G	RAFVR	24.08.43	19
Thomson, BA (Cantab), John	P/O	A/G	RAFVR	18.09.41	40
Thornton, John	P/O	Pilot	RAFVR	27.08.42	Unk.
Tickle, Dalton	F/S	Nav	RNZAF	23.06.43	24
Tilley, Arthur	F/S	Pilot	RAFVR	02.03.43	20
Tipping, Gerald	F/O	Nav	RAFVR	25.07.44	27
Tofty, Norman	F/O	Nav	RAFVR	15.02.44	31
Town, Joseph	Sgt	A/G	RAFVR	23.09.43	Unk.
Towse, DFM. Wilfred	P/O	Pilot	RAFVR	26.07.43	29
Tree, Raymond	Sgt	W/AG	RAFVR	12.08.42	20
Trezise, Eric	Sgt	Pilot	RAFVR	11.04.43	22
Tuck, Douglas	Sgt	F/E	RAFVR	09.03.42	22
Tucker, Eugene	F/S	Obs	RAF	23.05.40	24
Turley, Raymond	Sgt	W/AG	RAFVR	03.09.42	22
Turner, Jack	F/O	Nav	RAFVR	25.05.44	22
Turner, John	F/S	Nav	RAAF	08.06.44	23
Turner, Ronald	P/O	B/A	RAFVR	03.03.43	20
Tvrdeich, Ivan	P/O	A/G	RNZAF	24.03.44	32
Tyler, Frank	F/S	A/G	RAFVR	08.05.44	Unk.
Tyler, George	Cpl	Arm	RAFVR	14.04.44	31
Upton, James	W/O	Pilot	RAAF	16.07.44	30
Vasil, George	Sgt	W/AG	RAFVR	19.09.42	21
Venton, Peter	Sgt	Nav	RAFVR	29.06.43	21
Vincent, James	P/O	Nav	RAF	01.10.42	27
Vivian, John	S/L	Pilot	RAF	08.08.41	27
Wade, John	Sgt	A/G	RAFVR	12.12.44	Unk.
Wadman, Lester	F/O	A/G	RCAF	08.03.43	23

Waite, Henry	Sgt	F/E	RAFVR	24.05.43	18
Wakefield, Harry	Sgt	A/G	RAFVR	11.04.43	21
Wakefield, Kenneth	F/S	Obs	RAFVR	28.08.42	20
Walker, Bryan	P/O	W/AG	RAFVR	16.09.42	27
Wallace, Alexander	Sgt	W/AG	RAFVR	16.09.41	22
Wallen, Emanuel	Sgt	W/AG	RAFVR	31.08.43	26
Walrond, Arthur	Sgt	W/AG	RAFVR	29.06.43	29
Warbey, Terence	Sgt	F/E	RAFVR	26.06.43	Unk.
Ward, Dennis	Sgt	F/E	RAFVR	08.08.44	23
Wareham, Bernard	Sgt	W/AG	RAFVR	13.10.41	21
Warner, John	P/O	W/AG	RAFVR	23.07.41	Unk.
Warrell, Ronald	Sgt	W/AG	RAFVR	04.07.43	21
Watson, Cecil	F/S	B/A	RAAF	08.06.44	29
Watson, Reginald	F/S	Nav	RAAF	12.05.44	26
Watson, Robert	Sgt	A/G	RAFVR	28.04.44	19
Watson, William	Sgt	W/Op	RAF	04.08.40	19
Watts, Bernard	Sgt	F/E	RAFVR	28.04.44	Unk.
Watts, Cyril	LAC	W/Op	RAF	18.05.40	21
Waylan, John	Sgt	W/AG	RAFVR	16.07.42	31
Weaver, Ronald	Sgt	A/G	RAFVR	19.02.43	21
Webber, Harold	F/S	A/G	RAFVR	01.10.42	22
Webber, Norman	Sgt	Obs	RAFVR	03.06.42	22
Webster, Morven	Sgt	A/G	RAFVR	23.06.43	Unk.
Weir, James	F/O	Nav	RAFVR	15.06.44	Unk.
Weir, John	P/O	A/G	RAF	03.06.42	26
Wellesley, Charles	F/S	A/G	RAAF	19.02.43	23
Wells, Francis	Sgt	W/Op	RAFVR	24.03.44	Unk.
Wells, William	Sgt	W/Op	RAFVR	31.07.43	Unk.
Werner, Raymond	P/O	Pilot	RAF	11.06.40	27
West, Harry	Sgt	A/G	RAFVR	15.02.44	30
Wheeler, George	F/S	W/AG	RAFVR	25.07.44	21
Wheeler, Leslie	F/S	Pilot	RAFVR	24.03.44	21
Whitcher, Arthur	Sgt	A/G	RAFVR	23.07.41	22
White, AFM. Charles	F/S	W/AG	RAFVR	18.07.41	23
White, Godfrey	W/O	B/A	RCAF	27.01.44	37
Whiting, Geoffrey	Sgt	A/G	RAFVR	25.07.44	Unk.
Whittaker, Gordon	Sgt	A/G	RAFVR	27.04.43	22
Whittaker, John	Sgt	A/G	RCAF	12.05.44	20
Wigley, Horace	Sgt	F/E	RAFVR	06.11.42	21
Wilkins, Leonard	F/S	B/A	RAFVR	17.01.45	22
Willbourn, Bertram	Sgt	F/E	RAFVR	19.02.43	Unk.
Williams, David	F/S	Pilot	RAFVR	05.01.45	23

Williams, Francis	Sgt	F/E	RAFVR	23.06.43	22
Williams, Henry	Sgt	Obs	RAFVR	11.09.42	25
Williams, Ivor	Sgt	A/G	RAFVR	08.04.43	20
Williams, DFC. John	F/O	A/G	RAFVR	19.02.43	31
Wilson, Donald	Sgt	F/E	RAFVR	12.05.44	Unk.
Wilson, Jack	F/S	Pilot	RAAF	26.05.43	21
Wilson, Matthew	S/L	Pilot	RAF	11.04.42	28
Wilson, Patrick	Sgt	A/G	RAFVR	04.12.44	19
Wilton, Raymond	F/O	B/A	RAFVR	13.06.44	20
Winchurch, John	P/O	F/E	RAFVR	31.08.43	21
Wood, George	Sgt	A/G	RAFVR	28.04.44	Unk.
Wood, Thomas	Sgt	Obs	RAFVR	17.10.42	22
Woodford, Alan	F/S	W/Op	RAAF	20.02.44	20
Woodhams, John	Sgt	W/AG	RAFVR	29.06.41	22
Woodhouse, Charles	Craftsman	Elect.	US Army	20.05.42	27
Woodley, Charles	F/O	Pilot	RCAF	08.06.44	24
Woodruff, DFC, Dennis	F/L	Pilot	RAFVR	29.01.44	28
Woods, Dennis	LAC	Obs	RAF	12.05.40	19
Woodward, Arthur	F/O	B/A	RAFVR	26.06.43	22
Wooldridge, Wilfred	F/S	W/AG	RAF	18.12.41	20
Woollard, Peter	F/S	A/G	RAFVR	02.11.44	20
Wootten, Thomas	P/O	Obs	RAF	13.10.41	Unk.
Worling, John	Sgt	Obs	RAFVR	13.04.42	20
Wratten, Jack	Sgt	F/E	RAFVR	26.02.43	22
Wrenshall, Bernard	F/O	B/A	RCAF	08.08.44	31
Wright, Edward	Sgt	W/AG	RAFVR	01.09.43	19
Wright, Sidney	Sgt	F/E	RAFVR	12.06.43	21
Yeomans, Oswald	Sgt	Pilot	RAF	14.09.40	26
Young, William	F/O	Nav	RAFVR	05.01.45	Unk.

APPENDIX III

List of Wartime Commanding Officers

S/L	J. G. Llewelyn	02.05.38–21.05.39

(S/L Llewelyn became deputy commanding officer on appointment of J. L. Wingate who was promoted to the rank of Wing Commander.)

W/C	J. L. Wingate	21.05.39–21.12.39
S/L	Ralph W. Lywood	21.12.39–02.06.40

(Promoted to the rank of Wing Commander on 1 January 1940.)

W/C	Joseph 'Joe' Cox, DFC	02.06.40–14.12.40
W/C	Herbert R. Dale	14.12.40–10.05.41
W/C	Patrick B. Ogilvie, DSO, DFC	10.05.41–07.01.42
W/C	John C. MacDonald, DFC, AFC	07.01.42–06.06.42
W/C	Douglas J. H. Lay, DSO, DFC	06.06.42–07.12.42
W/C	Stewart W. Menaul, DFC, AFC	07.12.42–??.04.43
W/C	John D. Stephenson, DFC	07.04.43–30.08.43
W/C	A. J. Elliot	03.09.43–15.04.44
W/C	William D. Watkins, DFC, DFM	15.04.44–16.11.44
W/C	Nigel G. Macfarlane, DSO	21.11.44–12.03.46

APPENDIX IV

List of Second World War Airfield Locations

Betheneville	France	September 1939
Conde-Vaux	France	September 1939
Wyton, Cambridgeshire	England	December 1939
Alconbury, Cambridgeshire	England	April 1940
Wyton, Cambridgeshire	England	May 1940
Bourn, Cambridgeshire	England	August 1942
Mildenhall, Suffolk	England	April 1943

Bibliography

Bowyer, M. J., *The Stirling Bomber* (England: Faber & Faber, 1980)

Ford-Jones, M. R., *Bomber Squadron: Men Who Flew with XV* (England: William Kimber, 1987)

Ford-Jones, M. R., *Desert Flyer: The Log and Journal of Flying Officer William Marsh* (USA: Schiffer Military History, 1997)

Ford-Jones, M. R. and Ford-Jones, V. A., *Oxford's Own, Men and Machines of No. 15/XV Squadron, Royal Flying Corps/Royal Air Force* (USA: Schiffer Military History, 1999)

Franks, N., *Sky Tiger* (England: William Kimber, 1980)

Johnson, B., *The Secret War* (BBC, 1978)

Lowe, T., *Finding Leonard* (USA: Privately Published, 2005)

Middlebrook, M., *The Battle of Hamburg* (England: Viking, 1980

Middlebrook, M. and Everett, C., *The Bomber Command War Diaries* (England: Viking, 1985)

Middlebrook, M., *The Nuremberg Raid (Rev. Ed)* (England: Allen Lane, 1980)

National Archive, *No. XV Squadron Operational Record Book, Form 540, Air 27* (London, England, 1939/45)

RAF Museum, *RAF Loss Cards 1939–1945* (Hendon, London, Various Dates)

Roberson, N. J., *The History of No. 15/XV Squadron* (Privately Published, 1975)

Carter, N. and C., *The Distinguished Flying Cross and How It Was Won 1918–1995 Volumes I & II* (England: Savannah Publications, 1998)

Tavender, I., *The Distinguished Flying Medal Register for The Second World War Volumes I & II* (England: Savannah Publications, 2000)

Index